The Autonomous Administr:
East Syria: Between A Rock

Publication of this book is partially funded by:

Group of the Progressive Alliance of
Socialists & **Democrats**
in the European Parliament

GERECHTIGKEIT FÜR ROJAVA

MEP Andreas Schieder

The Autonomous Administration of North and East Syria

Between A Rock and A Hard Place

Edited by

Thomas Schmidinger

TRANSNATIONAL PRESS LONDON

2020

Society and Politics Series: 3

The Autonomous Administration of North and East Syria:
Between A Rock and A Hard Place

Edited By Thomas Schmidinger

First Published in 2020 by TRANSNATIONAL PRESS LONDON in the United Kingdom, 12 Ridgeway Gardens, London, N6 5XR, UK.
www.tplondon.com

Transnational Press London® and the logo and its affiliated brands are registered trademarks.

Requests for permission to reproduce material from this work should be sent to: sales@tplondon.com

Paperback
ISBN: 978-1-912997-51-0

Cover Design: Nihal Yazgan
Cover Photo: Thomas Schmidinger
All photos in this book are by Thomas Schmidinger

www.tplondon.com

CONTENTS

ABOUT AUTHORS

Nazan Bedirhanoğlu is a political scientist and a Freedom Project post-doctoral fellow in the Political Science Department at Wellesley College in Massachusetts (USA).

Contact: nbedirha@wellesley.edu

Rosa Burç is a PhD researcher at the Center on Social Movement Studies as part of the Scuola Normale Superiore in Florence, Italy. She specialises in the political sociology of statelessness, with a current focus on bottom-up articulations of democracy in the Kurdish Middle East.

Contact: rosa.burc@sns.it

Sebastian Maisel is Professor for Arabic linguistics at the University of Leipzig (Germany) and author of *Yezidis in Syria – Identity Building among a Double Minority* (2017). Contact: sebastian.maisel@uni-leipzig.de

Francesco Marilungo has a PhD in Kurdish Studies from the University of Exeter (UK). While completing his PhD, he was appointed by an Italian NGO to coordinate and monitor cooperation and development projects in the Kurdish regions of Iraq and Syria.

Contact: marilungo.francesco@gmail.com

Thomas McClure is a freelance journalist and founding member of the Rojava Information Center (RIC). He works for RIC as a researcher, spokesperson and point of liaison for foreign press seeking to report on North and East Syria.

Contact: thomas@rojavaic.com

Christoph Osztovics is an Austrian political scientist and co-editor of the *Vienna Kurdish Studies Yearbook*.

Contact: christoph.osztovics@posteo.de

Thomas Schmidinger is a political scientist and social anthropologist at the University of Vienna and the University for Applied Sciences Oberösterreich and Co-editor of the *Vienna Kurdish Studies Yearbook* and author of *Rojava - Revolution, War and the Future of the Kurds* (2018) and *The Battle for the Mountain of the Kurds* (2019).

Contact: thomas.schmidinger@univie.ac.at

Nina Steinhardt is a researcher with Rojava Information Center (RIC). Coming from an academic background, she conducts field research along with RIC´s team of local and international researchers to contribute to RIC´s in-depth coverage of the situation in North and East Syria.

Contact: contact@rojavaic.com

Jordi Tejel is a historian specialising in modern history, state/society relations, and state-building in the Middle East and the Syrian Kurds. He is Professor at the University of Neuchâtel (Switzerland) and author of *Syria's Kurds. History, politics and society* (2009).

Contact: jordi.tejel@unine.ch

Konstantin Truevtsev is a senior researcher at the Institute of Oriental Studies, Russian Academy of Sciences, an expert of the Valdai Club, an expert of the Russian Council for International Affairs, Assistant Professor at the Russian University of Friendship of Peoples.

Contact: hrrc@mail.ru

Wladimir van Wilgenburg is a political analyst, journalist and co-author of *The Kurds of Northern Syria – Governance, Diversity and Conflicts* (2019). Contact: vvanwilgenburg@gmail.com

Arzu Yilmaz has a PhD in International Relations from Ankara University in Turkey, where she wrote her dissertation on Kurdish refugees and the political identity of the refugee agent. She is currently Alexander von Humboldt Foundation fellow in the AAI at University of Hamburg (Germany).

Contact: yilmaza02@gmail.com

FOREWORD

Andreas Schieder, MEP

Rojava is a synonym for the diverse political and socio-political change in the region of western Kurdistan. It is here that religious tolerance and gender equality are lived. It gives the Kurds a modern, cosmopolitan structure. Rojava is a beacon of hope for democracy, with its secular polity, and its stability in a multi-ethnic society.

The Autonomous Administration of North and East Syria was born out of the Kurdish struggle for autonomy in Syria, as well as the fight of the Syrian population against the so-called Islamic State (IS). The region is the last with a civilian administration not ruled by the authoritarian Syrian regime, controlled by jihadist forces, or occupied by Turkey. Despite this, it is under pressure from both the invasion of Turkey and its Islamist allies, as well as the Syrian regime, which does not allow any substantial autonomy within its borders.

The Turkish military offensive is contrary to international law and was clearly motivated by Turkish domestic politics. The consequences were the mass flight of civilians, Kurds, Christians, Syrians, Armenians, and Yezidis. Hundreds of thousands are on the run, and there is a clear threat that the

1

Islamic state will regain strength.

The situation in Rojava is becoming increasingly critical, and the Kurdish autonomous regions in northern Syria are under pressure from the Turkish intervention. Without the Kurds, however, the Islamic state would probably not be defeated today; Europe also owes them a great deal. The Kurdish militias, who had, with the support of the USA, defeated the Islamic terror in the region, are now not being treated as freedom fighters, but as terrorists. Recent developments show how important it is for the European Union to ensure stability in the region. The humanitarian catastrophe in Idlib and on the EU's external borders requires rapid humanitarian aid and a long-term political solution.

In December 2019 I travelled to Rojava to gain a clearer perspective. Our delegation sought to investigate the situation after the Turkish invasion. I crossed the border river Tigris, between Iraq and Syria to venture into to the Autonomous Administration of North and East Syria. When I visited a camp for internally displaced persons (IDPs) near Derik, the tense situation in the region became evident. Hundreds of thousands have had to flee their homes, due to the recent attacks by the Turkish military, but also due to IS terror or the Assad regime. The people here feel like a pawn in world politics, torn between the big power blocs USA, Russia, and Turkey. Families have been forcibly expelled from their ancestral and legal homeland, who—in contrast to refugees in the legal sense—did not cross a state border when they fled and remained in their own country, Syria. These people long for peace and security.

I was in Qamishli, a city in the Autonomous Administration of North and East Syria, to meet with Rojava's top foreign affairs official, Abdulkarim Omar. We spoke about the conditions after the Turkish attacks. The aim was not only to deliver humanitarian aid, but also secure the region and show solidarity with this multi-ethnic administration.

In the beginning of March 2020, I organised the Under Attack! conference in Vienna, at which international experts discussed with political representatives from Europe and the region the establishment of Rojava as a Kurdish autonomous area in northern Syria and its development towards the multi-ethnic Autonomous Administration of North and East Syria. It is at this point especially important to note the great support of Thomas Schmidinger, to whom I would like to extend a heartfelt 'Thank you'.

The EU is now, more than ever, called upon to act as a pragmatic mediator. We must use all diplomatic means to ensure that ill-considered sabre-rattling does not turn into a large-scale, warlike conflict. We must not allow players like Turkey or the USA to risk the stability of the entire region, only to make short-term, domestic political points. In Europe, too, we are urged to be particularly careful; Iranian acts of retaliation could also affect us here. Only a strong, common European foreign policy can establish the EU as a diplomatic and multilateral peace power, which is now absolutely necessary to bring calm to international relations.

The Turkish invasion of northern Syria was a deliberate attempt to destroy the self-autonomous administration project in the Kurdish region. The deployment of peacekeeping troops is immensely important. Europe must be much more present in the military sphere. We need a real ceasefire, a diplomatic offensive, a demilitarised zone, humanitarian aid, an arms embargo, sanctions against Turkey, and the discussion whether we should not put the accession negotiations on hold, and above all we need solidarity with the Autonomous Administration of North and East Syria.

INTRODUCTION

Thomas Schmidinger

Introduction

In July 2012, Syrian Kurds started to organise themselves through councils and armed forces after the Syrian army withdrew from areas of Kurdish settlement and started to establish another Kurdish autonomous region next to the Iraqi part of Kurdistan. Since the Battle of Kobanê in 2014, the world became increasingly interested in this autonomous region. The Syrian government has never officially recognised the de facto government, now known as the Autonomous Administration of North and East Syria, which controls almost a quarter of Syria's territory. Turkey has increasingly harassed this area after occupying the westernmost Kurdish region of Efrîn.

Armed units of the Kurdistan Workers' Party (Partiya Karkerên Kurdistanê, PKK) founded in Turkey took over Kobanê and finally also Cizîrê and Efrîn between 19 and 14 July 2012. At that time, the biggest military problems for the newly founded People's Defence Units (Yekîneyên Parastina Gel, YPG) was the fragmentation of the Kurdish settlement into three enclaves. Jihadist groups from the so-called 'Islamic State' (IS) posed a growing threat to the areas now under Kurdish control.

Thus, local military defence units needed be quickly established. When the official Syrian army withdrew, soldiers left behind much of their equipment and ammunition. In addition to the YPG, which acted as a volunteer militia until 2014, a separate women's unit, the Women's Defence Units (Yekîneyên Parastina Jin, YPJ), was organised and still exists today.

Already in 2003, Syrian Kurds had formed the Democratic Union Party (Partiya Yekitîya Demokrat, PYD), a sister party to the Turkish Kurdish PKK. In 2012, the PYD formed mutually beneficial relations with the Syrian official regime that urgently needed its own soldiers in the summer to fight the Arab opposition in central Syria and wanted to ensure that the Kurdish areas did not fall into the hands of the Arab opposition. In this way, the PYD could create its own autonomous territory and also push back the rival party alliance of the Kurdish National Council in Syria (Encûmena Niştimanî ya Kurdî li Sûriyeyê, ENKS)[1] supported by the Kurdistan regional government in Iraq.

---

[1] For the establishment and members of the Kurdish National Council, see: Allsopp 2014: 201ff.

The struggle for autonomy

The emergence of Kurdish-dominated autonomy in northern Syria, initially referred to as Rojava (Western Kurdistan), culminated longstanding political struggles by Kurdish parties and civil society movements for political freedoms and autonomy in Syria. This struggle had been directed against an extremely authoritarian regime controlled by the Arab-nationalist Baath Party since the 1960s. Although members of religious minorities heavily dominated this regime, when Hafez al-Assad came to power within the Baath Party, the ideology of Arab nationalism, authoritarianism, and strictly centralised state power formed the basis for suppressing ethnic and linguistic minorities. The largest of these minorities, the Kurds, make up almost 10 per cent of the population of Syria; they had to struggle both with economic and political marginalisation and also with the non-recognition of linguistic and cultural rights. After an extraordinary census in 1963, 120,000 Kurds even lost their citizenship.[2] By 2011, their descendants, who by then had grown to over 300,000 people, still had not yet become naturalised Syrian citizens.[3]

The Kurdish areas of Syria lie on the south-western periphery of the entire Kurdish settlement area and have always been home to other population groups. In particular, northeast Syria, as part of the Iraqi-Turkish-Syrian border triangle, the so-called Jezire (Arabic for 'island', meaning between the two rivers Euphrates and Tigris), has always been a multi-ethnic area that hosted, in addition to the Kurdish population, Arabs, Aramaic-speaking Christians (Assyrians, Arameans, Syriac), Circassians, Chechens, and Dom (a group related to the European Roma). Further west, in the region around Manbij, the descendants of those adopting Turkish ethnicity in the Ottoman Empire, Turkmen, can still be found in Aleppo and parts of northwest Syria. They lived alongside Arabs, Kurds, and Circassians.

The region also contains incredibly diverse religions: in addition to a Sunni-Islamic majority population containing both Kurds and Arabs, more than a dozen different Christian denominations spread all over the region, Yazidi communities in Efrîn north of Hasaka, south of Amuda around Serê Kaniyê and near Tirbespî,[4] and, up until the 1990s, a Jewish community in Qamishli.

Thus, the Kurdish autonomy, which developed from 2012 onwards, could not be understood as an ethnic project, but as an autonomous project inclusive of all inhabitants of the region. This was finally expressed in the renaming to the Democratic Federation of Northern Syria in 2016 and then

---

[2] Tejel 2009: 50.
[3] Schmidinger 2018: 62.
[4] Maisel 2017: 18ff.

the Autonomous Administration of North and East Syria in 2018.

From the Kurdish Supreme Committee to democratic confederalism

After the Syrian army withdrew, a dispute emerged on how to govern the area. On 11 July 2012, a newly founded 'Kurdish Supreme Committee' (Desteya Bilind a Kurd) became a kind of transitional administration of the Kurdish areas and included both the PYD and its allies as well as the heterogeneous alliance of the Kurdish National Council ENKS. The ENKS as a whole and the PYD and its front organizations divided their seats equally, which meant that the PYD became the single strongest party in the newly formed committee. Kurdish intellectuals close to the ENKS interpret this as a shift in power in favour of the PYD.[5] The long-term, more important, factors for the rise of the PYD, however, is likely to be the PYD's new armed forces and security organs, the PYD's ability to gain recognition far beyond its own partisans in the fight against IS, and the disunity of the ENKS.

Although the joint body included all major Kurdish parties, the new institution became permanently paralysed by power struggles between PYD and ENKS. The two sides could agree on little other than granting positions to five members of the ENKS and five members of the PYD. Agreements were often not implemented and each side blamed the others for the lack of implementation.

After protracted negotiations between the PYD and the Kurdish National Council, the PYD unilaterally proclaimed three autonomous cantons in January 2014, whose administration has since not been recognised by the ENKS.[6] Representatives of ethnic and religious minorities were successfully integrated into the new system. However, a substantial minority of the Kurdish population continues to fundamentally reject the new system and only very small and insignificant opposition Kurdish parties have been persuaded to participate in the autonomous administration since 2014.

Although the ENKS has lost importance in recent years compared to 2012/2013, serious steps towards reconciliation have only been taken since 2019. On 17 June 2020, the US diplomat William V. Roebuck, the Deputy Special Envoy to the Global Coalition to Defeat ISIS, mediated an agreement in principle between PYD and ENKS.

In contrast to the Democratic Party of Kurdistan administrating the autonomous region of Kurdistan in Iraq, the forces in Syrian Kurdistan do not seek statehood. The concept of 'democratic confederalism' propagated

---

[5] Seyder 2017: 50.
[6] Schmidinger 2016: 12.

by the PKK and its sister parties is, in the eyes of its supporters, a form of self-government opposed to the Western concept of a state.[7]

Syria's PYD has therefore explicitly abandoned nationalism and the nation state by following the concept of 'democratic confederalism' developed by Abdullah Öcalan in prison after his capture and abduction to Turkey, and with which the Turkish Kurdish movement, PKK, ideologically changed from a Marxist-Leninist party to its own form of libertarian communalism.[8] Even though some of the Kurdish population of Syria still support ethnic nationalism and hope for a Kurdish nation state, the Autonomous Administration of North and East Syria has followed Öcalan's ideas and explicitly renounced ethnic Kurdish nationalism. This new approach facilitated the integration of Arab, Assyrian, and Armenian communities in northern Syria into the new political system, but at the same time other Kurdish parties criticised PYD as too deferential with the Arab population. In particular, some Kurds criticise the political inclusion of the Arabs who settled on Kurdish land during the 'Arab belt' project in the second half of the 1960s in the province of al-Hasaka on the Turkish and Iraqi borders.[9]

In any case, 'democratic autonomy' for Rojava has a strictly territorial base rather than ethnic autonomy. At least in theory, the political system in Rojava relies on a strong decentralisation, with the municipality being the smallest unit and centre of social organisation.

As in the PKK's entire sphere of influence, the Syrian PYD's gender policy, a very essentialist feminism, plays an important role in propaganda and in the party structure. In principle, the so-called *hevserok* (co-leadership) system, a dual leadership, applies at all levels: Whether in a local government, in a court, whenever two people share coordination then one of them must be a woman.[10] In fact, each municipality has two co-mayors, the PYD has two co-chairs, all councils have co-chairs, etc.

The public presence of YPJ-armed women also transforms perceptions of the traditional role of Syrian Kurdish women. However, this does not mean that the traditional role model has changed everywhere. The overwhelming majority of women in Syrian Kurdistan continue to live as housewives, heavily dependent on their husbands. The intrinsic connection of Öcalan's ideology and feminist women´s liberation also 'alienate women who wished to avoid ideological indoctrination from participation in

---

[7] Ayboğa/Flach/Knapp 2015: 102.
[8] Öcalan 2000: 129.
[9] Kader 2002: 44.
[10] Ayboğa/Flach/Knapp 2015: 123.

communes and women´s institutions.'[11] However, the new political and military structures at least offer alternatives for some young women and girls. This leads to conflicts in some families, but undoubtedly also leads to a stronger position of women and girls in society.

The autonomous administration also tries to create economic opportunities for women. Numerous women's cooperatives have been founded and efforts have been made to ensure possibilities through training and work opportunities so that women who have lost their relatives can support themselves.[12] Despite these groundbreaking women's cooperatives in a strongly rural and patriarchal society, it must not be overlooked, however, that these projects reach only a relatively small number of women in economic niches.

On the one hand, the region has a kind of politically controlled war economy for war-essential goods and, on the other hand, it continues to be a market economy characterised by small traders and craftsmen, although this also includes relatively large farms with industrialised agriculture. Until the civil war, the region served as Syria's granary that supplied large parts of the country with agricultural products. Although agricultural trade came to a partial standstill in the early years of the civil war, this has since changed. Syrian Kurdistan exports meat or sheep and cattle across the border to Iraqi Kurdistan. Cereals and vegetables from the Cizîrê now can be sold again to Damascus, Aleppo, and other Syrian cities. However, international economic sanctions also affect the population in north-eastern Syria. The Caesar Syria Civilian Protection Act passed by the USA in December 2019, massively fuelled the already rampant inflation in Syria, which also affects north-east Syria. In spring, prices for basic foodstuffs had doubled within a few weeks. The collapse of the Syria currency accelerated the changeover to the Turkish lira in the Turkish-occupied areas, but the Autonomous Administration of North and East Syria continues to use Syrian pounds. Hyperinflation increased in the summer of 2020 under the economic impact of the corona pandemic, which spread in Syria from spring 2020.

From Rojava to the Autonomous Administration of North and East Syria

The Kurdish para-state finally gained political legitimacy mainly through the military successes against the attacks of the so-called 'Islamic State', especially through the Battle of Kobanê in winter 2014/15, when the fighters of YPG and YPJ, supported by international volunteers, secular Arab units, Iraqi-Kurdish Peshmerga, and the US Air Force, managed to defend the city

---

[11] Allsopp/Wilgenburg 2019: 156.
[12] Dirik 2015: 44.

9

after heavy losses and massive destruction.[13] With this battle, the Kurdish autonomous administration of Rojava not only received considerable international attention and prestige, but also gained legitimacy among its own population.

The three cantons had no common political structure until finally, on 17 March 2016, an assembly of Kurdish, Assyrian, Arab, and Turkmen delegates in Rumaylan proclaimed a Democratic Federation of Northern Syria – Rojava. They did not declare secession from Syria but claimed very extensive autonomy within Syria. In December 2016, it was renamed the Democratic Federation of Northern Syria (Kurdish: Federaliya Demokratîk a Bakûrê Sûriyê). Its co-president Hediya Yusuf explained that the Kurds took an inclusive action for their non-Kurdish fellow citizens in order to integrate them into the new federation. Rojava would now only be a small part of the big federation.[14] While the previously sceptical Arab and Assyrian-Aramaic groups partly welcomed this move, the Kurdish opposition parties strongly criticised the removal of the Kurdish name Rojava.

The military protection of the Kurdish areas, but above all the expansion to the south in the fight against the so-called 'Islamic State', was based on a military alliance with the USA, which at the beginning of 2015 initially acted as a secret military advisor, but from autumn 2015 onwards increasingly operated openly as an ally. However, the USA found itself in the delicate situation of cooperating with the PYD while continuing to support Turkey against the PKK.[15] To circumvent this problem, the USA pushed to create a new umbrella organisation, which could then be classified as a more 'neutral' ally. The founding of the Syrian Democratic Forces (Hêzên Sûriya Demokratîk, SDF) on 10 October 2015 can be explained not only by the need to gain Arab allies, but also by the US need to find a politically less suspicious partner. Arab fighters became the majority of the SDF's fighters, although the Kurdish YPG certainly still represents the strategic core of the troops.

The establishment and increasing institutionalisation of the autonomous administration, however, concerned not only the Syrian regime, but above all Turkey, whose government sees any form of Kurdish self-government— even if it is only in a neighbouring country—as a threat to its own state integrity, especially if it is ruled by a party close to its own opponent, the PKK.

A humanitarian and political catastrophe for the autonomous area

---

[13] Schmidinger 2015: 245.
[14] Interview with Hediya Yusuf, 7.12.2017.
[15] Kaya/Lowe 2017: 287.

resulted from the Turkish attack on the Efrîn region in early 2018 and the subsequent occupation by the Turkish army and allied Syrian-Islamist militias. It led not only to a mass flight and expulsion of the Kurdish (including Yezidi) population of the region,[16] but eventually to a renaming of the entity. After the loss of the north-west and the conquest of further Arabic-speaking areas of the so-called 'Islamic State', the autonomous administration changed its name to Autonomous Administration of North and East Syria in December 2018. The administration uses Aramaic and Turkish in addition to Kurdish and Arabic to clearly make an inclusive and non-nationalistic administration. [17]

Further attacks by Turkey

However, after the Turkish occupation of Efrîn, Turkey continued to increase the pressure on the Autonomous Administration of North and East Syria despite the clear involvement of Syrian Turkmen in the local councils of the autonomous administration. In October 2019, Turkey invaded north-east Syria and probably posed the greatest threat to the Autonomous Administration of North and East Syria since the establishment of de facto autonomy in the Kurdish-populated regions of Syria.

After a telephone call to Erdoğan, on 7 October 2019, the erratic US President Donald Trump declared that the US Army would completely withdraw from Syria thus giving the Turkish army the green light for an invasion of the Kurdish areas, which began two days later under the name 'Operation Peace Spring' (Turkish: Barış Pınarı Harekâtı).

As in the occupation of Efrîn in 2018, the Turkish army collaborated with various Syrian militias, including the jihadist-oriented Ahrar al-Sharqiya, which also includes many former IS fighters, the Turkmen nationalist Sultan Murad Division, and former Free Syrian Army (FSA) units such as the Hamza Brigade. The invasion mainly targeted Girê Sipî (Arabic: Tal Abyad) and Serê Kaniyê (Arabic: Ra's al-ʿAin). The Christian and Yazidi population in this area feared the jihadist militias' brutality directed against religious minorities.

On 12 October 2019, members of the Ahrar al-Sharqiya militia viciously murdered Hevrîn Xelef, a prominent Syrian-Kurdish politician who, as a young woman and civilian, had no involvement in the fighting. Hevrîn Xelef

---

[16] Schmidinger 2019: 101ff.

[17] Missing languages include Armenian, Chechen, Circassian and Domari, the language of the Dom (Sometimes called Dome or Domba: a group related to the European Roma), although Armenians and Dom make up a similar proportion of the population to that of the Turkmen. It can be assumed that using Turkish as an official language intended to send a signal to Turkey's foreign policy and to make it clear to Turkey that self-administration does not have an anti-Turkish orientation and also involves the local Turkmen.

subsequently became a symbol of resistance against the Turkish invasion and war crimes against civilians in the region. Her image bedecked protest placards in the region and also in Rojava solidarity demonstrations initiated by the Kurdish diaspora scattered around the world.

The primarily Arabic-speaking city of Tal Abyad had already fallen into the hands of the Turkish army and the pro-Turkish militias on 10 October 2019. However, the Syrian Democratic Forces (SDF) initially repulsed attacks on Serê Kaniyê and continued to offer resistance in the multi-ethnic city despite being surrounded by the Turkish forces.

In contrast to Tal Abyad, Serê Kaniyê has a Kurdish-majority population and a significant Christian-Aramaic and Armenian minority. In addition, some Chechen families remain from those who founded the town in 1878 after fleeing from Russian expansion in the Caucasus. Sixteen villages with the Yezidi ethnicity lie close to the city, from which several inhabitants had moved to the city. The presence of Arabs make the city a microcosm of Syria's diversity. The SDF concentrated on defending the city, which had already been contested with the Jabhat al-Nusra jihadists in 2013.

Other fierce battles took place around Tal Tamr (Kurdish: Girê Xurma), founded by Christian-Assyrians in the 1930s, whose Christian population has declined in recent years because of the general situation in Syria and IS attacks.

After unsuccessful talks, in which US President Trump again threatened to destroy the Turkish economy, Russia increasingly took over the role of regional regulatory power. Russian President Vladimir Putin agreed on 22 October in Sochi to facilitate the withdrawal of the YPG/YPJ to 30 kilometres from the border and to allow a Turkish occupation of a region of about 3700 square kilometres, starting west of Tal Abyad and ending east of Serê Kaniyê. Those people who live in the region and most affected by the agreement did not have any input in the Sochi negotiations. Despite bravely clearing jihadists from Serê Kaniyê, the fighters of the YPG/YPJ still had to leave according to the Russian-Turkish agreement. Turkey and its allies gained, without a fight, the area between the eastern border of the Kobanê region and the suburbs of Tal Tamr. However, the Sochi Agreement allowed Tal Tamr to remain outside the Turkish occupied zone.

In the other regions, the Syrian-Turkish border would be secured by the Syrian government army, together with the Russian military police. The YPG withdrew from these border areas. However, the SDF's local military councils are still present and cooperate with the Syrian army and Russia. The Sochi Agreement only provided for the withdrawal of the YPG and not the withdrawal of other remaining units from the border regions. This allowed the local SDF military councils to remain stationed in Kobanê and the area from Dirbêsiyê to the Iraqi border.

The presence of many very different, sometimes rival military units in the same region complicates the situation. In particular, the line of demarcation between the Russian-Syrian and US spheres of influence inside the SDF held territories remains unclear. Russian units tried to move further east until they met with US resistance. This resulted in several small skirmishes between the various international troops, in which the SDF sometimes acted as a mediator. A firefight lasting several hours between Syrian government troops and US soldiers took place on 14 February 2020 in a village south of Qamishli. Finally, a Russian unit rushed in to stop the fight after the death of a Syrian.

The US allies in the region noted their concern over the partial withdrawal of the US military. To prevent a takeover of the region by the Assad regime and in particular by Iranian forces, Saudi Arabia also started to provide increased support to the SDF in December 2019, which, together with the continued presence of some US troops, increased the difficulty of negotiations between the Kurdish autonomous administration and Syria's central regime.

Meanwhile, more than 250,000 civilians have fled from the Turkish-occupied areas around Tal Abyad and Serê Kaniyê. Most of them found shelter in makeshift tent camps within the remaining self-governing area. The largest camp, Waşukanni near the city of Hasakah, already had over 9,000 displaced people in February 2020 with hardly any international support. Instead, Erdoğan demands support for the 'repatriation' of Syrian refugees to the newly occupied territories. However, most of these 'returnees' come from completely different regions of Syria. Therefore, the Kurdish side accused Turkey of ethnic cleansing, a war crime which did not prevent German Chancellor Merkel from announcing, during a visit to Ankara in January 2020, that Germany would consider supplying funds to help settle refugees in the Turkish-occupied territories of north-eastern Syria.

By summer 2020, several thousand Syrian refugees from other parts of Syria had already been settled in Serê Kaniyê, Tal Abyad, and the villages between the two cities. Not all of these refugees have returned to Syria voluntarily. Kurds who could contact these people occupying their houses and flats report that many displaced persons claim to have been settled against their will.

Debates on the region

When Turkey attacked northeast Syria in October 2019, scientists, journalists, and intellectuals concerned with developments in the region had little choice but to try once again to raise public awareness of the humanitarian and political consequences of the invasion. Reports from the region itself, however, were even rarer than usual, because from October to November the regional security was so precarious that even very experienced war correspondents became doubly concerned about risking their lives. From March 2020, after both Iraq and Syria announced a lockdown to counter the coronavirus pandemic, it became again impossible to cross borders from Iraq into the region. The border crossing at Semalka between the Kurdistan Regional Government in Iraq and the Autonomous Administration of North and East Syria remained closed.

Between these two phases, I travelled twice to northern and eastern Syria. In December, I accompanied the Austrian MEP Andreas Schieder to the region, who wanted to get a direct view of the situation after the Turkish attack. Schieder, who had repeatedly defended the Kurds, then agreed with his group in the EU Parliament to finance a conference on the current situation in northern and eastern Syria, which could take place in Vienna on 6 March 2020 shortly before the coronavirus-related lockdown.

This book is based on papers presented at the conference. However, it is not a typical publication of academic conference proceedings because the topics are not completely congruent with those of the conference. Some lectures that could not be held due to travel restrictions related to the coronavirus pandemic were submitted as book contributions. In addition, I also wrote a short contribution on the Jewish history of the region, which has been often neglected in previous presentations of the region.

The various authors for this volume have been intensively involved with the region in recent years. However, the authors do not only focus on the situation on the ground, but also on the international context of the autonomous administration. The conflict in Syria is no longer just a civil war, but a transnational conflict with important roles played not only by actors such as Russia or the USA, but also Turkey or Iran.

Given the transnationality of the conflict and the role of the hegemonic powers, these authors share thoughtful analyses from very different perspectives. It is important to share these diverse views with the world so that the tragic conflict might become more comprehensible. This does not mean, however, that I necessarily advocate each particular position taken by the varied contributors to this book. The intent is to offer you multiple perspectives and certainly not a common narrative.

Of course, a volume like this can only remain fragmentary, and thus some topics do not receive enough attention. For example, more detailed consideration should be given to the role of Iran and Saudi Arabia. Also, the situation of the smaller ethnic minorities in the region, such as the Circassians, Chechens, Turkmen, and Dom, would also have deserved closer examination. The most severe flaw, however, is certainly the lack of a separate contribution on gender relations.

The autonomous administration's gender policy attracts a lot of attention, especially in progressive circles. After all, its emancipatory claim, in many ways, exactly opposes the repressive ideology of various Islamist and jihadist militias in Syria. The previously mentioned conference had had a very interesting and critical presentation on gender. However, the late cancellation of a written contribution on gender made it impossible to get an adequate replacement. Finally, this topic is too important to ask for a quick, token contribution. As editor of the volume, I can only refer to this problematic void and hope that future publications will give the necessary space for the issue of gender.

Despite these omissions, the articles collected here provide important insights into the structure, hopes, and difficulties of the Autonomous Administration of North and East Syria. They represent contributions from committed academics, journalists, and activists who, with very different styles of writing and analysis, have entered into a fruitful exchange with each other based on their intensive engagement with the region for many years. With the knowledge they have gained, they have also begun a dialogue with politicians, including those in Europe. This book will surely not end these discussions but we hope it will help to pave the way for further action that increases understanding of and solidarity with the diverse peoples seeking a better future in north-eastern Syria.

Bibliography

Allsopp, H. (2014). *The Kurds of Syria. Political Parties and Identity in the Middle East.* I.B. Tauris: London / New York.

Allsopp, H. and van Wilgenburg, W. (2019). *The Kurds of Northern Syria. Governance, Diversity and Conflicts.* I.B. Tauris: London / New York.

Ayboğa, E., Flach, A., Knapp, M. (2015). *Revolution in Rojava. Frauenbewegung und Kommunalismus zwischen Krieg und Embargo.* VSA: Hamburg.

Dirik, D. (2015). "Die Frauenrevolution in Rojava" in: Küpeli, I. (ed.), *Kampf um Kobanê. Kampf um die Zukunft des Nahen Ostens.* edition assemblage: Münster, pp. 38-50

Kader, A. (2002). *The Kurdish Cause in Western Kurdistan Which is occupied by Syria.* Western Kurdistan Association and Kurdistan National Congress: London.

Kaya, Z. and Lowe, R. (2017). 'The Curious Question of the PYD-PKK Relationship' in: Stansfield, G. and Shareef, M. (eds.), *The Kurdish Question Revisited.* London: Hurst & Company, pp. 275-287

Maisel, S. (2017). *Yazidis in Syria. Identity Building among a Double Minority.* Lexington Books: Lanham, Boulder et.al.

Öcalan, A. (2000). *Zur Lösung der Kurdischen Frage.* Kurdistan Informations-Zentrum: Berlin.

Schmidinger, T. (2015). "Zwischen Türkei und IS – Militärische Erfolge der Kurden gegen den so genannten, Islamischen Staat' in Rojava" in: Hennerbichler, F., Osztovics, C., Six-Hohenbalken, M.A., Schmidinger, T. (eds.), *Wiener Jahrbuch für Kurdische Studien 3/2015*. Caesarpress: Wien, pp. 245-250

Schmidinger, T. (2016). *Rojava*. Mandelbaum: Wien.

Schmidinger, T. (2018). *Rojava. Revolution, War, and the Future of Syria's Kurds*. Pluto Press: London.

Schmidinger, T. (2019). *The Battle for the Mountain of the Kurds. Self-Determination and Ethnic Cleansing in the Afrin Region of Rojava*. PM Press: Oakland.

Seyder, F. I. (2017). *Die syrischen Kurden: Auswege aus dem Bürgerkrieg*. LIT: Berlin.

Tejel, J. (2009). *Syria's Kurds. History, Politics and Society*. Routledge: London, New York.

Memorial plaque for the fallen internationalists in the ranks of the YPG and YPJ at the border station of Semalka, February 2020

Protest against the Syrian regime in Amûdê by different Kurdish parties and civil society
groups, January 2013.

Meeting of the Women conference of the Democratic Union Party (Partiya Yekîtiya
Demokrat, PYD) in Qamishli, February 2014.

Fighters of the Women´s Protection Units (Yekîneyên Parastina Jin, YPJ) in Afrin, February 2015.

Kobanê after the attack of the so-called 'Islamic State', November 2015.

Monument for the killed YPJ-fighter Arin Mirkan in Kobanê, January 2019.

Prison Camp in Ain Isa, where female supporters of the so-called 'Islamic State' were detained until the war with Turkey in October 2019, when the inmates could escape, January 2019.

Waşukanni Camp erected at the end of 2019 for the displaced persons from Serê Kaniyê, February 2020.

Statue of the Free Woman at the entrance of Amûdê, February 2020.

CHAPTER 1

HISTORY OF SYRIAN KURDS AND THEIR POLITICAL PARTIES

Jordi Tejel

As the Syrian army pulled out of several towns in the north and northeast of the country in July 2012, Kurds found themselves masters of their own destiny after more than 40 years of dictatorship and political marginalisation. In the face of the sudden retreat of the state security apparatus, the Democratic Union Party (PYD), the Syrian offshoot of the Kurdistan Workers' Party (PKK), and the Kurdish National Council, composed of sixteen political parties, signed a political agreement providing for the creation of a joint Supreme Kurdish Council and the establishment of 'popular defence forces' in order to secure Kurdish gains. However, despite the apparent unity, the operational capacity of the Supreme Kurdish Council was hindered by an unbalanced power relationship between the PYD and the Kurdish National Council, in favour of the former, as well as their uneven representation in the three main Kurdish enclaves in northern Syria (Allsopp 2014: 194–200).

Ever since, the PYD and its military force, the People's Defence Units (YPG), have been exercising state-like power in the Kurdish regions of Syria. In 2017, the YPG within the Syrian Democratic Forces (SDF)—a coalition of Kurdish, Arab, and Assyrian militias—actively participated alongside the USA in military operations against the Islamic State (IS) around Raqqa, the 'capital' of its self-proclaimed caliphate. In sum, between 2012 and 2017, the Kurds had become key actors in the Syrian conflict (Gunter 2014; Barfi 2016; Allsopp and Wilgenburg 2019: 167–198).

Understandably, amid these unprecedented developments, observers and scholars attempted to account for the 'success story' of the PYD following the partial withdrawal of Syrian security forces from northern Syria. While some of them attributed PYD's rapid success to a possible secret deal with the regime (Savelsberg 2014: 85–108), others saw the achievements as resulting from a 'long struggle for autonomy' (Schmidinger 2018: 1–9). Regardless of the accuracy of these assessments, this paper seeks to provide a historically informed analysis of PYD's rapid ascent in Syria by paying particular attention to a series of complementary factors. As briefly discussed elsewhere (Tejel 2012), this paper emphasises that the consolidation of the PYD as the main broker in the Syrian Kurdish arena after 2011 is better explained by historical (the consolidation of three separated Kurdish enclaves since the establishment of the Syrian state), regional (the alliance between Syria's regime and the PKK), and political factors (traditional weakness of the other Kurdish political parties).

A single Kurdish territory?

Since the establishment of the Syrian state in the early 1920s, the Kurdish populations of Syria occupy three narrow zones isolated from one another, along the Turkish border: the Upper Jazira, Jarablus, and Kurd Dagh, with their respective main urban centres; namely Qamishli, Kobane, and Afrin. Besides these northern enclaves, Kurds also constituted important urban communities in Aleppo, Damascus, and Raqqa (Fuccaro 2003: 206–24; Ababsa 2010). Despite the largely negative consequences for local populations when new borders emerged following the collapse of the Ottoman Empire, some Kurdish tribes of the Upper Jazira kept alive, through marriages and trade, their kin relations beyond the Syrian territory, especially in Tur Abdin (Turkey) and Dohuk province (Iraq).

Linguistic similarities also facilitated transborder relations between Syrian Kurds and their relatives in Turkey and Iraq. Most Syrian Kurds speak Kurmanji (a Kurdish dialect with its own sub-dialects in Syria) as do Kurds in south-eastern Turkey and north-western Iraq. Finally, Syrian Kurds are Sunni Muslims, except for the Yazidis, who have traditionally been dispersed between the Upper Jazira, the Jabal Siman region, and Kurd Dagh. However, recent events in the Kurd Dagh region and Jabal Siman have had dramatic consequences on the Yazidis' numbers, religious networks, and usual settlements (Maisel 2016).

At least until the 1980s, Kurdish politics have been more connected with the Upper Jazira region and less associated with the Kurd Dagh and Jarablus areas. Under the French Mandate, the Upper Jazira along with Damascus became the centre of Kurdish politics due to the arrival of numerous tribal chiefs as well as Kurdish intellectuals escaping from Turkish repression. Thousands of Kurdish refugees from Turkey and Iraq during the 1920s and 1930 dramatically increased the Kurdish population of the Upper Jazira. Before 1927, only 47 Kurdish villages existed in this region; by 1939, between 700 and 800 villages had a Kurdish majority. According to the official census of 1939, the Upper Jazira had a population of 158,550, comprising 81,450 Muslim Kurds and 2,150 Yazidis.[1]

---

[1] Centre des Archives Diplomatiques de Nantes [Hereafter CADN], *Fonds Beyrouth, Cabinet Politique, No. 1367*, 'Répartition de la population de la Haute Jézireh.' Beirut, April 1939.

In 1927, Kurdish activists established the Khoybun League, (literally 'Be yourself'), the first Kurdish nationalist committee in Syria. The Khoybun League followed two different albeit not exclusive trajectories. While Turkey remained the target of its political and military activities since it was the country of origin for most of its members, the Khoybun League also favoured the participation of Kurdish representatives in Syrian political life.

However, before the Khoybun League was established, some Kurdish notables had already advanced some political claims. Thus, for instance, the first demands for local autonomy came in May 1924 from the deputy Nouri Kandy representing Kurd Dagh, who submitted to the French Mandate authorities a memorandum demanding administrative autonomy for all the regions with a Kurdish majority. Nouri Kandy had a clear idea of the role that the Kurds could play in favour of the French Mandate, such as fending off the Arab nationalists who, left to their own devices, would 'influence the Arab Union and bring down the Mandatory administration'. A similar petition in favour of Kurdish autonomy came from the chiefs of the Barazi Confederation, Bozan and Muhammad Shahin.[2]

Yet, these claims aimed mainly at establishing local power around a tribal group, not the entire Kurdish nation in Syria. The political character of Kurdish demands changed after the Khoybun League developed. Former leaders of Kurdish clubs in Istanbul succeeded in winning over a large part of Kurdish tribes, notably those having found refuge in Syria since 1920, to generally back their political and cultural demands. Thus, in August 1928, the French authorities received a memorandum based on the Mandate Charter and on the stipulations relative to the Mandatory Power's obligations to favour local autonomy.[3]

The French eventually rejected the petition. However, the free hand of the French Intelligence Service in the Mandatory Administration produced some surprising results in the Upper Jazira. Its officers were granted 'carte blanche' to a region previously little known to the French. Among these officers, Lieutenant Pierre Terrier distinguished himself by realizing his projects in the Upper Jazira. After leaving Jazira in 1927, Pierre Terrier was attaché to the Political Cabinet of the High Commissioner where he centralised all affairs affecting Franco-Kurdish relations in Syria.

Faced with increasingly pressing demands for independence from the

---

[2] Respectively, *CADN, Fonds Beyrouth, Cabinet Politique*, No. 1054. Petition addressed to General Billotte. Aleppo, May 9, 1924; *CADN, Fonds Beyrouth, Cabinet Politique*, No. 1054. Petition addressed to General Billotte. Aleppo, April 1, 1924.

[3] *Ministère des Affaires Etrangères (Paris), Quai d'Orsay, série Levant 1918–40*, No. 181. Memo presented by Sureya Bedir Khan to Philippe Berthelot, general secretary to the Ministry for Foreign Affairs. Paris, August 7, 1928.

three Kurdish enclaves in northern Syria, Terrier launched a counterproposal. For Lieutenant Terrier, the geographical disposition of the Kurdish territories rendered the constitution of an autonomous province across these regions untenable. He proposed therefore that Kurdish leaders and notables concentrate all their attention on Jazira, where 'one could hope to see the evolution of an autonomous Kurdish centre. As for the Kurd Dagh and Jarablus districts, one must be content with certain prerogatives.'[4] The implementation of this plan established the effective division between different Kurdish enclaves and their political and social evolution for years to come.

Thus, the autonomous movement in Jazira, often referred to as the Kurdish-Christian bloc, partly resulted from French endeavours to halt the devolution of powers to the Syrian nationalist bloc in 1936. The principal demands of the autonomist movement in Jazira can be summarised as: 1) a special statute with guarantees from the League of Nations comparable to that of the Alawites and the Druzes; 2) a support from French troops to guarantee the security of the minorities; and 3) the nomination of a French governor under the control of the League of Nations.[5] In addition, the well-known members of the nationalist committee eventually became deputies in the Syrian Parliament and some, including the sons of both Ibrahim Pasha (Milli tribe) and Hasan Hajo (Heverkan tribe), kept their seats throughout the 1950s.

At the same time, Kurdish leaders in Syria organised a military revolt in north-eastern Turkey (1927-1930)—the Ararat Revolt or Agri Dagh revolt (Nouri Pacha 1986)—aiming at the establishment of a Kurdish autonomous state in Eastern Anatolia.[6] Later, their leaders became deputies in the Syrian Parliament where they mainly asked for further autonomy as well as for infrastructural projects in northern Syria, such as roads, schools, and hospitals. Finally, the French authorities supported the core of the Khoybun League—Jaladat and Kamuran Bedirkhan—in laying out the foundations of a cultural renaissance movement using the Kurmanji Kurdish dialect (Tejel 2014: 839–855).

Collaboration between French and Kurdish intellectuals was also important to the 'creative nation-building' of the Kurds (Tejel 2009).

---

[4] *Service Historique de l'Armée de Terre (Paris), 4H 319*, No. 3, 'The Kurds,' No. 465/C.E/R. Beirut, January 19, 1943.

[5] *Archives Dominicaines, SAULCHOIR (Paris), Haute Jazira*, No. 45, Vol. II, 'The Manifesto from Jazira'. April, 1938.

[6] The Khoybun League coordinated its political and military activities with the Armenian Tashnak party. In 1927, both parties agreed to establish two autonomous states in eastern Turkey, an Armenian entity in north-eastern Turkey and a Kurdish state in south-eastern Anatolia, as per the Sèvres accord of 1920 (Bozarslan 1997: 182–186).

Influenced by European literature on folk culture, Kurdish intellectuals no longer lamented the 'backwardness' of Kurdish society, but instead, adapted a new narrative, which sought to highlight and romanticise the noble folk culture of the Kurds. Turning the tables on the narrative of Turkish nationalism, they labelled the Turks as the 'enemy' and true 'barbarians', while declaring themselves the 'martyr nation' (Tejel 2006). This narrative was, in turn, taken up by French Kurdologists who helped to legitimise and spread the cultural discourse of Kurdish nationalism to the West.

Those initial political endeavours did not generally involve the Kurd Dagh and Jarablus regions and, more importantly, in the mid-1930s the Kurd Dagh area witnessed the only anti-French revolt among Kurds in Syria (Lescot 1940/1988: 101–126). Although religious in character, the Murud movement challenged both the French and Kurdish landlords who had been co-opted by the Mandatory Power. As a result, rebels not only freed themselves from the economic and social influence of big landowners but also put an end to tribal structures in Kurd Dagh (Lange 2010: 401–428). Ultimately, according to local narratives on this uprising, Kurds from Kurd Dagh would become more 'modern' than in the Upper Jazira where tribal and clannish dynamics remained untouched.

Kurdish parties at the age of Syrian independence

The departure of the French troops from Syria in 1946 opened the door to a period of social, economic, and political upheaval that would continue unchecked for nearly two decades. First, Khoybun's diplomatic failures during World War II led to a crisis in the Kurdish nationalist movement in Syria. The committee's old members slowly withdrew from the Kurdish political scene, while Kurdish deputies to the Syrian Parliament maintained the status quo by abandoning all autonomist demands for their respective regions. Consequently, by the late 1940s, the Kurdish movement lacked both a leader and a plan to bring together the diverse political factions.

Faced with this void, some of the more militant Kurds sympathised with the Syrian Communist Party (SCP). Young, politically active Kurds perceived the old Kurdish nationalist elite to be the enemy of the people and a vestige of a bygone era. Significantly, in some cases, the Communist movement's leaders were the sons of the old nationalist leadership. According to British sources, in the early 1950s, the main centre of Communist activity in northern Syria was at Qamishli, while there were less important branches in towns such as Ras al-Ayn, Derbessiya, Amude, and Derik.[7]

In addition to the party itself, there were also branches of two

---

[7] National Archives in London (Hereafter NA), FO 195/2650. Political report No. 7885 'Kurdish Affairs'. Damascus, 25 September 1950.

Communist-controlled organisations, the Democratic Youth Organisation and the World Peace Movement. The involvement of Kurds in the SCP reached such a high level that it was known in the north of Syria as the 'Kurdish Party'. Furthermore, from 1933 Khalid Bakdash, a Kurd from *Hayy al-Akrad* or Kurdish quarter, who used his ethnic background to spread the party's propaganda among Kurds in Damascus, led the SCP and won a deputy seat in 1954, in large part thanks to the mobilisation of this electoral stronghold (Tejel 2009: 42–45).

Meanwhile, the rise of Pan-Arab nationalism generated increasing pressure on ethnic minorities in Syria. The sentiment of a real threat amid Syrian Kurds spread accordingly. In addition, regional developments also had an impact on the Kurdish political movement: the end of the monarchy in neighbouring Iraq and the strategic alliance between Iraqi strongman General Abdul-Karim Qassem, on one side, and the Communists and Kurdistan Democratic Party led by Mustafa Barzani, on the other, led to a renewal of Kurdish political activity in Syria.

As a result, and in contrast to the 1920s and 1930s, Kurdish activists in Syria now looked to Iraqi Kurdistan for inspiration, establishing a sister organisation, the Kurdish Democratic Party of Syria in 1957. As in the past, however, tensions between a pan-Kurdist programme and a much more 'Syrian-oriented agenda' plagued the Kurdish movement. According to Osman Sabri, he founded the Kurdish Democratic Party in Syria in 1957 together with Abdul Hamid Hajj Darwish (a law student), Rashid Hamo (a teacher), and Shaykh Muhammad Isa Mahmud. A year later, the founding members chose Nuredin Zaza, who had returned from Europe in 1956, as president (Tejel 2009: 48–49).

At the insistence of the Iraqi KDP, the name of the party was changed to Kurdistan Democratic Party in Syria at the beginning of 1960 (Jemo 1990: 33–34). This name change was significant, for it implied that the Kurdish enclaves of northern Syria were also part of Kurdistan. Accordingly, Kurdish aspirations could include the potential annexation of these Syrian territories by an autonomous or independent Kurdistan. As a result, on 5 August 1960, the Syrian government arrested and tortured the leaders of the executive committee (Zaza 1982: 181).

Political connections between the Syrian Kurds and the Iraqi KDP were not, however, the only perceived threat to 'national security' in those years. During the French Mandate, tens of thousands of Christians and Kurds had settled in the province of Hasaka and began to cultivate new crops and build new towns (Velud 1991; Tatchjian 2004). After World War II, Upper Jazira became the richest cotton-growing region of Syria. In addition to its agricultural wealth, the province had oil in a commercially exploitable form.

Economic growth was paralleled by an increase in population: the official Syrian figures showed that between 1954 and 1961 the population of the province had increased from 240,000 to 305,000.

According to a British report, the rapid increase of population was partly due to Jazira's 'magnetic attraction' for the 'poor and unemployed' who lived in the surrounding areas, that is Kurds from Turkey and Iraq.[8] As a reaction, Syrian media outlets as well as politicians began to denounce a supposedly massive 'infiltration' of Kurds from neighbouring countries and to make proposals to strengthen the 'Arabism' of the province in order to avoid the establishment of 'another Israel' (Vanly 1968). Consequently, during the first week of October 1962, a special census in the province of Hasaka tried to identify 'the real inhabitants' and the 'foreigners'. After the special census, the government arbitrarily declared more than 100,000 Kurds, mostly peasants, as 'non-Syrians' and denied them all the rights attached to citizenship (McGee 2014: 171–181).

Finally, Turkey raised concerns about Kurdish trans-border relations and the survival of cross-border networks that traded contraband. Since the French Mandate period, Turkey's porous border with Syria witnessed the proliferation of smuggled goods either circulating through or produced in Syria in large-scale operations. Turkish authorities, as well as newspapers, sometimes employed a very aggressive tone to regularly denounce French permissiveness regarding smuggling activities along the border during the 1930s.[9]

Likewise, in the mid-1950s, tensions rose across the Turkish-Syrian border, including some clashes not only between smugglers and border authorities but also between Syrian and Turkish border guards.[10] In July 1956, the Turkish Ministry of Foreign Affairs published a communiqué about thirty-eight smugglers captured during an armed encounter with Turkish frontier guards and involving local villagers near Nusaybin.[11] In 1957, Turkey and Syria dispatched troops to its border and the same year Ankara unilaterally planted mines along the boundary line.[12] Ultimately, Turco-Syrian border incidents were used by Syrian elites to reassert the need to protect

---

[8] NA, 371/164413. Report on the census taken in the province of Hasaka. Damascus, 8 November 1962.

[9] *Yenilik*, 'Kaçakçılara Ogut: Kaçakçılar Vatana duşmandır' (Smugglers are the enemies of the nation), 30 June 1936; *Tan*, 'Bir kaçak merkezi daha: Amude' (A new contraband center: Amude), 13 January 1937.

[10] NA, FO 371/121868. Turco-Syrian relations. Damascus, 25 June 1956.

[11] NA, FO 371/121868. Turco-Syrian Frontier Incident. Damascus, 13 July 1956.

[12] While twenty-eight smugglers had been found dead at the border by 1955, two years later ninety-six smugglers had died trying to cross the international boundary (Çelik 2018: 61). The mining of the border area in 1957 is certainly a key factor to understand the increase of fatal incidents along the Syrian-Turkish border.

national sovereignty over Upper Jazira, an 'Arab land'.

On 12 November 1963, Lieutenant Muhammad Talab al-Hilal, former chief of the intelligence services in Hasaka, published a study of Jazira aiming at countering Kurdish territorial claims in Syria. More importantly, the report suggested a dozen measures to eliminate the 'Kurdish threat' among which the displacement of Kurds from their lands to the interior and the colonisation of Kurdish lands by Arabs settlers. Of all the points proposed by Hilal, Damascus focused on creating an 'Arab Belt', a long strip of arable, well-cultivated land that would extend 280 kilometres along the Turkish-Syrian border; from Ras al Ayn in the west, to the Iraqi border on the east, which was to be between 10 and 15 kilometres wide (Vanly 1968). However, the plan was only partially implemented in 1973. This delay in establishing the 'Arab Belt' seemed to be related to technical constraints; notably the construction of the Tabqa dam on the Euphrates basin. According to some estimates, in 1975, around 4,000 Arab families of the Walda tribe, whose own lands had been drowned by the dam, were settled in 41 of the model farms in Upper Jazira (Meyer 1990: 245–278).

In 1967, all mention of Kurds in Syria was erased from school texts (HRW 2009). Meanwhile, the state was proclaimed the Syrian *Arab* Republic, while the constitution of 1973 explicitly stated that 'the people in the Syrian Arab Region are a part of the Arab Nation'.

Political and socio-economic pressures from Damascus were accompanied by inner disputes within Kurdish organisations. Thus, in 1970, the Kurdish Democratic Party of Syria witnessed its first split due to generational and ideological (left/right) differences and, more significantly, paved the way for endless divisions so that by the late 1980s there were no less than ten Kurdish parties for a population of one million people. In reality, the differences in the agendas of the various Kurdish parties were minimal. Most professed Marxist and anti-imperialist ideologies and demanded a certain degree of autonomy as well as equal rights vis-à-vis the Arab majority (Allsopp 2014: 72–98). In the face of pointless ideological disputes, many of which were driven by personal rifts, numerous Kurds left the parties and the latter were condemned to live in a state of political lethargy.

The emergence of Hafiz al-Assad's game

It was within this context that Hafiz al-Assad became interested in the Kurdish nationalist movement in Turkey. The conflict between Turkey and Syria was rooted in the transfer of sovereignty from the Sanjak of Alexandretta in 1939 during the French Mandate to the benefit of Turkey. Besides this territorial dispute, by the late 1970s, the Turkish dams on the Euphrates threatened Syria's water supply (Bullock and Darwish 1993). Henceforth, Hafiz al-Assad allowed the Kurdistan Workers Party (PKK) to establish bases on its territory, from which Kurdish fighters launched military operations against the Turkish army. Thanks to the cooperation of the Assad's regime, northern Syria became a breeding ground for PKK militants during the 1980s and 1990s (McDowall 1998: 65).

The PKK's success can be thus explained, at least to a certain extent, by the complicity of Syrian's regime. However, additional reasons lie behind the engagement of thousands of Kurds in this movement. Firstly, the slogan of a united and independent Kurdistan aroused great sympathy across all social classes in the Syrian Kurdish community in the 1980s. As in Turkey, many Syrian Kurds, whether allied with or opposed to the PKK, acknowledged that the PKK's discourse of the 'new Kurd', which implied renouncing his or her former personality in order to become a 'real Kurd', helped to restore, and even reinvent, Kurdish identity and place the 'new Kurds' on equal footing with Arabs (Grojean 2008). The armed struggle led by the PKK also aroused sympathy because it brought the possibility of real political achievements, in contrast to the clandestine activities of other Syrian Kurdish parties, which rarely bore fruit.

Secondly, the role played by Abdullah Öcalan, the charismatic leader of the PKK, should not be underestimated. To engage with the guerrilla movement increasingly translated into engagement in Öcalan's army, as he imposed himself as the embodiment of a certain political myth, which could only be challenged by another mythical figure, Mustafa Barzani, who was a *post-mortem* national hero. Thirdly, in regions such as Kurd Dagh and Jarablus, the PKK filled a vacuum left by other Kurdish organisations mainly based in Upper Jazira and Damascus. Well organised and supported by the Syrian regime, the PKK's officials created a highly effective network in those areas and managed to accumulate significant financial resources from Kurdish-owned businesses (Allsopp 2014: 137; Tejel 2009: 94).

Finally, certain youngsters from poor areas such as Darbasiyya and Kobane may have seen engagement in the PKK as a potential means of economic and social advancement. On the one hand, the complicity of the Syrian authorities with the PKK allowed organised gangs, trained by the PKK, to control the illegal traffic in drugs and weapons across the border. On the other, belonging to armed bands allowed some young Kurds to emerge as key local players, set apart from the older generations within their communities. Military engagement offered Kurdish youngsters an opportunity to challenge the traditional social order and to renegotiate their status in it.[13]

---

[13] The experience of youngsters' involvement during the First Intifada in the Occupied Territories (1987–1993) presents some similarities in that regard (Larzillière 2004: 18–19).

The alliance between the Syrian government and the PKK was not, however, costless. The relative freedom of action available to PKK representatives led to a revival of Kurdish identity and to the strengthening by proxy of Kurdish nationalism in Syria. The most obvious political consequence of this dynamic was new parties such as Yekitî (Unity) adopting the expression 'Syrian Kurdistan' referring to northern Syria, as opposed to the traditional phrase 'Kurdish regions of Syria'. In addition, this party 'stepped up the visibility of Kurdish protest' by organizing diverse demonstrations and public gatherings despite the regime's ban of such activities (Allsopp 2014: 191).

However, the strategic cooperation between 'minority clients' and 'patron states' also turned out to be extremely risky for the PKK. Threatened by the Turkish-Israeli alliance of 1996 and dependent on water supply from the Euphrates, Syria eventually succumbed to Turkish pressure to withdraw all support for the PKK and expel Abdullah Öcalan from Damascus. In January 1999, Öcalan began a long journey across Europe in a prolonged, and unsuccessful, search for asylum before reaching Kenya where he was arrested and transferred to Turkey. Although his delivery to Turkish jurisdiction raised questions about the international processes to bring alleged transnational fugitive offenders before the courts, Abdullah Öcalan was sentenced to death under Article 125 of the Turkish Penal Code (Gilbert 1999: 565–574). The sentence was, however, commuted to life imprisonment, as Turkey abolished the death penalty in support of its bid to be admitted to membership in the European Union.

New realities, old strategies?

As relations between the new Turkish Prime Minister Recep Tayyip Erdoğan and Bashar al-Assad improved throughout the 2000s, dozens of PKK activists based in Syria were handed over to Turkey and former PKK fighters returning to Syria were given prison sentences ranging from one to ten years. Despite this adverse backdrop, some Syrian PKK members established the PYD in 2003 with the double objective of escaping state repression while maintaining support from its thousands of members and sympathisers. In so doing, the PYD strengthened its position as successor to the PKK, with only Wifaq, a new party established in 2004 following a split within the PYD, as a potential challenger.[14]

Relations between the Syrian regime and the PYD have been ambiguous since then. While Damascus vowed to fight PKK's presence in Syria, Bashar al-Assad never sought to sever completely its channels of communication

---

[14] Kamal Shahin, founder of Wifaq, was murdered in February 2005 by PYD members who were arrested and sentenced in Iraqi Kurdistan. Subsequently, other members of Wifaq were assassinated or subject to murder attempts. As a result, the splinter organisation slowly faded away.

with the PYD. However, relations became strained between 2004-2005, in the aftermath of the Qamishli uprising. The events had begun specifically on 12 March 2004. During a football match between Qamishli and Deir ez-Zor (a traditionally Sunni Arab city), fans from both sides were reported to have begun chanting ethnically charged insults and chants. Inside the stadium, the situation disintegrated into chaos as the two sides battled each other with knives, stones, and sticks. As the riot escalated, the major of Qamishli gave permission for security forces to fire upon the crowds, killing an estimated seven Kurds. (Allsopp 2014: 35)

Rather than stifling the unrest, the killings—exacerbated by the false rumours that three children were among the slain—ignited an unexpected explosion of anger within the Kurdish community. At the funerals of the victims, thousands of mourners and protestors—mainly Kurdish but also Arab and Syrian—joined the procession. Once again, the security forces fired on the crowd, killing five. This time, rumours of a massacre in Qamishli spread across the region. Thousands of Kurdish protesters in Kurdish towns and big cities took to the streets. Within days, the protests became increasingly defiant against the regime, with Kurdish protestors openly flying the Kurdish flag and chanting slogans of Kurdish nationalism. As the violence settled at the end of March, 43 people were dead, some 2,500 were arrested and hundreds were wounded according to official figures, thought the actual numbers may have been much higher (Gauthier 2005: 97–114).

The uprising was significant for the Kurdish movement in Syria in several ways. First, it was a watershed moment in breaking through decades under the regime's tight grip on the Kurdish Syrian political space. For the first time in contemporary Syrian history, the Kurdish masses openly defied the state's red lines on Kurdish cultural and political expressions. The event also raised the profile of the 'Kurdish issue', both inside Syria and in the world. Henceforth, the Kurdish populations including PYD members, largely maintained heightened levels of awareness, mobilisation, and commitment (Allsopp 2014: 29).

However, these new attitudes were not necessarily reflected in the political sphere. Instead, renewed pressure from the regime forced the Kurdish parties to shift activities from the political to the cultural sphere. Subsequently, a growing rift emerged between the larger Kurdish population, increasingly eager for social and political change, and the traditional parties, seen as inept in bringing about genuine change.

As the Syrian uprising erupted in March 2011, Bashar al-Assad allowed PYD leader Salih Muslim Muhammad to return to Syria. More importantly, the PYD avoided taking a clear stance against the regime in the first months of the uprising, as the PKK was under increasing military as well as judicial pressure in Turkey. On 26 October 2011, 'after long negotiations and under the mediation of Masud Barzani, the parties that came out of the historical KDP agreed on the founding of a Kurdish National Council (KNC) in Erbil' (Schmidinger 2018: 88).

Nevertheless, the PYD refused to participate and, more importantly, stayed away from any attempt to associate itself with the Syrian opposition. The partial withdrawal of the Syrian security forces from northern Syria in summer 2012 only served to strengthen PYD's political role, as its militias took over the control of main roads, border crossings, and some administrative services in Afrin, Derik, and other small towns and villages. In sum, thanks to its financial resources, popular support in Kurd Dagh, pre-existing networks, and early establishment of armed militias, the PYD recovered its centrality within the Kurdish arena in Syria.

References

Ababsa, Myriam. 2010. Raqqa, territoires et pratiques sociales d'une ville syrienne. Damascus: IFPO.

Allsopp, Harriet. 2014. The Kurds of Syria. Political parties and identity in the Middle East. New York: I.B. Tauris.

Allsopp, Harriet & Willgenburg, Wladimir van. 2019. The Kurds of Northern Syria. Governance, diversity and conflicts. New York: I.B. Tauris.

Barfi, Barak. 2016. Ascent of the PYD and the SDF. Washington: The Washington Institute for Near East Policy.

Bozarslan, Hamit. 1997. Histoire des relations kurdo-arméniennes. In Hans-Lukas Kieser (ed.), Kurdistan und Europa, Zürich: Chronos, pp. 182–86

Bullock, John & Darwish, Adil. 1993. Water wars, London: Rowland.

Çelik, Adnan. 2018. La contrebande: un défi aux frontières étatiques. Etudes Kurdes 8, pp. 47–78

Fuccaro, Nelida. 2003. Ethnicity and the city: The Kurdish quarter of Damascus between Ottoman and French rule, c. 1724–1946. Urban History 30 (2), pp. 206–224

Gauthier, Julie. 2005. Les événements de Qamichli: irruption de la question kurde en Syrie? Etudes kurdes 7, pp. 97–114

Gilbert, Geoff. 1999. The arrest of Abdullah Öcalan. Leiden Journal of International Law 12 (3), pp. 565–574

Grojean, Olivier. 2008. La production de l'Homme nouveau au sein du PKK. European Journal of Turkish Studies 8. http://ejts.revues.org/2753 (accessed 22 April 2020).

Gunter, Michael M. 2014. Out of Nowhere. The Kurds of Syria in Peace and War. London: Hurst.

Human Rights Watch. 2009. Group Denial: Repression of Kurdish Political and Cultural Rights in Syria. https://www.hrw.org/sites/default/files/reports/syria1109webw cover_0.pdf (accessed 22 April 2020).

Jemo, Mamed. 1990. Osman Sebrî, Apo. Analyse bio-bibliographique. Paris: University of Sorbonne nouvelle.

Lange, Katharina. 2010. Peripheral experiences: Everyday life in Kurd Dagh during the Allied occupation in the Second World War. In Heike Liebau (ed.), The World in World Wars. Perspectives, experiences and perceptions from Asia and Africa, Leiden: Brill, pp. 401–428

Larzillière, Pénélope. 2004. Être jeune en Palestine, Paris: Editions Balland.

Lescot, Roger. 1940/1988. Le Kurd Dagh et le movement Mouroud. Studia Kurdica 1–5, pp. 101–126

Maisel, Sebastian. 2016. Yazidis in Syria: Identity building among a double minority. Lanham: Lexington Books.

McDowall, David. 1998. The Kurds of Syria. London: KHRP.

McGee, Thomas. 2014. The Stateless Kurds of Syria, Tilburg Law Review 19, pp. 171–181

Meyer, Günter. 1990. Rural development and migration in Northeast Syria. In Muneera Salem-Murdock and Michael M. Horowitz (eds.), Anthropology and development in North Africa and the Middle East, Boulder: Westview Press, pp. 245–278

Nouri Pasha, Ihsan. 1986. La révolte de l'Agri-Dagh. Geneva: Editions kurdes.

Savelsberg, Eva. 2014. The Syrian-Kurdish movements: Obstacles rather than driving forces for democratisation. In David Romano and Mehmet Gurses (eds.), Conflict, democratisation, and the Kurds in the Middle East: Turkey, Iran, Iraq and Syria, New York: Palgrave/Macmillan, pp. 85–108

Schmidiger, Thomas. 2018. Rojava: Revolution, war and the future of Syria's Kurds. London: Pluto Press.

Tatchijan, Vahé. 2004. La France en Cilicie et en Haute-Mésopotamie. Aux confins de la Turquie, de la Syrie et de l'Irak. Paris: Karthala.

Tejel, Jordi. 2006. Les constructions de l'identité kurde sous l'influence de la 'connexion kurdo-française' au Levant (1930–1946). European Journal of Turkish Studies 5. https://journals.openedition.org/ejts/751 (accessed 22 April 2020).

——. 2009. Syria's Kurds: History, politics and society. London: Routledge.

——. 2012. Syria's Kurds: Troubled Past, Uncertain Future. Carnegie Endowment for International Peace. https://carnegieendowment.org/2012/10/16/syria-s-kurds-troubled-past-uncertain-future-pub-49703 (accessed 22 April 2020).

——. 2014. The Kurdish cultural movement in Mandatory Syria and Lebanon: An unfinished project of national renaissance, 1932–1946. Iranian Studies 47(5), pp. 839–855

Vanly, Ismet Chérif. 1968. Le problème kurde en Syrie. n.l: Publication du comité pour la defense des droits du peuple kurde.

Velud, Christian. 1991. Une expérience d'administration régionale en Syrie durant le mandat français: conquête, colonisation et mise en valeur de la Gazîra, 1920–1936. Unpublished doctoral thesis, University of Lyon II.

Zaza, Nouredine. 1982. Ma vie de kurde ou le cri du peuple kurde. Lausanne: Favre.

CHAPTER 2

CHRISTIANS IN NORTH SYRIA: SYRIACS, ASSYRIANS, ARMENIANS, AND KURDISH CONVERTS

Thomas Schmidinger

In Efrîn and North and East Syria, Christians of different ethnicities have had a home next to Muslim, Yazidi, and Alevi Kurds. Especially the Jazira region (Kurdish: Cizîre) has one of Syria's largest Christian minorities. The attacks by jihadists and the Turkish army threaten these Christians. Before the war, more than 200,000 Christians lived in the region. However, that number might have dropped to less than 100,000 people, because many Christians became victims of attacks by the so-called Islamic state (IS) in 2014 and 2015 and by the Turkish-led invasion of October 2019. Others fled to Europe in the years of civil war.

While Christian communities of Syro-Aramaic and Armenian origin still live in the Jazira region, the Armenian Christian communities in Efrîn and Kobanê have disappeared. The remaining Christians in these regions are converts who are particularly vulnerable because both the jihadists and the different Islamist militias cooperating with Turkey consider them apostates.

This paper will give an overview of the different Christian ethnic and religious groups in northern Syria, their present social and political situation, and their relationship to the Autonomous Administration of North and East Syria, the Syrian regime, and the Turkish occupation and its Islamist militias.

Christians in the Jazira Region

The Christian minority in North and East Syria represent extremely diverse ethnicities and denominations. Many Christians speak a dialect of the Eastern Aramaic language. Other Christians have descended from Armenian survivors of the Ottoman Genocide of 1915. Furthermore, some Orthodox and evangelical Christians also have Kurdish and Arabic identities.

The Aramaic-speaking Christians identify themselves as Assyrians, Arameans, Chaldeans, or Syriac people and belong to distinct denominations. These different denominations can also have varied ethnic self-perceptions.

The oldest Christian ethnic group in the Jazira region are the Suryoye who traditionally lived north of the Turkish-Syrian border with their main traditional centres in the Mardin Province and the region of the Tur Abdin mountains that includes the eastern half of the Mardin Province with the city of Midyat, and parts of Şırnak Province west of the Tigris river. After the First World War, many of these Christians moved south to the French-administrated parts of the Jazira. This area later became part of independent Syria after the Second World War. Although the Suryoye of the Tur Abdin were not annihilated like the Armenian and Assyrian Christians in 1915, the atrocities against Christians in the late Ottoman empire led to a migration of Suryoye towards regions south of the border, where a significant Suryoye population already lived. Centuries-old churches like the Bara Baita church in the village of Khan Yunis/Birabê near Dêrik demonstrate the continuous presence of Christians in the region. However, after the establishment of the French protectorate, many Suryoye north of the new Turkish-French Mandate border decided to move south to live under French and not Turkish rule. The Suryoye speak Eastern Neo-Aramaic, a language with strong differences to Western Neo-Aramaic, the historic language of Jesus and still spoken today in a version in the villages of Maaloula, Jubb'adin, and Bakh'a in the Anti-Lebanon mountains in western Syria.

The classical version of Eastern Neo-Aramaic, often called Syriac, emerged in the first centuries after Christ in the theological school of Edessa. It has its own alphabet and serves as a ritual language. However, this form of classical Syriac used by religious texts also differs from the currently spoken forms of Eastern Neo-Aramaic. The Jews, Christians, and Mandeans historically spoke different variations of Eastern Neo-Aramaic. Most Jewish variations are disappearing. However, two of the Christian variations are still spoken in North and East Syria. The Suryoye Christians of Tur Abdin and the Jazira region speak the Turoyo dialect. The North-eastern Neo-Aramaic, originally spoken in a region in present day Hakkari (Turkey) and Urmiya (Iran), remains alive with its main dialect Assyrian Neo-Aramaic (also popularly called Assyrian).[1] The Turoyo and Assyrian Neo-Aramaic dialects are clearly distinct but mutually intelligible.

Another version of Eastern Neo-Aramaic was spoken in Qamishli by some Christians who migrated from the villages of Mlaḥsô (Turkish: Yünlüce, Kurdish: Mela) or the village of ʿAnṣa near Lice (Turkey). This form of Eastern Aramaic called Mlaḥsô or Mlahsö is now considered to be extinct.

The region's largest denomination is the *Syriac Orthodox Church*, a very ancient Christian church tracing its history to Saint Peter and Saint Paul and their time in Antioch in the 1st century. The *Syriac Orthodox Church* separated

---

[1] Talay, 2008: 41.

from the church of the Roman Empire[2] due to the Christology controversies in the 5th century. The Syriac Christians were labelled the Monophysites, meaning that they believed that Jesus Christ had only a single nature rather than being both divine and human. The Patriarch of Antioch rules the church. The patriarch moved his seat after the Genocide of 1915 from Antioch to the Cathedral of Saint George in the Christian quartier Bab Tuma in Damascus. North and East Syria has large communities of this church in Qamishil, Derik, Sere Kaniye, and many other towns close to the Turkish border.

In the 17th century, a split in this church resulted in the formation of the *Syriac Catholic Church* as one of the Uniate churches of the *Roman Catholic Church*. Although they have distinctive liturgical rites, they accept the Bishop of Rome, the Roman Catholic Pope, as their superior. The Archeparchy of Hasakah and Nusaybin has 8 parishes and about 5,000 believers. Its leader Archbishop Jacques Behnan Hindo oversees the Syriac Catholic Church of the region.

Another important church in the region, the *Assyrian Church of the East*, also split from the church structure of the Roman Empire during the Christology controversies of the early Christianity. The condemnation of the teachings of Nestorius by the Archbishop of Constantinople during the Council of Ephesus in 431 led to one of the early splits in Christianity.[3] Nestorius taught about two distinct hypostases (the fundamental realities supporting all else) in the Incarnate Christ, one divine and the other human. However, his main rival, Cyril from Alexandria taught that the Incarnate Christ has a single hypostasis, God and man at the same time. In fact, both agreed upon a double nature of Christ in one person. However the main difference was that Nestorius saw these two natures unified in the person (prosopon) while the other theologians saw them unified in the hypostasis.[4] The latter view serves as the basis for Catholic, Orthodox, Protestant, and most Middle Eastern churches. However, the *Assyrian Church of the East* still accepts the idea of Nestorius. Unlike most churches participating in the Council of Ephesus in 431, the *Assyrian Church of the East* did not condemn Nestorius. However, they also refuse the term Nestorians used by other Christians to accuse them of following Nestorius.

The *Assyrian Church of the East* became for political reasons the major church of the Persian Empire and proselytised large parts of central Asia including China and Kerala in southern India. Most people in these regions

---

[2] The church of the Roman Empire developed into the present-day Orthodox churches of the Patriarchate of Constantinople, the Roman Catholic Church and the churches of the Reformation.

[3] Baumer, 2006: 46f.

[4] Ibid.: 51.

eventually converted to Buddhism and Islam. However, members of this church remained in Hakkari in present day Turkey until the genocide committed by the 'Young Turks' in 1915 killed and drove them out of that region. After resettlement in Iraq, they became victims in 1933 of the Semele massacre by the new Iraqi army that killed up to 3,000 Assyrians from 64 villages[5] between Dohuk and Mosul.[6] About 30,000 survivors fled once more to the French protectorate Syria where they established the towns of Hasaka and Tell Tamer and some villages on the Khabur river. They became an important part of the population of the region. However, many of them left when the so-called Islamic state attacked their villages in spring 2015. These Assyrians also speak the second Aramaic language of the region, the Assyrian Neo-Aramaic.

In 1968, the *Assyrian Church* split into two factions. The official conflict concerned the calendar reform implemented by Patriarch Shimun XXIII and the change to the Gregorian calendar used by the Western Christians. However, the division also had political backgrounds related to developments in Iraq. The Baath regime in Baghdad supported the *Ancient Church of the East*, which adhered to the old calendar, and the Patriarch of the *Assyrian Church of the East* left for exile in Chicago. Most Assyrians in Syria took the side of the *Assyrian Church of the East*, which was led from Chicago until 2015 and which also has a bishop residing in al-Hasaka, Bishop Aprim Athniel, ordained on 3 October 1999. Bishop Aprim Athniel, who comes from al-Hasaka, had responsibility for Syria. Some Assyrian villages in Syria, however, also sided with those who refused to accept the Western calendar and today belong to the *Ancient Church of the East*.

Also, the *Assyrian Church of the East* has a Uniate Catholic branch called the *Chaldean Church* that today is the largest church in Iraq and has some parishes in the cities of North and East Syria. They belong to the Chaldean Catholic Eparchy of Aleppo that had about 30,000 believers before the war. Less than 10,000 of them live in the region of North and East Syria today.

Another large group of Christians, the Armenians speak Western Armenian, the language of the Armenians in the Ottoman Empire. Armenian parishes still exist in Tal Abyad, Sere Kaniyê, Hasaka, Qamishli, and Derik. Some of these parishes operate their own schools in the Armenian language. Many of the Armenians remember their ancestors' stories of deportation by the Ottoman government in 1915, when 1.5 million Armenians perished in the genocide by the 'Young Turks'. Therefore, many Armenians viewed the attacks of Turkey in spring 2018 and fall 2019 as a continuation of the genocide of 1915. Most Armenians in North and East Syria belong to the

---

[5] Shairzid, 2004: 206.
[6] Schmidinger, 2019a: 115.

Armenian Apostolic Church. However, Qamishli has a parish of the *Armenian Catholic Church* as well. The Armenian Apostolic community of Tal Abyad fled when the so-called Islamic State took over the city in 2014 and returned after liberation by the Kurdish YPG in 2015. In October 2019, the Armenian consulate in Aleppo helped with a second evacuation.

Other Christian denominations include parishes of the *Greek Orthodox Church of Antioch* belonging to the Orthodox Church under the Ecumenical Patriarch of Constantinople and its Catholic splinter group, the *Melkite Greek Catholic Church*, as well as some evangelical churches largely made up of Kurdish and Arab converts. These evangelicals, as former Muslims who became Christians, face great danger from jihadist attacks.

Thus, the Christians in the Jazira region consist of indigenous Christians and descendants of refugees from Turkey and Iraq who came to the Jazira at about the same time some of the Kurdish tribes came from Turkey.

During the French mandate period, much of the urban population in the Jaziri region was Christian. In 1926, Assyrian- and Aramaic-speaking Christians created the town of Qamishli directly on the Syrian side of the Turkish border close to Nusaybin. In the following years, about two thirds of the population of Nusaybin resettled in Qamishli, which soon became more populous than the old Nusaybin. The whole Christian population as well as many of the Kurds moved into the town.[7]

The Christians who came from Turkey in the 1920s 'made up the backbone of the population of the small towns constructed under the Mandate after 1922. The essentially urban Christian immigrants became active in commerce, in craft industries, or employed in the local military auxiliary units.'[8]

In the 1930s, the Christians of the Jazira region allied with the Kurds in their quest for an autonomous Jazira region. Christians united with the *Roman Catholic church* and much of the Kurdish elite supported this movement for autonomy. The most important protagonists of the autonomy movement included the Syriac Catholic Archbishop of Aleppo and Patriarch of Antioch, Ignatius Gabriel I. Tappouni, and his vicar general for the Jazira, Msgr. Hanna Hebbé, as well as Michel Dôme, the Armenian-Catholic mayor of Qamishli.[9] The autonomy movement did not succeed and the region became part of the centralised Syrian state after the Second World War.

With the beginning of the civil war in Syria, many Christians started to

---

[7] Schmidinger, 2018a: 44.
[8] Velud: 72.
[9] Schmidinger, 2018a: 45.

emigrate from the region. Despite their gain of new cultural and linguistic liberties in the autonomous cantons created by the Kurds in 2012, many Christians felt threatened by the new jihadist militias. Especially the Christians in Sere Kaniyê (Arabic: Ras al-Ain), a city established by Chechen refugees from the Caucasus in 1878 came under fire of the jihadist Jabhat al-Nusra in the first battle of Sere Kaniyê between January and July 2013. In early 2015, the so-called Islamic State attacked the Assyrian villages at Khabur river near Tal Tamar. On 23 February 2015, after launching a large offensive against the Assyrian villages at Khabur river, the IS abducted 150 Assyrians from the villages in that region.

With the Turkish invasion against Tal Abyad and Sere Kaniyê (Arabic: Ras al-Ain) in October 2019, all Christians from these towns fled to the remaining territory still controlled by the Syrian Democratic Forces. That means that the Armenian-Apostolic communities of Tal Abyad and Sere Kaniyê do not exist anymore. Also, the Syrian Orthodox and other Aramaic Christian communities in Sere Kaniyê have been erased. The Christians from these towns live today either as displaced persons within the remaining territory of the Autonomous Administration of North and East Syria or they fled to regime-held territories like the cities of Aleppo or Damascus or they fled abroad. Some now live in Europe, some of the Armenians fled to the Republic of Armenia.

Assyrian Cathedral of Our Lady, the episcopal see of the Bishop of whole Syria of the Assyrian Church of the East in Hasaka.

The Syriac Catholic Church in Sere Kaniyê/Ras al-Ain was one of three churches in this town that were in use until the Christians had to flee because of the Turkish attacks in 2019.

Armenian Apostolic (right) and Syriac Orthodox Church (left in the background) in Dêrik.

Chaldean Church in in Dêrik with Christmas decoration.

Bara Baita Church in Khan Yunis/Birabê near Dêrik ist the oldest church in Northern and Eastern Syria that is still in use.

Christians from Afrin published a Youtube-Video with their Pastor Diyar calling for help against the Turkish invasion in 2018.

Christians in Efrîn

In the most western part of the Kurdish inhabited territory of Syria, Efrîn, Christianity emerged at the same time historically as in the Jazira region. However, other than migrants to the Jazira region, the older Christian communities have no link to contemporary Christians in Efrîn.

Early Christian ruins indicate that the region of Efrîn formed part of the core lands of early Christianity. The most important ruin is probably the Qal'at Sim'ān, a large Byzantine monastery where, according to legend, Symeon Stylites the Elder (389–459) lived atop a pillar for several decades. From the beginning of the Syrian civil war until 2018, these ruins have been at the frontline between the YPG/YPJ and the Islamist rebel organisations. Today's city of Cindirês had a Christian diocese at the time of the First Council of Nicaea in 325.

The mystical monk Maron, revered as the founding father of the Maronite branch of the Roman-Catholic Churches, retreated to the Taurus Mountains near the ancient town of Cyrrhus in the north of Efrîn, where Muslims venerate the tomb of the prophet Huri. Until the start of the civil war, Maronite Christians from the Lebanon made the pilgrimage to the Tomb of Maron near the village Beradê (Arabic: Brad) in the south of the region of Efrîn..

In the years before the civil war, the Maronites constructed a small new church and placed, in 2010, a statue of St. Maron from Lebanon. However, the church only served Maronite pilgrims, since there has not been any Maronite community here for quite a while. The early Christian communities of the region have no continuity with later Christian communities. Under Islamic rule, the early Christians, who spoke Greek and Aramaic, may have migrated to the larger cities or converted to Islam. However, no detailed records exist about any of this.

Survivors of the genocide against the Armenians in 1915 settled in Efrîn and founded an Armenian-Apostolic church and an Armenian school. Most of the small community emigrated to the U.S., Armenia, or Aleppo in the second half of the 1960s.

In 2018, the editor of the Armenian newspaper *Kantsasar* published in Aleppo, Zarmig Chilaposhyan-Poghigian, claimed that three Armenian families still lived in Efrîn. One of the last Armenians of Efrîn died during the battle of Efrîn at the end of February 2018.[10]

However, the decline of the Armenian community did not mean that Christianity has disappeared from Efrîn. In 2012, an evangelical missionary moved from Aleppo to Efrîn and established a new evangelical church called *Church of the Good Shepherd* (*Şivanê Qanç*) made up of Kurdish converts. The secular atmosphere of Efrîn allowed conversions from Islam to Christianity. By 2018, this Kurdish Christian community had increased to three hundred families. Apart from the city of Efrîn, much smaller churches also developed in the small towns of Cindirês and Reco. However, most Christians of the region of Efrîn live in the city of Efrîn. Following the Turkish invasion of the region, members of the Christian communities of Cindirês and Reco fled to the city of Efrîn. Their church buildings may not have survived the Turkish army's bombardment that did severe damage, particularly in the city centre of Cindirês. Most Christians from these two communities found a provisional haven in the Church of Efrîn, until they had to flee once more following the conquest of Efrîn.[11]

While converts face severe problems in many Islamic communities, conversion to Christianity did not create problems in secular Efrîn. The conversions to Christianity since 2015 seems partially due to reacting against the jihadist militias, particularly the IS, but probably also represents a form of 'cultural conversion'. The middle and upper strata of society particularly want to 'Europeanise,' to try standing apart from their Islamic surroundings. They frequently see Christianity as 'modern' and 'secular,' while they regard Islam as 'backward' and 'fanatical.' These perceptions of both the self and

---

[10] http://asbarez.com/170050/armenian-man-killed-by-turkish-shelling-in-afrin/
[11] Schmidinger 2018b: 29.

other seem to play an important role in the conversion to Christianity. These Kurds do not convert to one of the traditional Syrian Churches but to an actively proselytizing evangelical church community under the charismatic Kurdish pastor Diyar. Pastor Diyar spoke out against the Turkish attacks on Efrîn several times and expressed his fear that a Turkish victory could prove particularly dangerous for Christians in Efrîn. 'If these gangs enter Efrîn, before all, they will kill Christians,' a Kurdish news agency quoted him saying in early February 2018.

A year after the Turkish invasion, I met Pastor Diyar in the evangelical church in Kobanê where he started to preach after the fall of Efrîn. He told me that most members of his community found refuge in one of the IDP camps in the Shehba region around Tal Rifaat. The community continues to conduct religious services in a tent in these camps.[12] He also showed me WhatsApp messages of remaining Christians inside Efrîn, who told him about their daily dread of being recognised as Christians. They wrote him that they live in fear and try to hide their religious identity.

Evangelicals in Kobanê

The evangelical church in Kobanê, where the pastor from Efrîn is active now, was established at the end of 2015 after the liberation of Kobanê from the so-called 'Islamic State' under the name of the *Brother Church* (*Kenîseya Biratiyê li Kobanê*). Contrary to some reports in international media (for example, a Christian Orthodox news site reported on the newly opened church in September 2018,[13] NBC in February 2019, and Newsweek in April 2019[14]), the church had been established since 2015. In the more conservative Kobanê, the Kurdish self-government immediately accepted the Christian church, but society was not as welcoming as in the much more liberal and secular Efrîn. The church leadership in Kobanê, unlike in Efrîn, argues that some believers had Christian ancestors and now they found their way back to Christianity after these ancestors were forced to become Muslims. In fact, two of the forty-five member-families descend from Armenian Christians forced to convert to Islam in the context of the 1915 genocide.[15] The relatively small church community received support from Christian refugees from Efrîn in 2018. The services take place every Friday and Tuesday in Kurdish and Arabic. However, the Christians of Kobanê also perceive a constant threat of an invasion of Turkey into the remaining Kurdish areas. At the same time, the former pastor of the Church of Efrîn, now preaching

---

[12] Interview with Pastor Diyar, 12 January 2019.
[13] http://theorthodoxchurch.info/blog/news/brethren-christian-community-opens-first-congregation-in-kobane-aleppo/
[14] https://www.nbcnews.com/news/world/life-under-isis-led-these-muslims-christ-n963281
[15] Schmidinger 2019b: 202.

in Kobanê, realises that the Turkish regime's Islamic orientation increases the attractiveness of Christianity among the Kurds:

> If Turkey invaded Kobanê, Christians would do the same thing here as in Efrîn. Then there would be no more Christians here. This also applies to the many Christians in Qamişlo. Ultimately, the cruelty of the Islamist militias and the hatred preached by pro-Turkish Muslims are also one of the reasons why the Kurds are now interested in Christianity. Turkey also harasses the pastors in Turkey who preach the message to the Kurds. They put secret service agents in the parishes and harass the pastors. Recently a pastor named Muhammed had to flee from Turkey to Belgium. However, Rojava has religious freedom. We can live and preach freely here and when Erdoğan sees this, he loses his temper because he doesn't want the Kurds to learn about Christianity.[16]

The authoritarian state-Islam of the Turkish AKP regime poses a real threat but also presents an important argument for the Christian mission. With a conversion to Christianity, one also declares a religious and cultural distinct from Turkey and its president Erdoğan and additionally emphasises a westward orientation.

Another reason for converting to Christianity, closely linked to the idea of a westward orientation, is a kind of 'back-to-the-roots' trend in parts of the community. Kobanê once had an Armenian Christian community of survivors of the Genocide of 1915 much bigger than the one in Efrîn. In 1915, around 15,000 Armenians from Sivas were deported to a camp near Kobanê.

Three Armenian churches existed in Kobanê until the 1960s. Two Armenian schools existed in the 1950s. In the school year 1958/59, 253 pupils attended the schools employing 15 teachers.[17] In the politically troubled 1960s with the boom of Arab nationalism in Syria, most emigrated to the Armenian Soviet Socialist Republic. The Avedis Sarafian School, the last Armenian school in the city, finally closed its doors in 1975.[18] When the Syrian civil war began in 2012 and the so-called 'Islamic State' attacked the Kurdish enclave in September 2014, only a few Armenians still lived in the city and none had a Christian community. However, some Christians that established the evangelical Church at the end of 2015 had Armenian ancestors and argued that they did not convert to Christianity, but rather

---

[16] Interview with Pastor Diyar, 12 January 2019.
[17] Migliorino 2008: 120.
[18] Schmidinger 2015: 148.

'returned' to their true religion.[19]

Christian policemen of the Sutoro in Dêrik.

Memorial of the Armenian Genocide in the courtyard of the Armenian Apostolic Church in Qamishli.

---

[19] Interview with a woman of the church leadership, 12 January 2019.

Ishow Gowriye, the leader of the Syriac Union Party, in his office in Qamishli.

Political affiliations of Christians in North and East Syria

The Baath regime always manipulated religious identities to enforce its rule over Syria. The regime used fears of Sunni-Muslim dominance to gain support from religious minorities such as Alawis, Druze, Ismailis, and Christians. Christians accepting the rule of the Baath Party and their Arabic-nationalist doctrine had a relatively comfortable life in the secular dictatorship of the Syrian Arab Republic. At the same time, the church hierarchies carefully excluded from higher positions those clerics inclined to oppose the Baath regime. Until now the hierarchy of most Christian churches in Syria remain very loyal towards the regime of Bashar al-Assad. The opposition's Islamisation even strengthened many Christians' support for the regime.

However, loyalty towards the Arabic-nationalist regime meant identifying as an Arab Christian and denying a different ethnic background. The regime could soon cause trouble for groups who insisted on an ethnic identity other than Arab or in an official role of languages other than Arabic.

At the beginning of October 2005, in opposition to the ruling Baath-Party, progressive supporters of a Syriac identity established the Syriac Union Party in Syria (Syriac: ܓܒܐ ܕܚܘܝܕܐ ܣܘܪܝܝܐ, Gabo d'Ḥuyodo Suryoyo). The Syriac Union Party comes from the Syrian branch of the so-called Dawronoye movement, a left-wing Syriac political movement with origins in the 1980s in the Syriac town of Midyat in Turkey. The Dawronoye movement has an ideology based on left-wing secular nationalism. Sister organisations exist in Turkey, Iraq, and Europe.

When public protests began against the regime, the party, led by Ishow Gowriye, joined forces with the Kurdish Democratic Union Party (Partiya Yekîtiya Demokrat, PYD). After the withdrawal of the Syrian army from the Kurdish areas in summer 2012, the Syriac Union Party became the main Christian ally of the PYD. Similar to the PYD, it established military forces, the Syriac Military Council and a Christian police force called Sutoro. However the party was not only active in the Jazira, but also in territories still controlled by the regime where the party participated in the civilian protests, but could never act freely and open official offices as it did in the areas of the Autonomous Administration. The party has a strong commitment for the project of the Autonomous Administration and sees itself as the main representative of all Aramaic-speaking Christians in the region. It considers all these Christians with different denominations and different varieties of eastern Aramaic languages as a single unified ethnic group and considers a Turkish invasion as the biggest threat for the future existence of Christians in the region.[20]

The Assyrian Democratic Party (Syriac: ܓܒܐ ܐܬܘܪܝܐ ܕܡܩܪܛܝܐ, Gabā Aṯurāyā Demoqraṭāyā) as an ethnic party of the Assyrians from the *Assyrian Church of the East* had already been established in 1978. Unlike the Syriac

---

[20] Interview with Ishow Gowriye, 8 February 2020.

Union Party, the Assyrian Democratic Party always had a strict confessional understanding about their own ethnic identity. They considered real Assyrians as only their church members who speak their specific form of Aramaic. Thus, they only seek to represent this particular group. Party president, Ninos Isho, wants a recognition of the Assyrians as an indigenous people of Syria by the Syrian constitution.[21] In the 1990s, the party had a relatively good relationship with the ruling Baath-Party. However, when the regime could not protect the Assyrian villages and towns on the Khabur river from jihadist attacks of 'IS', the party and their affiliated armed groups, the Assyrian People's Guard–Nattoreh and later the Khabour Guards, searched for new allies and found them in the PYD and the Kurdish armed forces and the People's Protection Units (YPG) and the Women's Protection Units (YPJ).

Today both parties belong to the Autonomous Administration of North and East Syria and united their forces in fall 2019. Although both parties represent a large part of the Aramaic-speaking Christians in the northern and eastern fractions, many clerics, who generally still support the government in Damascus, do not approve of the parties' support for the Autonomous Administration.

The Syriac Union Party has three representatives and the Assyrian Democratic Party has one representative among the forty-three representatives constituting the Syrian Democratic Council, a kind of proto-parliament of a future Syria established in 2015 and supported by the Syrian Democratic Forces.

Another party, also known as Mtakasta, the Assyrian Democratic Organization (Syriac: ܬܢܛܝܡܐ ܐܬܘܪܝܬܐ ܡܬܟܣܬܐ), was established already in 1957 and led by Gabriel Moushe Gawrieh. Unlike the Syriac Union Party and the Assyrian Democratic Party, the Assyrian Democratic Organisation does not belong to the Autonomous Administration of North and East Syria. In October 2011, it became a part of the Syrian National Council that serves as an umbrella organisation of the predominantly pro-Turkish Arab and Islamic opposition. Because the Assyrian Democratic Organisation never recognised the Autonomous Administration, it also never asked for the permission to open offices. Therefore, the authorities of the Autonomous Administration then closed two offices of the party in Qamishli and Dêrik in March 2017. Although the Assyrian Democratic Organisation cooperated with the pro-Turkish opposition and not with the Autonomous Administration, it became increasingly critical of Turkey when Turkey invaded Syrian territory with the help of Islamist militias. During the Turkish

---

[21] Interview with Ninos Isho, 11 February 2020.

invasion in October 2019, it announced that it 'strongly condemns the Turkish incursion into Syria, in which, wouldn't have taken place without a green light from the US President who disavows the responsibility and commitments promised earlier, as well as, implication of other countries in the Syrian conflict that serve its own interest that are contrary to interest of the Syrian people.'[22] It also announced a renewed 'call to the Autonomous Administration and PYD to review and reconsider their political position and experience to include or widen the participation of all segments of the people of Al Jazira to further serve their interests in peace, freedom, and democracy.'[23]

Christian military forces

As previously mentioned, both parties participating in the Autonomous Administration of North and East Syria have established their own militias, the Syriac Military Council and the Assyrian People's Guard–Nattoreh led by Robert Ichou. Another Assyrian militia, called Khabour Guards, formed in the Khabour valley. While the Syriac Military Council participated as a founding member of the Syrian Democratic Forces (SDF) in 2015, the Khabour Guards and Nattoreh only joined in early 2017.

The Khabour Guards first tried to be an independent militia of local Assyrians but could not defend themselves against the jihadist Islamic State; therefore, they accepted support by the Syriac Military Council and the Syriac Union Party. On the evening of 21 April 2015, some group abducted, blindfolded, shot and left for dead David Gindo and Elias Nasser, two leading Khabour Guard commanders. Elias Nasser managed to survive and crawled to a main road where someone picked him up and took him to a hospital in Qamishli. Although this appeared to be an assassination attempt by IS, Nasser later accused the Kurdish YPG for the attack.[24] A Kurdish court convicted four YPG fighters for assassinating David Gindo and the assassination attempt on Elias Nasser in July 2015. Two of the perpetrators received a twenty-year sentence while one received a four-year and the other a one -year sentence. Nevertheless, the relationship between the Khabour Guards and the YPG and the SUP worsened, and the Khabour Guards instead allied themselves with the Assyrian Democratic Party

In April 2017, YPG forces completely handed over the Khabour valley to Khabour Guards and Nattoreh. In 2018, Nattoreh joined the Khabour Guards. On 6 July 2019, the Syriac Military Council and Khabour Guards announced the formation of a joint Syriac-Assyrian Military Council.[25]

---

[22] http://aina.org/news/20191010182817.htm
[23] Ibid.
[24] http://www.aina.org/news/20150522205619.htm
[25] https://www.youtube.com/watch?v=A-RDapHwhG8

However, on the ground, militia still use the term and symbols of the Khabour Guards.

Like the YPG, the Syriac-Assyrian Military Council also has a female branch, the Bethnahrain Women's Protection Forces, set up in September 2015. The Bethnahrain Women's Protection Forces has only one military base with about hundred fighters and has more political than military significance. Like the Kurdish Women's Protection Units YPJ, they see themselves as a protector of women and the movement's feminist positions.

Inside the SDF, an Armenian militia called Martyr Nubar Ozanyan Brigade (Armenian: Նահատակ Նուպար Օզանեան Գումարտակ) was established on 24 April 2019. The small brigade with less than 100 fighters is named after Nubar Ozanyan, an Armenian Marxist-Leninist revolutionary from present day Turkey, who was commander of the Army of the Workers and Peasants of Turkey (TİKKO), the armed wing of the Communist Party of Turkey/Marxist-Leninist (TKP-ML). Nubar Ozanyan was killed in action during the 2017 battle of Raqqa against the IS. The brigade was founded on the very symbolic date of 24 April, the Armenian Genocide Remembrance Day, when all Armenians except Armenians in Turkey commemorate their victims of the Genocide of 1915. Unlike the much larger Syriac-Assyrian Military Council, the Martyr Nubar Ozanyan Brigade led by Masis Mutanyan has more political than military importance.

Besides these Christian military forces affiliated with the SDF, some Christian forces have affiliated with the Syrian regime. The Gozarto Protection Forces (GPF) is stationed in Qamishli and is part of the pro-government National Defence Forces (NDF).[26] This militia fought with the Kurdish YPG in the city of Qamilshli in 2016.

Kurdish Autonomous Administration and Christian minorities

Already with the establishment of the first political structures of what became the Autonomous Administration of North and East Syria, the leading Kurdish political actors tried to include minorities into their new political system. The core of the new ideology of Abdulla Öcalan and his followers since about 2003 involves the idea of 'democratic confederalism', a territorial and decentralised autonomy and not ethnic nationalism. For ideological, but also for practical reasons, the region's autonomous structures tried to include minorities of all kinds into their new political system. The 'Social Contract of the Democratic Federation of Northern Syria' serves as the de facto constitution of the Autonomous Administrations was accepted in 29 December 2016 declares: 'We, peoples of Rojava-northern Syria, including

---

[26] Allsopp/Wilgenburg, 2019: 67.

Kurds, Arabs, Syriacs, Assyrians, Turkmen, Armenians, Chechens, Circassians, Muslims, Christians, Yezidis, and the different doctrines and sects, recognise that the nation-state [...] has brought problems, serious crises, and agonies for our peoples.'[27]

The Jazira's large Aramaic-speaking Christian minorities and its Armenian minorities were especially seen as a constitutive people of the autonomous cantons established in January 2014. Along with Kurdish, the Syriac variety of Aramaic became a de facto official language in the Jazira. All administrative buildings in the Jazira have trilingual inscriptions in Kurdish, Arabic, and Syriac. Even Jazira's vehicles have trilingual licence plates. However, the Armenian language does not have a similar status and further to the west, where no Christians with Syriac as their native language live, Syriac is not used as an official language. Kobanê and Efrîn were bilingual and not trilingual. Now, wherever Syriac Christians live, the public sphere includes their language the same as Kurdish and Arabic.

In autumn 2018, the alliance between Christians and Kurds faced tests. The Syriac Union Party wanted to change the curricula of Christian schools: All subjects should be taught in Syriac and the excessively pro-Assad content should be removed. High-ranking clerics opposed this change as did their church leaders in Damascus. Finally, many parents of Christian students protested the decision of the Autonomous Administration to change these curricula. Assyrians in Europe and the US accused the Autonomous Administration of seeking to 'kurdify' the Christian schools. However, the different Christian group resolved the conflict between the many parents sought official governmental certificates that could help their children's later studies at the universities and the Christian political parties that wanted to change the curricula. The conflict finally ended in a compromise. Most schools continued to teach the official Syrian state-curricula but added a few hours of Syriac-Aramean language. However, Christians close to the Assad regime used the issue to denounce the Kurds and the Autonomous Administration as authoritarian and against Christians.

A future for the Christians in North and East Syria?

Many Christians in North and East Syria have left the country since 2011. The displaced Christians from the Turkish-occupied territories Efrîn, Tal Abyad and Serê Kaniyê increasingly try to leave Syria. The remaining community is politically split between more pro-regime clerics and the Gozarto Protection Forces, on one side, and the supporters of the Syrian Democratic Forces and the Autonomous Administration, on the other side. During my travels to the region, all Christians I talked with told me that they

---

[27] https://mesopotamia.coop/social-contract-of-the-democratic-federation-of-northern-syria/

fear Turkey and the Turkish allies as much as the jihadists. Most Christians could come to an understanding with the Assad regime or the Autonomous Administration set up by the Kurds. Regime supporters may say their pro-regime opinion freely in the territory controlled by the Syrian Democratic Forces. On the other side, Christians who support the Autonomous Administration say that they would also stay if the regime would take over and that they would prefer the Assad regime over Turkey or the jihadists.

A future for Christians in this region is only imaginable with continued governance of the Autonomous Administration or a return of the central regime, but not if Turkey and its allies would take over the remaining territories in northern Syria. Also, a return of at least some Christians to Serê Kaniyê, Tal Abyad, or Efrîn could only happen if the Turkish troops and their allied militias would leave these regions.

References

Allsopp, H. and van Wilgenburg, W. (2019). *The Kurds of Northern Syria. Governance, Diverstiy and Conflicts*. London/New York City: I.B. Tauris.

Baumer, C. (2006) *The Church of the East: An Illustrated History of Assyrian Christianity*. London/New York City: I.B. Tauris.

Migliorino, N. (2008) *(Re)Constructing Armenia in Lebanon and Syria. Ethno-Cultural diversity and the state in the aftermath of a refugee crisis*. New York City: Berghahn.

Schmidinger, T. (2015). Westarmenien in Kurdistan: Überleben und Exil armenischer Gemeinden hundert Jahre nach dem Genozid. In: Hennerbichler, F., Osztovics, C., Six-Hohenbalken, M.A., Schmidinger, T. *Wiener Jahrbuch für Kurdische Studien 2015, Bd. 3: 100 Jahre Völkermord an ArmenierInnen und die KurdInnen. Komplexe Vergangenheit und Nachwirken in der der Gegenwart*. Wien: Caeserpress. pp. 137-184.

Schmidinger, T. (2018a). *Kampf um den Berg der Kurden. Geschichte und Gegenwart der Region Afrin*. Wien: Bahoe books

Schmidinger, T. (2018b). *Rojava. Revolution, War, and the Future of Syria´s Kurds*. London: Pluto Press.

Schmidinger, T. (2019a). Christians in Iraq. In: Sevdeen, Bayar Mustafa/Schmidinger, Thomas: *Beyond ISIS. History and Future of Minorities in Iraq*. London: Transionational Press. pp. 113-124.

Schmidinger, T. (2019b). Mission und Migration: Kurdische ChristInnen im 20. und 21. Jahrhundert. In: Schmidinger, T., Brizić, K., Grond, A., Osztovics, C., Six-Hohenbalken, M.A., *Wiener Jahrbuch für Kurdische Studien 2019*, Bd. 7: Religion in Kurdistan. Wien: Praesens Verlag. pp. 131-156.

Shairzid, T. (2004). Von Semele bis zur Anfal-Kampagne. Verfolgung und Widerstand der Assyrerinnen und Assyrer. In: Kreutzer, M., Schmidinger, T., *Irak. Von der Republik der Angst zur bürgerlichen Demokratie?* Freiburg im Breisgau: Ça ira Verlag. pp. 207-207.

Talay, S. (2008). *Die neuaramäischen Dialekte der Khabur-Assyrer in Nordostsyrien*. Wiesbaden: Harrassowitz.

Velud, C. (2000). French Mandate policy in the Syrian steppe. In: Mundy, M./Musallam, B. (Eds.), *The Transformation of Nomadic Society in the Arab East*. Cambridge: Cambridge University Press. pp. 63-81

CHAPTER 3

YEZIDIS IN SYRIA

Sebastian Maisel

Introduction

Yezidis, a Kurdish-speaking ethno-religious community, have historically lived in northern Mesopotamia stretching from Aleppo to Mosul. Today, they mainly live in northern Iraq. Smaller groups are found in Armenia, Germany, Syria, and Georgia. The community's religious centre is Lalish in the Sheikhan District west of Mosul, Iraq. The leaders of the Yezidis, Mir Tahsin Beg and the religious authority of the Baba Sheikh Ba'dhra, reside in a small town close to Lalish. Other significant religious sites such as temples, shrines, and centres of religious learning had been established in Efrîn (Syria), Achnalik (Armenia) and Tbilisi (Georgia). This chapter gives an overview of the Yezidi community in Syria, its origins, history, and current situation.[1]

Over the last decades, and especially since the turn of the millennium, all Yezidis have experienced dramatic political, cultural, and social changes in their historical settlements. Uniquely local circumstances shaped these changes; the Yezidis, as a group, did not experience much simultaneous and unilateral development. However, we have limited knowledge about these transformation processes in the various regions, because scholars have just begun to collect, process, and analyse information. Their research struggle with the general conditions of insecurity, war, and displacement that make general assessments difficult. Instead, this paper focuses on local and regional developments. A report on the religious customs of the Yezidis in Armenia could vary significantly from those of western Syria or the Sheikhan region. Only a small part of Yezidi dogma and rituals applies to the whole community. Usually, an individual's Yezidi identity is shaped by regional traditions and practices.

Most Yezidis consider themselves ethnic Kurds. Thus, when looking at historical processes among the Yezidis in Syria, one should also study the history and transformation of the Kurdish community. As part of the estimated 30 million Kurds, the 500,000 Yezidis live in the larger area of

---

[1] Parts of this paper come from the author´s book *Yezidis in Syria: Identity Building among a Double Minority*, Lexington Books, 2017.

Kurdistan, where they face similar conditions as non-Yezidis Kurds. Because of ethnic and political tensions, the number of Kurds living in Syria cannot be determined exactly. Estimates range between eight and fifteen percent of the total Syrian population of 20 million. The Kurds of Syria live in three separate areas, the region northwest of Aleppo, the Syrian Cizîrê (the provinces of Heseke and Qamişlo), and the urban centres of the country, Damascus, Aleppo, Homs, and Hamah. In addition, a large diaspora of Syrian Kurds live in Lebanon and Europe.

Probably less than 15,000 Yezidis live in Syria, making them one of the country's smallest minority groups. This small number of Yezidis, like the division of their living area, negatively affects their position in the Syrian minority context. Due to the arbitrary drawing of political borders after the First World War and the Mandate Administration's territorial swaps between Syria and Turkey, the Yezidis in Syria live in two isolated areas cut off from their community's religious centres in northern Iraq.

Some Yezidis live in an area west and northwest of Aleppo in Jabal al-Akrād, Kurdagh, or simply Efrîn. Geographically, the area connects to the region around Kilis, where Yezidis used to live, which initially belonged to Syria, but was ceded to Turkey in 1921.

The Yezidis in this area, Efrîn, live in a predominantly Muslim environment. Along with some Druzes, they are the only religious minority in the area. Because most of the population is Kurdish; the ethnic separation does not apply. The Yezidi villages within the area are spread over three enclaves: 1) Şikak with the villages of Qestel Cindo, Baftun, Qitmê, Sinka; 2) Cûmî with the villages of Feqîra, Ghezewiye, Qîbar, Turunde, Şadêrê, Çeqelê Cûmê, Iska, Endara, Ashq Sherqi, Keferzet, and 3) Şêrew with the villages of Basûfanê, Kimar, Gunde Mezin. In addition, Yezidi families live in the larger towns and cities, Efrîn, Ezaz, and Aleppo. Until recently, about 1,000 families lived in Efrîn. If a Yezidi family usually consists of five to seven members, this would suggest a total number of approximately 5,000 Yezidis in northwest Syria.

The second area for Yezidis in Syria is the Cizîrê Region and near the two administrative centres, Heseke and Qamişlo. Yezidi communities live in three small enclaves consisting of several villages: 1) Wadi al-Jarrah northwest of Qamişlo around Tirbespî (formerly known as Qubur Bid, or Qahtaniya) with the main villages of Otilje, Drecik, and Tell Khatun; 2) the area between Amûdê and Heseke with some 20 villages, and 3) near the city of Serê Kaniyê along the Khabur with 15 villages including Asadiye, Cava, or Mereykis. Some Yezidi families moved to the urban centres of the region which brings the total estimate of Yezidis in this area to approximately 5,000 individuals.

Finally, isolated Yezidi families reside in the large Syrian cities, Damascus, Aleppo, Homs, or Hamah.

Again, before the civil war, an estimated 15,000 Yezidis lived in Syria. Displacement and migration led to a sharp decline, which leaves around 5,000 Yezidis in Syria and approximately 15,000-20,000 abroad.

Most Syrian Yezidis work in the agricultural sector as farmers, pastoralists, or day laborers. In the towns and cities, others work in the service sector, restaurants, shops, and trade. In a very few cases, some Yezidis could enter public secular institutions such as the administration, military, or education sector.

Before the war, the location, either Efrîn or Cizîrê, was important in determining the position of individuals and the community in the social and economic hierarchy. The Yezidis in the Cizîrê had a significantly different status from those in Efrîn. Yezidis in the Cizîrê suffered constant discrimination due to their religious and ethnic origin. Yezidis in Efrin were largely supressed because of their Kurdish ethnicity and less so because of their religion.

Because Yezidis in Efrîn had lived in the area for several centuries, they integrated into the broader society. In contrast, the Yezidis in the Cizîrê have a weak social status because they settled there about a century ago and constantly faced changes among the local population. On one hand, the arbitrary political borders after the First World War cut them off from other Yezidi areas in Sinjar and Tur Abdin. On the other hand, they suffered from systematic Arabisation and Islamisation through the displacement of Kurdish/Yezidi families and the resettlement of Arab-Muslim farmers in the so-called Arab Belt in the Cizîrê.

Early History

Yezidi and non-Yezidi scholars have diverse opinions about the origin of Yezidis. Most suggest a relation to ancient Mesopotamian cultures and religions. Others still propagate the idea of a sectarian split from Islam. However, the latter argument has finally disappeared in Western publications. Most Western scholars now view the Yezidis as a system of pre-Islamic Kurdish traditions reformed by the Sufi Sheikh Adi bin Musafir. Under his successor Hassan Bin Adi, the transformation continued integrating additional pre-Islamic elements and rituals.

One of the two holy scriptures of the Yezidis, the Mashaf Resh, already mentioned a Yezidi community near Aleppo. During the annual round trip of Yezidi clerics, tawaf, one of the sacred objects they display is attributed to with this local group.

The written history of the Yezidi in Syria began around the year 1070 with the birth of Sheikh Adi in Beit Far (Khirbet Qanafir) in a small village in the Beqaa Valley that lies in today's Lebanon but was then part of Greater Syria (Bilad al-Sham). Other relatives, his parents, and his nephew also came from this region giving the area some significance. Another sacred text mentions that Sheikh Adi's family originally came from the Hakkari Mountains and his grandfather the first to move to Beit Far.

Sheikh Adi later moved to Baghdad and back to the Hakkari Mountains, where he founded the Sufi order of the Adawiya, which merged with local, sun-worshipping traditions to establish a religious movement that came to known as the Yezidis. First described as a heretical Islamic sect, it later recognised as a unique, independent ethno-religious community that still resembled a branch of Sufism. But the reforms introduced by Sheikh Adi laid the foundation of the religious community, which later was attacked and scattered by the Muslim rulers of that time. One group moved to Syria and established a base in the area of Aleppo. They retained Sufi characteristics until the seventeenth century.

Evidence of Yezidis in Syria during the medieval era can be found in Ottoman archival files from Raqqa as well as in the Kurdish chronicle, Sharafname, written by the Emir of Bitlis, Sharaf al-Din Khan. This chronicle describes the Yezidi community with information on their members, distribution, and history. The Hakkari sheikh Mend was awarded the region around the mountain of Qosai west of Aleppo. A sheikh caste by the same name, Sheikh Mend, still holds influential positions and belongs to the Yezidi leadership.

The next stage of studying or dealing with Yezidis in Syria began in the middle of the seventeenth century, when the first European scholars, French clerics, encountered the Yezidis in the vicinity of Aleppo. Detailed accounts[2] describe their social and religious structure with many features still practiced today including the marriage regulations and caste system.

The 19th century, however, saw the start of the settlement of Yezidis in the Cizîrê, mostly as a result of displacement or escape from Ottoman territories in the north. The community in Efrîn was targeted during several taxation and conscription attempts as well as intense Islamisation campaigns. At this time, the Yezidis became known as a separate community. Official reports, travel accounts, and oral narratives mention their numbers (10,000 – 15,000) and their growing discontent with their Muslim rulers and neighbours.[3]

---

[2] Fuccaro (1993): 241-53
[3] Lescot (1938), Lammens (1907)

Mandate period

After the dissolving of the Ottoman Empire and the establishment of British and French Mandates, conferences in San Remo, London, and Lausanne defined the political borders of Syria. These distant decisions divided Kurdish territories and separated western Yezidis from the main homeland.

French rule in Syria brought two new political concepts to the Kurds and Yezidis: independence and decentralisation. These two ideas played a major role in developing the Kurdish national identity that was further developed by the immigration of Turkish and Iraqi Kurds after failed revolts against their new political leadership. Yezidis in the Cizîrê were drawn into the events and started to nurture their own religious and political identity.

French rule allowed previously disadvantaged groups the opportunity to participate and self-organise. Like other religious minorities (Druzes, Alawites, Maronites), the Kurds/Yezidis readily served in special Mandate troops. This offered a unique way out from the economic misery and a rare chance to advance within the social hierarchy. Yezidis took advantage of this chance and were overrepresented in the military in comparison to their percentage of the total population. However, because most Yezidis were illiterate, only a few actually advanced in rank. Only members of the ruling Sheikh lineage were permitted to attend school. It took Yezidi activists many years to overcome this age-old custom. Community leaders feared that attending school would lead to further Islamisation or Christianisation of their children. The logical consequence was to establish their own Yezidi schools, which they did in Efrîn. However, since no official permit was issued and anti-Yezidi resentments grew, the school was closed a few years later. But this school represented a first step toward a distinct Yezidi approach to religious education, a struggle that would last for several decades.

French Mandate administration then conducted a new census indicating that the Yezidis were 10 per cent of the Kurdish population of 200,000.

During the first years of the Mandate, Syria became a haven for Kurdish refugees from Turkey and Iraq, who left because of failed nationalistic ambitions. These refugees included Yezidis from Sinjar. Similar to the situation in neighbouring countries, Kurdish intellectuals, aghas, and tribal leaders from the Cizîrê established a well-organised autonomy movement, which was not supported by Yezidi Kurds, mainly due to their lack of an educated leadership Only some individual Yezidis supported the national movements.

Despite the new political border, the Yezidis in the Cizîrê and Sinjar continued making limited contacts; however, mostly in form of a one-way street into the French territory after uprisings against the Iraqi central government. The French, who had their headquarters in Heseke, wanted to encourage large-scale resettlement of Yezidi groups. This would create another small and decentralised minority canton, but also offered economic stimulus to the area, because of the farming skills of Sinjar Yezidis.

After Turkey's government crushed several Kurdish nationalist revolts, other Kurds came to Syria. Here they continued their political and military activities. For many years, the largest Kurdish political organisation, Khoybun, had its headquarter in Damascus and branches in Aleppo and Heseke. Khoybun idealised the Yezidis as the only true religion of the Kurds, however, did not include prominent Yezidi members in the organisation. Haco Agha, the leader of the Heverkan tribal confederation, organised Khoybun activities in Heseke. He had close contact with Ismail Beg Chol, the Sinjar Yezidi leader, who tried several times to become the leader of the Yezidis in the name of Khoybun. After Haco returned from Turkey, France supported his settlement with his Syrian Yezidi fellows in Syria and built the city of Tirbespi.[4] Other Yezidi families from both sides of the border followed suit and added to the demographic, but not economic, growth of the community during this time.

Little has been recorded about the Yezidis in Efrîn. The region retained its character as a closed social-economic unit, whose inhabitants, such as the Yezidis, had been settled here for centuries. Kurds in Efrîn regarded the new French rulers differently, some supported them, and others rejected them. Some Yezidis fought actively against the French authorities and promoted Kurdish national interests, such as Darwish Shemo, leader of the village Ershe Qibar (Qîbar). The entire area witnessed an increasing Islamisation with forced conversions of individuals, families, and sometimes entire villages. Many Yezidis used the religious principle called *taqiya* that permitted the faithful to deny the true religion in case of danger. Others gave up their religion because they saw economic and social advantages beyond what Yezidism could offer. The lack of trained clerics made it difficult to maintain religious ceremonies and instruction. As mentioned earlier, this led to certain resentments among Iraqi Yezidis; even the young Mir Tahsin Beg doubted the seriousness of religious practice in Efrîn.

Until the end of the Mandate period, the growing Kurdish nationalistic movement and its temporary support of the French authorities helped both Yezidi communities to maintain their position as a Syrian minority. As a result, they drifted into a conflict of loyalties between nationalistic (Kurdish and Arabic), colonial (French and British), and Islamist movements. The Second World War had no immediate impact on the Yezidis, but the new

---

[4] Tejel (2008): 32-34

Syrian government's centralisation, as well as the further tightening of political borders, influenced the future instability of the religious and social Yezidi community. The growth of the Kurdish national movement in Syria and neighbouring countries, the often-militaristic response of their governments as well as the increasing Islamisation of the entire society led to a permanent weakening of the community's traditional, century-old structures, and brought them to the verge of extinction.

Independent Syria

During the early days of the republic, one could observe little informal or religious contacts between the two Syrian Yezidi areas. Many conservative and traditional Yezidis of the Cizîrê considered their brothers in faith as deviants who no longer adhere to the orthodox Yezidi doctrine and who assimilate to their Muslim environment. Yezidis in Efrîn had a better economic situation and they found a place in the social structure. Their concentration in larger villages help balance relations between Yezidi and Muslim Kurds. Both groups lived together in stable conditions for many centuries, which created a status quo of mutual tolerance. Usually, they left each other alone and did not worry about the affairs of the other. In certain economic and political questions, mostly related to problems with the Syrian authorities, they even cooperated on occasions.

All Yezidis faced religious pressure because of Islam classes in school, required for everyone except Christians. No degree was awarded without passing those Islamic religion classes. In addition, no Yezidi religious instruction was available or even permitted. Only the few Yezidi clerics in the area would sometimes during social gatherings address religious issues to the youth. Other members of cleric families left the country and immigrated to safer places.

In the 1960s and 70s, increased Arabisation policies had a particularly hard impact on the Yezidis in the Cizîrê. Many lost their citizenship, land, and other privileges, which led to a growing number of Yezidis leaving the country and migrating to better economic places, such as Germany, where they could practice their religions freely.

Syria under Bashar al-Assad

When Bashar al-Assad took over the Syrian government and before civil war broke out, Yezidis and other minority groups hoped that the country would transform towards a more inclusive society upholding the concept of a national identity not discriminating on ethnic or religious identification. In 2004, Assad quickly destroyed these hopes along with small attempts of reforms when he cracked down on the opposition, and especially hard on the Kurdish opposition.

After the tides of the civil war started to turn against the regime, officials began to implement small steps toward normalising the status quo by passing legislation to reverse the decisions of the infamous population census that deprived citizenship and its benefits from hundreds of thousands of Kurds and Yezidis. However, citizenship was not granted to all Kurds and only a few thousand accepted the offer. The gap of mistrust between the Kurds and the government was already too wide.

The Yezidis stuck in a lawless situation suffering both as Kurds and Yezidis also mistrusted the government. During the first decade of Bashar al-Assad´s rule, they suffered many cases of violent acts and crimes. The Yezidi Forum in Oldenburg documented these cases[5] that also included economic repression and severe infringements on land ownership and property. The general lack of security and widespread anti-Yezidi feelings led to a further depopulation of the Yezidi villages. Sometimes 80 per cent of a Yezidi village moved away, mostly to join relatives in Germany. However, the German court system initially did not grant them immediate or automatic asylum.

The first decade of Bashar al-Assad's rule brought no improvement for the Yezidi community. Concurrently, the relationship between the state and the Kurds deteriorated and left the two camps more polarised and divided. Since the Yezidis had not yet invested in the political struggle, they were easily ignored. Considered as a primary target, they felt the effects of stigmatisation and discrimination, which added up over time and pushed the community further back and to the fringes of society. From there, those who could go, left the country, while the others dug in trying not to expose their identity in order to wait for better times to come. And those better times were about to start.

Yezidis under the autonomous administration

Early on during the Syrian civil war, large territories in the north and northeast of the country came under the control of Kurdish militias and their allies. They battled hard and finally defeated radical Islamist groups, such as ISIS or Nusra. Those liberated areas set up a self-declared autonomous administration dominated by the Democratic Union Party (Kurdish: Partiya Yekîtiya Demokrat, PYD) and its military wing, the People Protection Units (Kurdish: Yekîneyên Parastina Gel, YPG). The autonomous area included all Yezidi villages in Syria thus bringing an end to the Assad regime's control. The new administration adhered to the principles of equality and democracy and granted its communities and individuals unprecedented liberties and rights.

Yezidis, both men and women, took part in the new autonomous

---

[5] Yezidisches Forum Oldenburg (2006)

administration, and the administration started to recognise and accept the Yezidis as an integral part of the larger community. Yezidi holidays were now celebrated publicly and with official support. Statutes were erected, support for Sinjar was expressed, and Yezidism was praised and integrated into the larger, overall identity discourse of the region. The general mood was cautiously optimistic.[6] However, it was also recognised that these freedoms were only gained with the help of the Kurdish militias, the PYD, and the autonomous administration. They contributed their own interpretation about Yezidi religion, identity, and origin, which they connected with Zoroastrians. The PKK/PYD had promoted this argument in the past and many Syrian Yezidis quickly accepted it.[7] Although this never became a significant part of the community's religiosity, they strongly support the idea as well as the ritual display and acceptance of certain Zoroastrian symbols.

This and the fact that the PYD ideology competed with the politics of the Iraqi Kurds became a problem for the relationship between the Yezidis in Syria and those in Iraq. Because of a brain-drain of scholars, political pressure, and the lack of security, the Yezidi community in Iraq examines its roots much more cautiously and does not make bold statements about the community's ancient past. The Yezidi leadership in Iraq did, however, dismiss the claims from Syria about a Zoroastrian-Yezidi connection.

Nevertheless, Yezidi religious representation flourished during those times with the establishment of schools, teacher seminaries, community centres, pilgrimage sites, and an active religious community life. The Yezidi renegotiated the role of women in society and religion and the participation of younger activists, regardless of their caste and origin.[8]

In the Cizîrê Region, one also noted the opening of Yezidi Houses, the organisation of large conferences, the public celebration of religious holidays, and the general active engagement of new social and religious leaders. The self-administration also included some Yezidis in their administrative and political ranks. In return, they fully supported the political agenda and demonstrated their support for Abdullah Öcalan. Through their complete embedding into the Kurdish movement, they hoped to strengthen their position within the local and regional society and ultimately become accepted as a non-Muslim, non-Arab community. After accomplishing this political goal, they focused on the two other important issues: religious revival and ending mass emigration.

---

[6] Shaykhū (2015)
[7] Following the guidelines from their sister organisation, the PKK, it became a controversial political argument. See Foltz (2017).
[8] Ali and Hosseini (2018): 1-4

The new Syria

When the civil war broke out, the Syrian Yezidi community had been divided spatially, religiously, and economically. The establishment of autonomous cantons by the self-administration extended a common political framework to all Yezidi villages situated within this geographical zone. Outside Syria, in the diaspora, the two groups also became more cohesive due to the activities of social and political organisations abroad who claimed to speak for all Syrian Yezidis. However, on the ground in Syria, the two Yezidi groups became closer after Turkey's Olive Branch military operation and Turkish-led militants occupied Efrîn. After the Yezidis were expelled from Efrîn, one can no longer describe the community as spatially divided. Only one Yezidi territory in Syria remained, the Cizîrê.

The representatives from Efrîn joined ranks with the Yezidi organisations in the Cizîrê, where Yezidi families and villages opened their doors for the distant relatives who became refugees. The slogan ´Solidarity with Efrîn´ became more than a slogan when large demonstrations showed their support for the Yezidis and other Kurds from Efrîn. From Kobane via Sinjar to Efrîn, powerful calls emerged for the liberation of Kurdish/Yezidi lands; unfortunately, the situation in Efrîn did not allow for a military struggle. Instead, solidarity took other forms including aid for the refugees, lobby work for the religious minorities, and formal unification of organisations and institutions such as the Yezidi House. They constructed with renewed fervour the idea of belonging to one community.

The road that led to the convergence of the Yezidi community was hard. Communication was difficult, resources were scarce. Those Yezidi families who fled from Efrîn to the city of Aleppo or the nearby Shahba refugee camp started to organise the community based on the experiences they had in the previous years. They started offering classes for religious instruction, established Mala Ezidiyan in Aleppo's Sheikh Maqsud District on 5 August 2018, collected and distributed aid, and other provisions, documented the migration, and coordinated the work with local and international NGOs.

The Yezidi organisations also continued their political activities for recognition and protection. While some representatives were invited to the Sochi Summit, the community was excluded from the process of drafting the new Syrian Constitution. The organisations located within Syria who call for Yezidi participation include the Ezdina Media Foundation, the Yezidi Association in Efrîn, the Yezidi House in the Cizîrê Region, and the Alliance of Syrian Yezidis. These groups coordinate and cooperate with other Syrian Yezidis organisations based in Germany.[9] Generally, although the

---

[9] See Call from the Yezidis of Syria… (2018)

community lost an important part of their homeland, it brought the community closer together as they opposed the military aggression and subsequent destabilisation of north-eastern Syria. Yezidi leaders and activists from all backgrounds jointly signed a letter expressing these concerns.[10]

The Turkish-led military operation Olive Branch in early 2018 led to the expulsion of almost all Yezidi families from Efrîn and another wave of migration. Most of the population temporarily settled in camps in the Shahba area held by the Syrian regime. However, their equally bad situation in the temporary camps has little support and growing resentments from the local population. This campaign seeks to erase the Yezidi identity and heritage from the area by destroying religious architecture, desecrating shrines and graves[11], and forcing the few remaining Yezidis to convert to Islam. For many, this and the recent events in Sinjar simply continues the age-old genocide against the Yezidis.

The second Turkish-led military campaign against Kurdish territories in northern Syria, Operation Peace Spring in October 2019, affected the Cizîrê community directly, occupying the villages around Serê Kaniyê and forcing its inhabitants to flee. Also, here we note a gradual process of retreat: first from the village to the next town, from there to Heseke, and finally some families moved to Iraq where they must await their fate.[12]

The diaspora community

Many Yezidi families still have a very strong desire to leave Syria. The lack of security, the difficult economic conditions, and the strong bonds to their relatives abroad made this decision easier for them. That is not to say that Yezidis were not loyal or connected to their homeland; but they miss the land and not the Syrian state. They fear another genocide, and little has been done in Syria to alleviate this feeling.

Germany remains the `promised land´ for the Yezidis even though the very complicated and dangerous journey to Germany has resulted in many dying on the way. Often local officials do not want them to leave and made the first step of the trip very difficult. On route, they had to deal with harsh conditions and anti-immigrant sentiments, but once they reached German soil, their physical and material situation almost immediately improved; and, so did their societal status.

Germans have a certain affinity to the Yezidis, and their legal system is

---

[10] Statement by Yazidi community leaders on Turkish invasion of northeast Syria and targeting of Yazidis published at https://www.yazda.org/post/statement-by-yazidi-community-leaders-on-turkish-invasion-of-ne-syria-and-targeting-of-yazidis

[11] Information about the destroyed shrines comes from McKeever (2019) and O´Connell (2018).

[12] Hagedorn (2019)

more welcoming to asylum seekers. In the 1990s, Yezidis from Turkey received the status of group asylum, which allowed everyone from that community to come to Germany. However, the rulings regarding Yezidis from Syria were less supportive and more inconsistent. Before the civil war, the German-Syrian agreement to repatriate refugees resulted in some deportations of Yezidis back to Syria. However, after the Sinjar genocide, Yezidis could easily receive the desired legal status. Public opinion, the media, politicians, and the legal systems all supported their case. The favourite rulings continued until July 2019, when a German court denied a Yezidi application and stated that the security situation in Iraq had improved.

Those who came to Germany found a well-organised community and a strong network of support. Although Germans view the Yezidis as a homogenous group, they have divisions along geographical, political, and social lines. The Yezidi Identity Inventory[13] showed a strong divide between the more secular and liberal Turkish and Syrian Yezidi on one side, and the more traditional and conservative Iraqi community on the other side.

Political views also divide the Yezidis. Some groups support either the PKK/PYD or the KDP and others try to remain non-partisan. The Syrian sector, due to its small numbers, had little representation. However, the Syrian Yezidis in Germany also have a political divide with most supporting the PYD.

Conclusion

The last two decades saw enormous changes in the perception of Yezidi identity in Syria both from those outside and within the community. How Yezidis viewed themselves, how they want to be regarded by others and how the others described them, all of these markers of identity were manifested in sometimes contradictory ways with highs and lows and little common ground. This makes the attempts to define or build identity a difficult undertaking; however, in times of increased focus on hierarchical societal structures, due to war and genocide, the Yezidi community must position themselves in the world of stricter ethnic, religious, economic, and social boundaries. Unique Yezidi markers that shaped these boundaries can be recognised in the field of rituals and public display of religiosity, the political affiliation, and the appropriation of the Sinjar genocide discourse.

The alternative to participating in this sometimes lethal and often violent interaction is leaving the area for good. While about half of the Syrian Yezidis have followed this path, the other half tries to strengthen their newly gained freedoms and rights under the Autonomous Administration in North and East Syria in order to form a new Yezidi identity different from classical or

---

[13] Tagay, et al. (2013)

mainstream forms of Yezidi identity in Iraq or the diaspora. But in the absence of a uniform, standardised Yezidi identity, local variants will emerge and subsequently influence the larger, general identity.

Many Yezidi voices call for accepting that there is no future for them in their homeland. These Yezidi activists say all Yezidis should emigrate to safer places to start a new life. With more than 50 per cent of the population currently living as refugees, one can see the source of this argument. Also, the return to their villages is highly unlikely in the immediate future due to the armed occupation, insecurity, destruction, and lack of reconstruction and services.

The people in Rojava still strongly intend to include the Yezidis in their community and this welcoming attitude represents one of the remarkable gains in the otherwise negative, desolate prospects for Yezidis. However, the fragile stability in the Cizîrê Region could disappear with the next military incursion either by the Turkish-led alliance or the Syrian government's troops. They could end the region's democratic experiment in self-administration and inclusion of all religious and ethnic components. Partially because of the events in Sinjar, the Yezidi community has earned trust, admiration, and respect from local and international actors. Over the past 10 years, the Syrian Yezidi community remained resilient in their battle for survival, recognition, and renewal. They are not ready to give up their last territory in Syria, although they struggle with growing numbers of Yezidi emigrants to safer countries. The developments of the 21st century led the community to a new level of self-consciousness and opened new avenues to redefine their faith and identity.

References

Ali, Majid Hassan and Seyedeh Behnaz Hosseini: Between Rights, Political Participation and Opposition: The Case of Yezidis in Syrian Kurdistan (Rojava). *Syrian Studies Association Bulletin*, vol. 23, no. 1, 2018, www.ojcs.siue.edu/ojs/index.php/ssa/article/view/3283/1313

Call from the Yazidis of Syria to the United Nations to involve them in the committee of rewriting the constitution. Published 27.08.2018 at www.ezdina.com

Foltz, Richard, 'The "Original" Kurdish Religion? Kurdish nationalism and the false conflation of the Yezidi and Zoroastrian traditions', in *Journal of Persianate Studies*, vol. 10 no. 1, 2017, pp. 87-106.

Fuccaro, Nelida: *A 17th Century Travel Account on the Yazidis*, Annali, vol. 53, no. 3, 1993, pp. 241-253.

Hagedorn, Elisabeth, 'Now we await our fate: Displaced Yazidis fear loss of land in Syria', *The New Arab*, 01.11.2019, www.alaraby.co.uk

Kreyenbroek, Philip: *Yezidism in Europe – Different Generations Speak about their Religion*. Harrassowitz, 2009.

Lammens, Henri: Le Massif du Gabal Sim´an et les Yézidis de Syrie, MFO, vol. 2, 1907, pp. 389-90.

Lescot, Roger: *Enquete sur les Yezidis de Syrie et du Djebel Sindjar*, Beyrouth: Librarie du Liban,

1938.

Maisel, Sebastian: *Yezidis in Syria: Identity Building among a Double Minority.* Lexington Books, 2017.

McKeever, Alexander: Afrin: Incidents of Desecration and Destruction Of Cultural Sites. July 11, 2019, www.bellingcat.com/news/mena/2019/07/11/afrin-incidents-of-desecration-and-destruction-of-cultural-sites/

O´Connell, James: Incident Report Feature: Intentional Destruction of Religious Sites in Afrin. www.asor-syrianheritage.org/incident-report-feature-afrin-religious-sites/, 2018.

Rojava Information Center: Report on the Displaced People from Afrin Canton in Shahba, Northern Syria and Surrounding Areas, June 2019, www.rojavainformationcenter.com/storage/2019/06/Report-on-the-Displaced-People-from-Afrin-Canton-in-Shahba-Northern-Syria-and-Surrounding-Areas.pdf

Shaykhū, Kamāl, al-Īzīdiyūn fī ʿAfrīn: Dhākira muthqila wa-khawf min al-majhūl (The Yezidis from Afrin: Heavy Memories and Fears from the Unknown), Deutsche Welle, 03.03.2015,   www.dw.com/ar/الايزيديون-في-عفرين-ذاكرة-مثقلة-وخوف-من-المجهول/a-18289607

Tagay, Sefik, et al.: *Ezidisches Identitäts-Inventar (EZI)*, Essen, 2013.

Tejel, Jordi: *Syria's Kurds: History, Politics and Society.* Routledge, 2008.

Yezidisches Forum Oldenburg: Stellungnahme zu der Situation der Yeziden in Nordostsyrien auf Anfrage des VG Magdeburg, Oldenburg, 2006.

Mala Êzîdîya in Afrin before it was destroyed by the Turkish invasion in 2018.

Cemetery of the Yazidi village of Feqîra in the Afrin region of Syria before its desecration by pro-Turkish militias in 2018.

The Yazidi village of Qitmê in the Afrin region in 2015.

Mala Êzîdîya in the Jezira region in the village Qislachuk south of Amûdê in 2020.

Exhibition in memorial to the fights between jihadi groups and the YPG/YPJ in Êzîdî villages around Serê Kaniyê in 2012/2013 in the Mala Êzîdîya in the Jezira region in the village Qislachuk in 2014.

CHAPTER 4

THE JEWS OF NORTH AND EAST SYRIA AND THEIR HERITAGE

Thomas Schmidinger

The religious history of north and east Syria includes not only Muslims, Christians and Yazidis, but also Jews, mainly connected with the Jewish community of Nusaybin on the Turkish side of the present Syrian-Turkish border crossing at Qamishli (Kurdish: Qamişlo). Although indigenous Jews no longer live in the Autonomous Administration of North and East Syria, the region's cultural and religious diversity include a Jewish heritage.

The Jewish community of Qamishli

Until a few years ago, a Jewish community still existed in Qamishli, a city founded in 1926 by Armenian survivors of the Genocide of 1915 and the Christian and Jewish population who moved across the border from the Turkish-controlled Nusaybin and into the French Protectorate of Syria. Qamishli still has one of the last synagogues of Syria and in all of Kurdistan. Most, but not all, of the region's Jewish population came from Nusaybin. In addition to Qamishli, these migrants also settled in the villages of al-Shuka and Tel Sha'ir[1], west of Kobanê and in the village of Awaija southeast of Qamishli. The rich Jewish family Rahina bought land and leased it to poor landless Jews and therefore the village became a hub for impoverished Jewish families. Until the 1960s, Awaija had mainly poor Jews who could not make their living in Qamishli and who lived off their land in the village. In 1927, a Jewish merchant established the Qamishli souk soon called 'Souk of the Jews', a name still used today by locals.

Around 3,000 Jews lived in the city of Qamishli in the 1930s.[2] Most spoke a Jewish-Aramaic language but they also learned Arabic and some of them Kurdish. The French authorities appointed the first leader of the community, Moshe Nahum. Besides him, various rabbis, such as Hakham Nissim Brahimo, played an important role for the community. By the late 1940s, the city had three synagogues and a beth midrash, a Jewish house of learning. In 1941, Iraqi Jews who had survived the Farhud, a pogrom following the pro-

---

[1] Laskier 2002: 323.
[2] Schmidinger 2014: 37.

71

Nazi coup of Rashid Ali al-Gaylani,[3] fled to Qamishli and were smuggled from there to Palestine.

However, the Israeli-Palestinian conflict also affected the Jews of Qamishli. In 1947, rioters partly damaged the great synagogue. A year later, the government seized it. In 1967, a mob killed about 50 members of the community.[4] Nevertheless, the community shrank but did not disappear until the 1990s. Since Syria, unlike most Arab countries, prohibited Jews from leaving and tried to keep them in the country with repressive measures, the Jewish community of Qamishli also existed until 1992, when the then Syrian President Hafez al-Assad finally allowed the Jews to leave the country.[5] Before 1992, local Kurds helped to smuggle Jews from Qamishli across the border to Turkey if they wanted to leave the region. Followers of the Kurdish Naqshibandi Sheikh Muhammad al-Khaznawi helped Jews from Qamishli to escape to Turkey and leave the region towards Europe, America, or Israel.[6] By 1992, the community had declined to about 200 members of whom about 150 emigrated after the end of the travel restrictions.

Although about ten Jewish families remained after 1992 in Qamishli and Damascus, the community did not have a rabbi and lacked a religious life. The last Jew from Qamishli left in autumn 2013, when Kurds controlled the city. An old Muslim Kurd has the key to the synagogue but he does not welcome visitors to the building. Only after repeated attempts and many preliminary talks with people over a span of several years, I had a chance to visit the synagogue in February 2020.

One of the last synagogues of Kurdistan

The remaining synagogue in Qamishli is one of the last synagogues existing in the whole Kurdish region of the Middle East. A few synagogues remain in the Iranian part of Kurdistan (in Sanandaj and Kermanshah) until today.

The synagogue in Qamishli has a large patio with a once beautiful garden and a fountain—today non-functional. A prayer room lies on the right and another on the left side of the patio. Until the last of the community left in 2013, they continued to use the smaller prayer room on the left side of the patio. Electricity has been cut off, but the small prayer room still looks as if it had been abandoned just the day before. The bema (the platform for reading the Torah) still has some sheets of papers with prayers in Hebrew, an Arabic list of (most probably) former community members, and a

---

[3] Ammann, 2019: 40.
[4] For this article, I could talk to a former member of the community who told me about these events but who wanted to stay anonymous.
[5] Ibid: 38.
[6] Interview with an al-Khaznawi family-member who wanted to stay anonymous, 5 January 2010.

twentieth-century artistic imagination of Shimon bar Yochai, a second-century Tannaitic Rabbi, referred to as simply 'Rabbi Shimon' in the Mishna. Shimon bar Yochai's popularity stems from his alleged authorship of the Zohar, the chief work of Kabbalah for many Orthodox Jews. When the Zohar first appeared in thirteenth-century Spain, its first publisher, Moses de León, ascribed the work to Shimon bar Yochai.[7] However, his picture on the synagogue's bema does not tell us much more about the Jewish community of Qamishli than that its last members obviously had some respect for Jewish kabbalist traditions.

The larger hall to the right of the patio seems to have been out of use for a longer period. Nevertheless, it also still contains a bema, a menorah, and a beautiful floor lamp with a bilingual inscription in Hebrew and Arabic in its base that commemorates a Benjamin Zion Elijahu 'who died before his time' in 1992.

The synagogue lies in that part of the old town under mixed control of the Syrian regime and the Syrian Democratic Forces. When I visited, a tattered photo of Hafez al-Assad still adorned the synagogue's entrance. The older population of Qamishli still have memories of the synagogue; however, younger folks and those who have migrated from the villages probably do not know about it.

View to the big prayer room from the patio of the synagogue in Qamishli.

---

[7] see Matt 2018.

Lamp with a bilingual inscription in Hebrew and Arabic in its base that commemorates a
Benjamin Zion Elijahu.

Menorah in the large prayer hall of the synagogue in Qamishli.

The small prayer room of the synagogue in Qamishli.

The bema in the small prayer room of the synagogue in Qamishli with some sheets of papers still lying around with prayers in Hebrew, an Arabic list, and a twentieth-century artistic imagination of Shimon bar Yochai.

Shops in the bazaar owned by Jews

Even though the city no longer has any Jewish residents, some shops in the Qamishli bazaar still belong to emigrated Jews. Today, Christians or Muslims operate these shops, but they continue to pay rent to the Jewish owners now living in Europe or Israel. A local lawyer collects the rent and makes sure that the owners receives the payments. Apparently, some of the Jews from Qamishli have not completely given up on the region and have kept their business premises to this day.

In the current situation, all questions about ownership remain very sensitive. Therefore, for ethical research reasons, I cannot provide sources for this information. However, the fact remains that Qamishli Jewish families, some of whom have left the country decades ago, still own some shops in the Qamishli bazaar. Both the old Baath regime and the current self-administration allowed this ownership.

A shop in the bazaar still has the Jewish name Ezra, which for many customers serves as proof of the quality of the goods offered there. The name Ezra obviously signals that a Jewish person owns the shop but a non-Jewish person operates it. However, the Jewish owner living outside of Syria receives rent.

Cemetery and the grave of Judah ben Bathyra

The old Jewish cemetery, located in the border area with Turkey, was almost completely destroyed in 1985 by the Turkish army, who built a watchtower there. Jews who died later were buried close to Qamishli near the tomb of the Jewish scholar Judah ben Bathyra. Judah ben Bathyra lived in Nisbis[8] (today´s Nusaybin) before the destruction of the second temple in Jerusalem where he was the head of the academy.[9] The Mishnah quotes 17 laws by him and the Baraita, the Jewish oral law not incorporated in the Mishnah, has about 40 of his laws.[10] However, a mystery surrounds the identity of the Judah ben Bathyra buried in the tomb because two different persons had the same name sometimes called Judah ben Bathyra I and, at other times, Judah ben Bathyra II. Allegedly, Judah ben Bathyra I lived in Jerusalem in his youth, but left before the destruction of the temple and settled in Nisibis, while Judah ben Bathyra II might have been his grandson born in Rome who studied in Palestine and settled down in Nisbis in the second century AD.[11]

Despite the mystery of who actually lies in the grave in the sensitive border area with Turkey, this site has clearly been the destination of pilgrimages for centuries and had a supra-regional importance for the

---

[8] Neusner: 1969: 47.
[9] Eisenberg, 2013: 148.
[10] Jewish Encyclopaedia: http://www.jewishencyclopedia.com/articles/2663-bathyra
[11] Cohn-Sherbok, 2005: 148.

Judaism of the upper Mesopotamia. The Italian Rabbi Moses ben Mordecai Basola, who visited the Middle East between 1521 and 1523, met 'four Babylonian Jews' in Beirut who told him about the tomb of Judah ben Bathyra near Nisbis and that it was a famous tomb in the region.[12] He spoke further of a pillar of cloud which appears on the 18th of Sivan and at Pentecost over the tomb and also that Jews from surrounding areas made pilgrimages to the tomb.[13]

The tomb of Judah ben Bathyra remains well preserved today. Unfortunately, its small prayer room has a hole in the roof and a hole in a wall.[14] If the building is not restored in the next few years, it could collapse. It is very dangerous to visit the tomb and the small new Jewish cemetery surrounding it because of its proximity to the Turkish border. Locals fear Turkish snipers. This makes the place practically impossible to visit.

The old Jewish cemetery of Nisbis/Nusaybin and Qamishli on the border has been destroyed by a Turkish watchtower. View from Nusaybin (Turkey) to the hill that was the former cemetery.

Is there a future for the Jewish heritage of the region?

In general, the historical memories of Kurds, Arabs, and Christians do not include history of the Jews of the region. Decades of anti-Zionist and anti-Semitic propaganda by the Syrian Baath-regime resulted in the topic of the regional Jewish heritage becoming highly sensitive, even for political

---

[12] David, 1999: 107.
[13] https://www.jewishvirtuallibrary.org/nisibis
[14] Schmidinger, 2019: 139.

groups who do not have any negative feeling towards the Jews. This makes a return of Jews to the region very unlikely. However, it may be possible to preserve the material heritage of the Jewish community of Qamishli, in particular the synagogue and the historic tomb of Judah ben Bathyra, one of the oldest Jewish pilgrimage sites in Mesopotamia.

Jewish-owned shop 'Esra' in the bazar of Qamishli.

The memories of the Jewish community of Qamishli are fading. In the 1990s, when I could first visit the city of Qamishli, individual Jews, with an open Jewish identity, still lived in the city. Today, mostly the older city dwellers retain specific memories of their Jewish former neighbours. Those younger than thirty years usually have no personal memories of the Jewish community. The city's Jewish material heritage remains invisible because no one can visit the synagogue hidden behind bland walls. The possibility of Turkish snipers keeps anyone from visiting the old Jewish cemetery and the tomb of Judah ben Bathyra. Perhaps the conflict-laden situation may even help preserve the material cultural largely hidden from jihadist attacks.

The current anti-Semitic Syrian regime has repeatedly accused the Autonomous Administration of North and East Syria of working with the 'Zionist enemy'. Thus, the Autonomous Administration finds it difficult to openly include the region's Jewish history in its view of a society shaped by diversity. However, should the political situation stabilise, it would be good if the region managed to preserve their Jewish heritage and make it accessible to the descendants of the former community as well as to the region's Muslims, Christians, and Yazidis. The Jewish history of Qamishli should be as much a part of their historical memory as that of the other religious communities in the region.

References

Ammann, B. (2019). The Jews of Iraq. In: Sevdeen, B. M. and Schmidinger, T. (eds.): *Beyond ISIS: History and Future of Religious Minorities in Iraq.* Transnational Press London: London. pp.: 33-56.

Cohn-Sherbok, D. (2005). *The Dictionary of Jewish Biography.* Continuum: London, New York

David, A. (1999). *In Zion and Jerusalem. The Itinerary of Rabbi Moses Basola* (1521-1523). Edited with Notes and an Introduction by Abraham David. C.G. Foundation of the Jerusalem Project Publications of the Martin (Szusz) Department of Land of Israel Studies of Bar-Ilan University: Jerusalem

Eisenberg, R. L. (2013). *Essential Figures in the Talmud.* Jason Aronson: Lanham, Boulder, New York et.al.

Matt, D. C. (2018). *The Zohar.* Pritzker Edition. Stanford University Press: Redwood City CA

Neusner, J. (1969). *A history of the Jews in Babylonia. I. The Parthian Period.* E. J. Brill: Leiden.

Schmidinger, T. (2014). *Krieg und Revolution in Syrisch-Kurdistan. Analysen und Stimmen aus Rojava.* Mandelbaum Verlag: Wien

Schmidinger, T. (2019). 'Das Ende des kurdischen Judentums und sein Nachleben zwischen Instrumentalisierung und Erinnerung' in: Schmidinger, T., Brizić, K., Grond, A., Osztovics, C., Six-Hohenbalken, M. (eds.), *Wiener Jahrbuch für Kurdische Studien 7/2019: Religion in Kurdistan.* Praesens Verlag: Wien, pp. 131-156

CHAPTER 5

ON THE KURDISH QUEST FOR AUTONOMY:
ROJAVA'S POLITICAL SYSTEM AND THE
STRUCTURES OF SELF-ADMINISTRATION IN NORTH
AND EAST SYRIA

Rosa Burç

Introduction

With the withdrawal of the Syrian government's military forces in 2012
from Syria's northern areas with a Kurdish-majority population, local political
forces not only achieved control but also became vanguards in building an
autonomous entity, widely known as Rojava, based on the principles of
decentralisation, pluralism, and grassroots organisation. Although the
autonomous Kurdistan Region of Iraq (KRI) came into being as the first
formalised and institutionalised form of Kurdish territorial autonomy, the
Rojava model manifests a developing, yet new, approach to the question of
self-determination for the Kurds and other minorities in the Middle East. It
shifts the focus from the non-existence of Kurdistan as a nation state towards
the role of bottom-up politics as a counter-hegemonic sphere built through
women's autonomy, radical self-governance, as well as the reinvention of
nationhood beyond ethnic dogmatism.

In 1993, Chantal Mouffe noted that the lack of democratic struggles with
which to identify triggered new forms of identification, mostly of ethnic,
nationalist, or religious natures; two decades later, Francesca Polletta defined
contemporary struggles for *more* democracy as a central characteristic of what
she called the 'participatory age' (2014: 79). Against the backdrop of closing
borders around the world, people turning their back on the displaced and
dispossessed, right-wing populisms dominating national politics,
particularistic nationalisms being on the rise, as well as authoritarian regimes
entrenching and deepening, social movements across the world have been
questioning the limits of the nation state, elaborated on alternative concepts
of democracy, and have claimed more direct democratic practices of
decision-making. In her (2004) study *Freedom is an Endless Meeting,* Polletta
already challenged the widespread idea that participatory democracy is
worthy in theory but insufficient in practice, by demonstrating how American
social movements have used bottom-up organising as a tool to bring actual

political change inside and outside their movements. The attempt, amid an ongoing war, at circumventing authoritarian statism in Rojava through bottom-up reorganising of society and redefining dominant categories, therefore promises to contribute to the wider academic discussions on alternative democracies that go beyond the specific context of the Kurdish Middle East.

This essay aims to serve as an overview on how the Kurdish freedom movement conceptualises self-governance and autonomy as an alternative to the neoliberal modality of democracy. To understand why, in this particular context of war and opportunity, a non-nation-state project was pursued and not ethnic autonomy in the classical territorial sense, this essay will contextualise Rojava within the question of how Kurdish experience with state(less)ness in and outside Syria has shaped the movement's ideological framework and its implementation in northern Syria. Hence, how a paradigmatic shift in the movement's objectives of liberation began with Abdullah Öcalan's reconsideration of dominant categories and wide-spread beliefs. This then leads to a discussion of how these ideas have shaped the building pillars of Rojava's political system today. Given Turkey's increasingly active military interventions in the region and interest in preventing at its border the establishment and recognition of a Kurdish-led self-administration instigated by a Kurdish democratic confederalist movement, informed by the ideas of Abdullah Öcalan, this essay will situate the role of Turkey as inherent to assessing the political system in northern Syria, as well as how Turkey threatens the Rojava model now emerging as an alternative in the region.

Divided by borders, united in ideas

As one of the largest stateless nations in the world and systematically denied self-determination and recognition, Kurds in the Middle East have two dominant tendencies in proposing solutions to the so-called Kurdish question. Some Kurdish political actors advocate for more classical nationalist solutions such as independent Kurdish statehood. Others, such as the Kurdish movement under the PKK, have advocated a transregional confederalist vision since the late 1990s that no longer seeks an independent nation state but a self-organised federative system. When the movement emerged in the late 1970s, it conceptualised liberation as mostly within the categories of nationhood. However, an internal transformative process took place in the following decades.[1] Rooted in the early 1990s and emerging

---

[1] With the disintegration of the bipolar world system in the early 1990s, Abdullah Öcalan believed that the PKK had to adopt strategic changes in order to respond to the changing dynamics in world politics, hence also, to survive this critical juncture. Formed in the late 1970s, the PKK was strongly informed by socialist ideas that had influenced revolutionary movements and national liberation

between 2002 and 2005, the PKK's paradigmatic transformation resulted in a pluri-national and confederal movement, which has been proposing decentralised municipal structures across the region since then. This movement established the Group of Communities in Kurdistan (KCK) in 2005 (Gunes 2017). The KCK was meant to serve as an umbrella group for Kurdish political parties committed to the democratic confederalist principles. With the new bottom-up approach, the KCK envisioned self-organised and on-the-ground representation of the Kurds living in Turkey, Iraq, Iran, Syria, as well as in places outside these countries. Other than the PKK, other organisations belonging to the KCK included the Democratic Union Party (PYD) active in Syria since 2003, the Free Life Party of Kurdistan (PJAK) in Iran, and the Kurdistan Democratic Solution Party (PÇDK) in Iraq, as well as associated civil society organisations. In addition to the parties, KCK also encompasses a youth council, a women's council, and five other administrative councils. The councils of the KCK send a total of 300 delegates to Kongra-Gel, which eventually functions as the legislative organ (Candar 2013). Guided by confederal principles of equal representation and consensual decision-making, this was the first step toward forming plural, decentralised, and confederal political bodies that cooperate with each other across the four different nation states of Turkey, Syria, Iraq, and Iran. Consequently, this was a first step in making the national borders irrelevant for the political articulation of the peoples of the region, as well as a first step in building a transregional and common political imaginary. Despite differences due to particular political constellations in all of the four parts of the geographical area unofficially known as Kurdistan, the majority of Kurdish parties committed to the principles of democratic confederalism and have almost identical demands. For example, Kurds in Turkey and Syria have fundamentally different political situations but in both countries they attempted to formally set up a confederal municipal system that allows cooperation and political articulation beyond nation-state borders and that do not challenge the territorial integrity of the already existing states. Nevertheless, political parties such as the Iraq-based Kurdistan Democratic Party (PDK) and party allies in Syria oppose the confederalist proposal for Rojava.

---

struggles across the world at the time. It had adopted a Marxist-Leninist approach to the question of national self-determination and conditioned national liberation with the formation of its own Kurdish state. With the changing global system, the PKK situated itself anew ideologically, which also led to reorganising its political and military wings. Along with the global developments triggered by the disintegration of the Soviet Union in 1991, as well as practical experiences in wider Kurdistan, PKK formed autonomous parties and organisations in the respective nation states of the Kurdish-majority region. Revising the need for Kurdish statehood as a precondition for freedom, it redefined the solution of the Kurdish question as an essential necessity to solve the democracy question in the Middle East. The strategic and ideological reconfiguration of the PKK's ideology sought to provide a comprehensive strategy for all systematically oppressed groups in society.

Beyond the commitment to the political principles of one or the other project, the geographical, historical, and cultural closeness of the regions—given that borders artificially separated entire villages and cities after the First World War—affects the potential to foster a common political vision for the region. For example, colonial mapmaking considered railroad tracks when drawing the Turkish-Syrian border and resulted in neighbours becoming citizens of Syria on the one side and citizens of Turkey on the other side of the border. The geographical interconnectedness and strong community ties between the two sides of the border is also reflected in a local Kurdish saying: 'You can brew a tea in Suruç and drink it in Kobanê.' After the Ottoman Empire, when Kurdish self-determination was denied at the beginning of the twentieth century, traditional Kurdish regions such as Kobanê were artificially named Ain al-Arab on the Syrian side and Suruç on the Turkish side.

Rojava has been widely acknowledged as the most prominent site of the implementation of the confederal idea; however, as already mentioned, the same principles have been driving forces behind the Kurdish political movement in Turkey. Decentralised politics aimed at circumventing the authoritarian state by establishing self-reliant municipal structures was most recently expressed by forming a bottom-up and grassroots left-alliance under the Peoples' Democratic Party, HDP in 2012. Informed by the paradigmatic shift of the Kurdish movement, activists in Turkey's Kurdish southeast have declared democratic autonomy several times, for example, in December 2015.[2] When Turkish military aggression against Kurdish populations had reached yet another peak, the movement proposed forming democratic autonomous regions throughout the whole country, aiming to build federal and genuinely democratic structures in highly centralised Turkey—very close and almost parallel to developments on the other side of the border in Rojava.

In 2015, HDP's vision of a radically democratised Turkey found an electorate and denied President Recep Tayyip Erdoğan the absolute majority needed for his attempts to establish a single-ruler system through constitutional amendments (Burç and Tokatlı 2019). Also, on the other side of the Syrian-Turkish border, the city of Kobanê's resistance against the Islamic State group explicitly exposed Turkey's foreign policy opposing the establishment of a new political system and self-reliant local structures in neighbouring Syria.

---

[2] One of these statements was issued at an extraordinary general assembly of the DTK, Democratic Society Congress (Demokartik Toplum Kongresi). The DTK was founded in 2007 as part of the paradigmatic re-organisation of the PKK and aims to implement the confederalist project in Turkey (Biehl 2016; DTK 2016).

The international community expected Turkey, as a bordering country, to actively provide a humanitarian corridor to Kobanê and prevent the Islamic State group from seizing the city. Instead, the Turkish government imposed strong conditions on their support: the Kurds in Syria should join the Syrian-Arab opposition, PYD should distance themselves from the PKK, the three cantons of Rojava should disintegrate, and, finally, a buffer zone on the Turkish-Syrian border should be established in northern Syria, which at the time would have led to a de facto Turkish occupation of Rojava (Landler et al. 2014). At the same time, after the 2015 general elections, Turkey had launched so-called 'cleansing operations' in its southeast against supposed PKK members. However, since these military operations were carried out in all Kurdish-majority cities with HDP as the strongest party, this kind of re-securitisation of the Kurdish question effectively targeted Kurdish civilians in collective punishment for 'deviant' electoral behaviour. The imposed politics of war inside Turkey amounted to 4,551 deaths since 20 July 2015, of which 478 were civilians and 223 individuals of unknown affiliation between 16-35 years old, entire districts destroyed, and a significant displacement of the local population (International Crisis Group 2019).

The interconnected and simultaneous Turkish military interventions in Kurdish areas inside and outside Turkey demonstrate how domestic politics translate into foreign policies. The nationalist state doctrine in Turkey denies any form of Kurdish self-determination inside Turkey, including the right for free education in the mother tongue. However, this Turkish nationalism also perceives any sort of Kurdish autonomy outside Turkish borders as an immediate threat to Turkish state integrity and thus a legitimate military target. This pattern continued when the Kurdistan Democratic Party in the Kurdistan Region of Iraq, known for its opposition of the non-nation-state project in Rojava, held a referendum for independence in 2017. Against the expectations of the party leaders in Kurdistan-Iraq, the Turkish government cooperated with Iraqi prime minister Haider al-Abadi and Iran's theocratic regime and opposed Kurdish aspirations of national independence from Iraq.[3] Northern Syria's political project, however, is fundamentally different from the one established in northern Iraq. This is also due to divergent conditions such as differing territorial and ethnic situations in northern Iraq and northern Syria. For example, Iraq's Kurdistan region can be considered homogenous in the ways the population identifies as ethnically Kurdish; however, northern Syria has very heterogeneous areas such as Cizîre (Arabic: Jezira) making the realisation of an explicitly ethnocentric project more difficult. Therefore, the non-nation-state project in northern Syria also reflects the given demographics and geographical context. Hence, it proposes

---

[3] https://www.bbc.com/news/world-middle-east-35830375
https://www.reuters.com/article/us-mideast-crisis-kurds-referendum-turke-idUSKCN1C1135

a more radical social structure and a regional settlement that neither challenges any of the existing nation-state borders nor imposes dominance of one ethnic group over another. Despite this, since 2012, the Turkish government continually attacks—increasingly by military means—the emerging polity and claims that it threatens Turkey's national integrity.

In this political atmosphere of unfolding calls for democratic autonomy across Kurdish regions in the Middle East, a two-day meeting in the northern Syrian town of Rimelan formed a constituent assembly with 31 parties and 200 delegates in March 2016. This meeting took place in the fifth year of the Rojava resistance against the Islamic State group in Syria. The three self-administered cantons at the time, Kobanê, Afrîn and Cizîre, were represented, as well as representatives of Arab, Assyrian, Syriac, Armenian, Turkmen and Chechen peoples of the regions of Girê Spî/Tal Abyad, Shaddadi, Aleppo and Shehba.[4] In this first declaration of its kind since the Syrian war began, a significant majority of the northern Syrian peoples expressed their will to not declare national independence in the classical sense, but to defend and build a confederal system as part of conflict resolution in Syria. The assembly drafted a new social contract based on the constitutive principles of grassroots democracy, women's liberation, and full representation of all societal groups organised in a council system (Rojava Assembly 2016). Further, since the territory of the self-administration was extended into regions with non-Kurdish majorities, the political entity known as 'Democratic Federation of Rojava' was renamed to 'Democratic Federation of Northern Syria'. The shift from organising under the name of 'Rojava', which is a direct translation from Kurdish language and means 'setting sun', therefore describes the Western part of the wider region known as Kurdistan, to 'Northern Syria' and at a later stage to 'North and East Syria' expressed the non-ethnocentric claim of the newly established political system. These name changes also raised awareness for the project's development as a modality of autonomy that incorporates all linguistic, ethnic, and religious groups within the region. The rejection of Kurdish-inspired naming conventions also recognised interests of larger Arab-majority regions such as Raqqa, Manbij, and Deir ez-Zor that joined the self-administration. Since 2017, these local councils have been operating as part of the political system yet at the same time independently. However, despite the attempt at building a political project based on inclusivity, not all Kurdish actors in northern Syria supported the developments, some explicitly opposing the non-ethnocentric claim. For example, the Kurdish National Council, mostly known with its Kurdish abbreviation ENKS, was founded in 2011 and includes various Syrian Kurdish parties that criticise the PYD's confederalist project because it does not advocate an explicitly Kurdish

---

[4] https://www.bbc.com/news/world-middle-east-35830375

autonomy. [5] These parties support the Iraqi Kurdish proposal for a Kurdish nation-state as promoted by the political elites in the Kurdistan Regional Government of Iraq (Gunes and Lowe 2015).

With the renaming of the polity into 'Autonomous Administration of North and East Syria', the Future Syria Party was founded on 27 March 2018 with the goal to establish a post-war order in Syria that grants maximum autonomy to the regions, while at the same time preserving the integrity of the already existing nation-state borders. The party tried to work for democratic renewal and the interests of all social groups, while forging acceptance and unity among Christians, Arabs, and Kurds. Hevrîn Xelef, known for her diplomatic skills, served as the party's secretary general (Aslan 2019). Turkish-backed militants executed her during the first days of the Turkish offensive into north-eastern Syria in late 2019 (Hendi 2019).

Until the strategic defeat of the Islamic State group in their de facto capital in Raqqa in October 2017, Turkey's proxy involvement in northern Syria was predominantly by forming an ideological and logistical backyard for ISIS militants. In early 2018, the Turkish army launched the military operation 'Olive Branch' in Afrîn and entered the Syrian conflict as an explicit aggressor and since then as an active actor on the ground against the Kurdish-led polity in the north. In line with domestic practices of ethnic-social engineering over a century of Turkish history, President Erdogan and his advisers stated that the area around Afrîn should be 'cleaned' and returned to its 'real owners', denying the existence of the local Kurdish population (McGee 2019). Since then, particularly after launching 'Operation Peace Spring' in October 2019, followed by targeted drone attacks in early 2020 in the city of Kobanê, the Turkish army and its proxy militias have occupied parts of the northern region in Syria. This occupation not only threatens the region with demographic engineering, persecution of minorities, and forced migration but also endangers the experiment in alternative democracy.

Kurdish experience with state(less)ness in Syria and beyond

Selahattin Demirtaş, the imprisoned former co-chair of Turkey's left alliance HDP, best described statehood and its absence in a statement after the state-orchestrated assassination of human rights lawyer Tahir Elçi (Forensic Architecture 2018). According to Demirtas, "not the state killed Tahir Elci, but statelessness".[6] This expresses the two dimensions of statelessness for Kurds in the Middle East: the simple lack of a Kurdish nation state and, more important, the lack of fundamental protection of

---

[5] Unity talks that started in late 2019 and aimed to foster a rapprochement between the PYD and ENKS for a joint future in northern Syria, turned fragile after initial success when the ENKS rejected core principles of the Rojava model such as the co-chair system in October 2020.

[6] https://www.bbc.com/turkce/haberler/2015/11/151129_elci_cenaze_hatice_kamer

human and minority rights by any of the states that Kurds inhabit and are citizens of.

Therefore, while state authoritarianisms in Turkey, Syria, Iran, and Iraq have had their particularly distinct manifestations throughout time and region, Kurds and other minorities share a common history and collective consciousness of subjugation to necropolitical violence imposed by nation states trying to preserve state sovereignty through assimilation policies and enforced national homogenisation (Mbembe 2003; Burç and Tokatlı 2021).

The early manifestations of the new non-nation-state paradigm shifted the focus from the nation-state level and political claim-making to the local level and shaping an ethical and politically inclusive society. While amid the developing Syrian civil war, the new paradigm became the driving force behind the emergence of self-governance structures in Syria, as well as oppositional politics in Turkey (Gunes 2017; Burç 2018; Celep 2018), one cannot assume identical articulations of the shared paradigm in all regions mobilised by the Kurdish movement. The new polity in northern Syria must be contextualised within its previously mentioned close interconnectedness with Turkey and Syria's history of state authoritarianism against minorities in the north.

During the 1960s and 1970s, the Syrian government's Arabisation policies, like the 'Arab Belt' project of Hafiz al-Assad in 1973, resettled Kurdish populations and exchanged them for Arab populations. Already in 1962, hundreds of thousands of Kurds in Syria were stripped of their legal citizenship, rendering the Kurdish population in the north stateless by definition (Taştekin 2016; Burç and Oveisy 2019). This policy has an integral connection to Turkification policies that were in face after the establishment of the Turkish Republic in 1923. Among those stripped of Syrian citizenships were also families of former refugees who came from Turkey when Kurdish populations fled the violent state-homogenisation policies in Turkey during the 1930s and settled on the other side of the border in Syria (Burç and Tokatlı 2021; Çağaptay 2004).

The proposals for Kurdish self-determination started with the interconnectedness of the region, the arbitrariness of nation-state borders that divide traditional Kurdish homeland, and a shared experience of dominant nation states. However, the Kurdish movement proposes in the Rojava project something different from the classical approaches of minority nationalisms that claim nation-statehood, ethnic federalism, or simply the protection of minority rights, which eventually all function within the categories of the dominant nation-state paradigm. Rojava's political system has the distinctive goal of undoing the monocultural and hierarchical one-state/one-nation/one-flag principle.

Many note that the PKK founder Abdullah Öcalan's presence in Syria in 1979 critically shaped the mobilisation of northern Syrian populations for the politics of the Kurdish movement (Tejel 2011; Taştekin 2016; Schmidinger 2018). Öcalan (2016: 452) himself describes his presence in Syria as a significant memory in the collective consciousness of Kurdish people in the north. Thomas Schmidinger (2018) argues that the impact of the PKK during the 1980s and 1990s in Syria, has been mainly due to the movement's ability to fill the vacuum of a collective vision for minorities in the region, given that traditional and conservative Kurdish parties failed to offer a strategy out of the state authoritarianism imposed by the Ba'ath regime at the time. Fehim Tastekin (2016) emphasises that the Marxist approach on the minority question and the Kurdish issue was attractive in particular to young students in Damascus, as well as for populations in ethnically heterogenous border regions like Afrîn and Kobanê that later became key regions for building today's autonomous self-administration. The strong support for the PKK in Afrîn and Kobanê also derived from the de facto absence of other parties, which were mostly present in the region of Cizîre. As discussed previously, considering history and geographical proximity helps analysts understand the evolution of Kurdish politics in the region and the different quests for autonomy. Both Afrîn and Kobanê are located at the Turkish-Syrian border, while the region of Cizîre has been closer to the Iraqi side of Kurdistan and situated in the border triangle of Syria, Turkey and Iraq.

Following the PKK's paradigmatic reconceptualisation that reconstructed territorial and societal demands away from the undertones of the nation-state paradigm toward a more emancipated and self-reliant understanding of society, the PKK guerrillas—initially only considered as an armed threat to the nation states—became more focused on their social impact in the region. The guerrillas introduced conflict resolution through village assemblies that replaced traditional feudal mediators (Jongerden and Akkaya 2011). Women started relying on all-women guerrilla units that taught self-defence, both practically and ideologically (Üstündağ 2016). Women started to organise themselves in collectives to defend themselves against violence, forced marriages, or honour killings; they also participated in education and leadership, as well as in building autonomous structures for women in society. This led to an increasing recognition of gender equality that became one of the main pillars of democratic confederalism and democratic autonomy as exercised today in northern Syria's political system (Burç 2020).

Democratic autonomy and democratic confederalism

Northern Syria's experience of autonomy has been drastically shaped by the loss of state authority, geopolitical proxy wars, the ongoing Syrian civil war, and Turkish imperialist involvement. However, this political model's conceptual framework comes from PKK founder Abdullah Öcalan's political thought on the twin concepts of democratic autonomy and democratic confederalism. He has been developing this framework for conflict resolution and bottom-up resilience since early 1990s, yet more materialised since the early 2000s and under the harsh conditions of solitary confinement.

In these proposals, the Kurdish question is conceptualised as a democracy question defined by deepening democracy and creating decentralised structures of local self-governance designed to involve all citizens in decision-making and empower communities as well as marginalized communities within. Therefore, autonomy does not simply feature territorial boundaries or introduces minority rights within the hegemony of the dominant nation, but rather requires the democratisation of the interrelation of state and society (Gunes and Bayır 2020).

Abdullah Öcalan intended to provide a counterproposal to the existing nation-state structures and focused on challenging the systems of subordination, such as the subordination of minorities and of women. Öcalan, in fact, rearticulated theories on deliberative democracy and radical democracy from within the context of the Middle East. He also introduced a novelty by taking the subordination of women as a main reference point and showing how the current democracy deficit results from nation states inherently functioning through minority-majority dichotomies and the subordination of women.

For instance, while academic literature mostly describes the Rojava model as radical democracy based on grassroots organisation, using these categories uncritically from a Western perception might lead to false assumptions about Rojava's political system. Western discourse explains radical democracy as part of a state-centred concept of autonomy and methodologically reduces it to direct democratic practices of participation, which is about 'taking over' councils following a majoritarian approach or, for example, constructing a more 'women friendly' environment (Lijphart 2012; Martin 2013; Singh 2019). However, the Rojava political system's radical democracy does not rely on the competitive principle that is inherent to majoritarian conceptualisations of direct democracy. Its idea of autonomy uses the terms of competences and social practices, hence cannot be simply called 'radical democratic' from a Western point of view: its practice as a form of autonomy aims to achieve a new ethos of citizenship and community. Radical democracy as proposed by democratic confederalism foresees the transformation and democratisation of city governments by rooting them in popular assemblies and then weaving them together into a confederation consisting of municipalities and not nation states.

In his writings, Öcalan insists that building a confederalist system would neither threaten the territorial integrity of already existing nation states nor disregard the central government (Öcalan 2016; 2017). However, the municipal structures would eventually make the nation state's physical and imaginative borders obsolete for the political realm of community life. Democratic confederalism, as put forward by the Kurdish movement, therefore provides a model of dual power, creating a situation that makes it possible for self-administered, municipal areas to exist autonomously despite the existence of the nation state. Self-administrated bodies on all levels allow the political space to open to all strata of the society and to politically integrate society with all its divergent ethnic, religious, and political groups. These groups, by no means, represent static formations, because the idea of localising political participation in an anti-hierarchical structure, also foresees building new associations, confederations, and groups according to the given needs and situation, as well their dissolution when necessary. This dynamic approach challenges the idea of attributed identities to certain groups, which also means the unmaking of dichotomies such as majority and minority in how society is constituted politically. Öcalan promotes the central pillars of democracy and autonomy as integrating all social and political groups in decision-making. This integration ensures society's capacity to solve everyday problems in society, without the need for centralised power.

Structures of the self-administration in Rojava

The practical manifestations and implementation of the democratic autonomy concept have been changed and adjusted during the ongoing conflict in Syria, hence the difficulty of a scholarly assessment of the strengths, weaknesses, as well as types of implementation. The institutionalisation of a confederalist project in northern Syria has developed within less than a decade, but more crucially, has suffered from constant attacks by the so-called Islamic State forces and jihadist militias assigned as proxies by regional powers, a strict embargo by neighbouring states, including the KRI, and also Turkish military operations against the autonomous administration. Nevertheless, the self-administration developed three basic administrative institutions along with autonomous security forces and an independent yet integrated women's structure .

The three main structures of self-administration in Rojava are (1) Autonomous Administration, (2) Syrian Democratic Council and (3) TEV-DEM. The society organises itself starting from the smallest political unit, the commune with approximately 150 to 1,500 inhabitants. From the bottom-up, all inhabitants find representation in councils of neighbourhoods, then sub-districts, districts, cantons, regions, and finally in the Autonomous Administration. However, democratic autonomy also facilitates society's parallel organisation outside the communes in so-called civil institutions through committees on specific issues in the Autonomous Administration.

The Autonomous Administration, responsible for coordination between the regions, exists next to what can be described as an executive body known as the Syrian Democratic Council (SDC). The SDC can be considered with its diplomatic character as a political umbrella providing the political framework to resolve conflicts among various groups in Syria. Political parties can participate in the council, as well as representatives from civil society or the autonomous administrations. The SDC has three main bodies, the executive council, the political council, and the general conference. It has several offices: The Organisational Office, Women's Office, Foreign Relations Office, Media Office, Youth Office, Finance Office, and Archive Office. While first constituted mostly by Kurdish and/or left parties in northern Syria, the SDC has now been joined by a broader spectrum of parties and individuals such as the Syrian National Assembly, which initially had opposed the confederalist project as proposed by the SDC. The Syrian National Assembly announced its decision to join in June 2020, emphasising the need for unity of the northern Syrian people (Syrian Democratic Council 2020).

While the Autonomous Administration aims to administer government services through locally elected bodies and ministries on issues such as health, education, or infrastructure, the SDC seeks to represent political parties. Hence, the SDC, as an umbrella, tries to integrate political parties in northern Syria into a federal, democratic, and women-led political entity.

The third major institution in the political landscape of the Rojava model is TEV-DEM, which was already established in 2011 and translates into 'Movement for a Democratic Society'. It is an umbrella body for civil society organisations and representative and serves as a counter-power to the other two bodies (Rojava Information Center 2019; Knapp and Flach 2016).

The establishment of political structures amid an ongoing war has been mainly possible by gaining, after 2012, the de facto monopoly over the use of force. With Kurdish fighters defending and securing Kurdish majority areas in northern Syria, the security forces became the primary institutions and facilitators of governance structures (Allsopp and Wilgenburg 2019). The security forces have two organizational levels: The internal security forces such as the security police Asayish and Civilian Defense Forces (HPC) and the external defence forces such as the People's and Women's Protection Units (YPG/J), Syrian Democratic Forces (SDF), and Self-defence Duty Forces (HXP) serving as the sole military power protecting the territory from outside threats. The defence forces, the YPG/J and, after 2015, the SDF, mainly acted as the self-administration's military force. However, the Asayish was established to fill a security gap and to maintain public order. They became one of the most visible security forces of the self-administration, concerned with checkpoints administration, anti-terror, organised crime, traffic, and intelligence. While initially being established by the PYD, their institutionalisation took place within the context of the democratic autonomy project. For instance, in areas of Assyrian majority, the main police forces were connected to the local political organisations, like the Sutoro police (Syriac Security Office) in Cizîre. Despite Asayish's claim of operating within the democratic autonomy framework, hence fostering autonomous local security forces, some criticise Asayish as an explicitly partisan force of the PYD because of its commitment to the confederalist project and ideology (Allsopp and Wilgenburg 2019).

Beyond the prominent visibility of women as female fighters in the Women's Defence Units (YPJ) against the so-called Islamic State, the same logic of fostering women's rights and gender equality facilitated the building of autonomous civilian structures for women. The two parallel set of structures consist of, on the one hand, institutions that include men and women and, on the other hand, women-only institutions. The latter is represented by the Kongreya Star, a women's confederation of all women's groups in Rojava. The women's confederation gathers every two years to assess past development and to make new plans for women's autonomous structures in the NES. All women involved in any of the self-administration's institutions automatically belong to the women's confederation. This includes all governance levels such as councils, communes, cultural and artistic collectives, families and workers committees, and service institutions (Kongreya Star 2018; Knapp and Flach 2016; Rasit and Kolokotronis 2020).

Along with representation in the women's confederation, all women continue to maintain their autonomy as members of their respective institutions. Consequently, women do not only organise on a supra-level, in the women's confederation, but in every commune by creating their own women's commune parallel to the mixed structure (Dirik 2018). On every administrative and institutional level, the women's body makes decisions binding on all structures, with an additional veto right reserved for decisions taken in the mixed bodies. Furthermore, all institutional bodies, ranging from collectives, communes to political parties, have a co-chair system with one seat reserved for a man elected by the mixed-gender bodies and one seat reserved for a woman elected by the women-only bodies (Kongreya Star 2018).

This political system with autonomous women's organizations as an essential component attempts to establish an institutionally grounded, self-defence mechanism against possible male dominance and centralised power deriving from the patriarchal social structures. Therefore, the self-administration has dynamic institutions that alter according to the societal context. However, it does not compromise an inherent feature of the political system: equal representation and participation.

Conclusion

This essay has argued that the political system unfolding in northern Syria after the withdrawal of the Syrian military in 2012 must be assessed within the context of the region's interconnected history, Turkey's involvement, and Kurdish statelessness as an unsolved conundrum in the Middle East. The dynamic structure of the twin concepts of democratic autonomy and democratic confederalism strongly emphasises women's self-reliance as a revolutionary act of emancipation, as well as equal representation and participation to provide inner autonomy to communities within dominant communities. This distinguishes the Rojava project from modalities of autonomy that exist within the paradigms of the nation state, which inherently reinstate hegemonic dichotomies such as majority-minority. Therefore, the political system in Rojava proves to be a fundamental contribution to the wider discussions on how pluri-national democracies can be conceptualised beyond nation-state paradigms. Starting by unpacking the intertwined subordination of minorities and women, the essay discussed the paradigmatic journey of the Kurdish freedom movement under the PKK from a nationalist to a confederalist movement, as well as the role of Abdullah Öcalan in developing the ideas that facilitated the experiment—implemented in the midst of a war—in grassroots democracy, decentralisation, women's autonomy, and minority protection. The political system constructed on firm ideological grounds and a transregional resonance remains fragile given the increased military interventions by Turkey in the past five years. Being stuck in a continuous situation of defence against attacks from the Islamic State group, jihadist militias, Syrian regime, and most recently Turkey, clearly constrains the extent to which the political system can freely develop and progress.

References

Allsopp, Harriet, and Wladimir van Wilgenburg. 2019. *The Kurds of Northern Syria: Governance, Diversity and Conflicts*. Bloomsbury Publishing.

Aslan, Azize. 2019. 'Hevrin Khalaf and the Spirit of the Democratic Nation'. *ROAR Magazine*. 24 October 2019. https://roarmag.org/essays/hevrin-khalaf-interview/.

Biehl, Janet. 2016. 'The DTK's Updated Democratic Autonomy Proposal'. *Ecology or Catastrophe* (blog). 20 February 2016. http://www.biehlonbookchin.com/dtks-autonomy-proposal/.

Burç, Rosa. 2018. 'One State, One Nation, One Flag—One Gender? HDP as a Challenger of the Turkish Nation State and Its Gendered Perspectives'. *Journal of Balkan and Near Eastern Studies* 21 (3): 319–334.

———. 2020. 'Non-Territorial Autonomy and Gender Equality: The Case of the Autonomous Administration of North and East Syria - Rojava'. *Filozofija i Drustvo / Philosophy and Society* 31 (3): 319–39.

Burç, Rosa, and Fouad Oveisy. 2019. 'Rojava Is Under Existential Threat'. *Jacobin Magazine*. 22 February 2019. https://jacobinmag.com/2019/02/rojava-united-states-withdrawal-syria-erdogan.

Burç, Rosa, and Mahir Tokatlı. 2019. 'Becoming an Autocracy Under (Un)Democratic Circumstances: Regime Change Under AKP Rule'. In *Erdoğan's 'New' Turkey Attempted Coup d'état and the Acceleration of Political Crisis*, edited by Nikos Christofis. Routledge.

————. 2020. 'A Second Foundation? Constitution, Nation-Building and the Deepening of Authoritarianism in Turkey'. In *Back to the 30s? Recurring Crises of Capitalism, Liberalism and Democracy*, edited by Jeremy Rayner, Susan Falls, George Souvlis, and Taylor Nelms. Palgrave Macmillan.

Çağaptay, Soner. 2004. 'Race, Assimilation and Kemalism: Turkish Nationalism and the Minorities in the 1930s'. *Middle Eastern Studies* 40 (3): 86–101.

Candar, Cengiz. 2013. *'Leaving the Mountain': How May the PKK Lay down Arms? Freeing the Kurdish Question from Violence*. Tesev Publication.

Celep, Ödül. 2018. 'The Moderation of Turkey's Kurdish Left: The Peoples' Democratic Party (HDP)'. *Turkish Studies* 19 (5): 723–47.

Dirik, Dilar. 2018. 'The Revolution of Smiling Women'. In *Routledge Handbook of Postcolonial Politics*, edited by Olivia U. Rutazibwa and Robbie Shilliam, 1st ed., 222–38. Routledge.

DTK. 2016. '14-Punkte-Resolution des DTK'. Civaka Azad. 3 January 2016. http://civaka-azad.org/14-punkte-resolution-des-dtk/.

Forensic Architecture. 2018. 'Investigation of the Audio-Visual Material Included in the Case File of the Killing of Tahir Elçi on 28 November 2015'. Goldsmiths University. https://content.forensic-architecture.org/wp-content/uploads/2019/03/FA-TE-Report_12_English_public.pdf.

Gunes, Cengiz. 2017. 'Turkey's New Left, NLR 107, September–October 2017'. *New Left Review*, no. 107. https://newleftreview.org/issues/II107/articles/cengiz-gunes-turkey-s-new-left.

Gunes, Cengiz, and Derya Bayır. 2020. 'Democratic Autonomy in Kurdish Regions of Syria'. In *Non-Territorial Autonomy and Decentralization. Ethno-Cultural Diversity Governance*, edited by Tove H. Malloy and Levente Sala, 115–33. Routledge.

Gunes, Cengiz, and Robert Lowe. 2015. 'The Impact of the Syrian War on Kurdish Politics Across the Middle East'. London: Chatham House.

Hendi, Ahed Al. 2019. 'The Dream of Syrian Democracy Was Killed by U.S.-Backed Jihadis'. *Foreign Policy* (blog). 11 June 2019. https://foreignpolicy.com/2019/11/06/hevrin-khalaf-murder-syrian-revolution-jihadis/.

International Crisis Group. 2019. 'Turkey's PKK Conflict: A Visual Explainer'. International Crisis Group. 3 January 2019. https://www.crisisgroup.org/content/turkeys-pkk-conflict-visual-explainer.

Jongerden, Joost, and Ahmet Hamdi Akkaya. 2011. 'Born from the Left: The Making of the PKK'. In *Nationalisms and Politics in Turkey : Political Islam, Kemalism and the Kurdish Issue*, 123–42. Routledge.

Knapp, Michael, and Anja Flach. 2016. *Revolution in Rojava: Democratic Autonomy and Women's Liberation in Syrian Kurdistan*. Translated by Janet Biehl. London: Pluto Press.

Kongreya Star. 2018. 'Kongreya Star and Its Committees'. https://rojavainformationcenter.com/storage/2019/12/Kongreya-Star-2018-Brochure.pdf.

Landler, Mark, Anne Barnard, and Eric Schmitt. 2014. 'Turkish Inaction on ISIS Advance Dismays the U.S.' *The New York Times*, 7 October 2014, https://www.nytimes.com/2014/10/08/world/middleeast/isis-syria-coalition-strikes.html.

Lijphart, Arend. 2012. *Patterns of Democracy: Government Forms and Performance in Thirty-Six Countries*. 2nd ed. New Haven: Yale University Press.

Martin, James. 2013. *Chantal Mouffe: Hegemony, Radical Democracy, and the Political*. Routledge.

Mbembe, Achille. 2003. 'Necropolitics'. *Public Culture* 15 (1): 11–40.

McGee, Thomas. 2019. 'Turkey's Occupation and Expansion in Syria'. OpenDemocracy. 11 November 2019. https://www.opendemocracy.net/en/north-africa-west-asia/turkeys-occupation-and-expansion-in-syria/.

Mouffe, Chantal. 1993. *The Return of the Political*. London: Verso.

Öcalan, Abdullah. 2016. *Demokratik kurtulus ve özgür yasami insa: (Imrali notlari)*. Neuss: Wesanen Mezopotamya.

———. 2017. *The Political Thought of Abdullah Öcalan: Kurdistan, Woman's Revolution and Democratic Confederalism*. London: Pluto Press.

Polletta, Francesca. 2004. *Freedom Is an Endless Meeting: Democracy in American Social Movements*. Chicago: University of Chicago Press.

———. 2014. 'Participatory Democracy's Moment'. *Journal of International Affairs* 68 (1): 79–92.

Rasit, Huseyin, and Alexander Kolokotronis. 2020. 'Decentralist Vanguards: Women's Autonomous Power and Left Convergence in Rojava'. *Globalisations* 17 (5): 869–83.

Rojava Assembly, Declaration. 2016. 'Final Declaration of the Rojava-Northern Syria Democratic Federal System'. *YPG International* (blog). 17 March 2016. https://ypginternational.blackblogs.org/2016/07/01/final-declaration-of-the-rojava-northern-syria-democratic-federal-system-constituent-assembly/.

Rojava Information Center. 2019. 'Report: The Political System of North and East Syria'. https://rojavainformationcenter.com/2019/12/report-beyond-the-frontlines/.

Schmidinger, Thomas. 2018. *Rojava: Revolution, War and the Future of Syria's Kurds*. London: Pluto Press.

Singh, Jakeet. 2019. 'Decolonizing Radical Democracy'. *Contemporary Political Theory* 18 (3): 331–56.

Syrian Democratic Council. 2020. 'The Syrian National Assembly Announces Its Joining to The Syrian Democratic Council'. 18 June 2020. http://m-syria-d.com/en/?p=2522.

Taştekin, Fehim. 2016. *Rojava: Kürtlerin Zamanı*. 1. baskı. İletişim Yayınları ; Bugünün Kitapları, 2375. 210. İstanbul: İletişim Yayınları.

Tejel, Jordi. 2011. *Syria's Kurds: History, Politics and Society*. Paperback ed. Routledge Advances in Middle East and Islamic Studies 16. London: Routledge.

Üstündağ, Nazan. 2016. 'Self-Defense as a Revolutionary Practice in Rojava, or How to Unmake the State'. *South Atlantic Quarterly* 115 (1): 197–210.

CHAPTER 6

STRUGGLE AGAINST ISIS AND THE INTEGRATION OF ARAB TERRITORIES IN THE AUTONOMOUS ADMINISTRATION

Wladimir van Wilgenburg

Introduction

The Autonomous Administration of North and East Syria (AANES) was formed in September 2018 (Wilgenburg 2018). The administration includes Arab majority areas such as Manbij, Raqqa, parts of Deir al-Zor province and Kurdish towns of northern Syria (Reuters 2018). Although the People's Protection Units (*Yekîneyên Parastina Gel* - YPG) initially only controlled Kurdish majority towns such as Derik, Efrin, Kobani and Amuda in 2012 (Reuters 2012), the Syrian Democratic Forces (SDF) spearheaded by the YPG by 2018 already controlled a quarter of the country (Reuters 2018). This essay will explain how the project of the Democratic Union Party (PYD) and the YPG initially had a more Kurdish focus on Rojava (West Kurdistan[1]) but increasingly focused on gaining a more 'Syrian focus' after the integration of Arab territories in the autonomous project from 2013 to 2019 during the fight against ISIS. As a result, the YGP became the SDF, and the Democratic Union Party (PYD) became the SDC. Also, the geographical focus changed from Rojava to the northeast of Syria.

The Rojava Revolution and self-governance (2012-2016)

The Democratic Union Party (Partiya Yekîtiya Demokrat, PYD) was formed in 2003 (Allsopp and Wilgenburg 2019: 61). The party operated within the umbrella structure of the *Koma Civakên Kurdistan*, the Kurdistan Communities Union (KCK), which was formed by the Kurdistan Workers Party (Partiya Karkerên Kurdistan, PKK) in 2005 to link affiliated armed and political organisations across Kurdish areas of Turkey, Iran, Iraq, and Syria (Allsopp and Wilgenburg 2019: 62), (Akkaya and Jongerden 2012: 7).

---

[1] Western Kurdistan is the term Kurdish nationalists use to describe Kurdish areas of northeast Syria. They argue that the greater Kurdistan was divided into four parts: the Kurdish areas of Turkey (North Kurdistan), Iraq (South Kurdistan), Syria (West Kurdistan), and Iran (East Kurdistan).

The KCK parties follow the democratic confederalism ideology of the imprisoned PKK leader Abdullah Öcalan that aims to build self-governing, non-statist bodies in the four separate parts of Kurdistan. Öcalan aspired not to build an independent Kurdish state based on the traditional nation-state model, but local autonomous administrations inspired by the ideology of the American anarchist Murray Bookchin (Allsopp and Wilgenburg 2019: 63). This project builds on the self-government of local communities and organises in the form of open councils, town councils, local parliaments, and larger congresses (Allsopp and Wilgenburg 2019: 7). Although Öcalan sought to build autonomous structures in areas where Kurdish communities live, he did not try to create a traditional Kurdish ethno-state build on homogenisation and with a one-language policy or society build on one common language, culture, market or history, similar to the nationalist projects of Arab, Turkish, and Iranian nationalist states (Komun 2018), (Knapp, Flach, & Ayboga, 2016: 157). According to the imprisoned PKK leader Abdullah Öcalan, the *democratic nation* in which ethnicities could co-exist was the alternative to state nationalism:

> Democratic confederalism presents the option of a democratic nation as the fundamental tool to resolve the ethnic, religious, urban, local, regional and national problems caused by the monolithic, homogeneous, monochrome, fascist social model implemented by modernity's nation-state. Within the democratic nation every ethnicity, religious understanding, city, local, regional and national entity has the right to participate with its own identity and democratic federate structure. (Öcalan 2016: 18).

The PYD first adopted Öcalan's 'democratic autonomy' project in 2007 (Allsopp and Wilgenburg 2019: 90). In December 2011, the PYD founded the People's Council of Western Kurdistan (*Meclîsa Gel a Rojavayê Kurdistanê* - PCWK) that later became the PYD representative in the Erbil power-sharing agreements (Allsopp and Wilgenburg 2019: XV). Moreover, in 2011, the PYD formed the Movement for a Democratic Society (*Tevgera Civaka Demokratîk* – TEV-DEM) that later played an important role in setting up local administrations in Syria (Allsopp and Wilgenburg 2019: XVII). This all formed the basis of the official establishment of the local Autonomous Administrations (AA) in 2014. The YPG also described itself as the 'Democratic Nation's Defence Force'. Although the YPG followed Öcalan's ideology, it emphasised its non-partisanship and non-affiliation with any political parties such as the PYD (YPG Rojava).

However, this self-government could not be established without territorial control and military dominance. Initially, there were plans to rule the Kurdish territories through the Supreme Kurdish Committee, (*Desteya*

Bilind a Kurd). An administrative committee formed in accordance with the Erbil power-sharing agreement of 12 July 2012 between the PYD-led PCWK and the Kurdish National Council (KNC) mediated under the auspices of Masoud Barzani, the leader of the Kurdistan Democratic Party (*Partiya Demokrat a Kurdistanê* - KDP) and the (now former) president of the Kurdistan Region of Iraq (*Hikûmeta Herêmî Kurdistan* - KRG) (Allsopp and Wilgenburg 2019: XVII, 72). On 1 July 2012, the different sides signed a supplementary agreement outlining the functions of the SKC and established on 9–10 July a committee with five representatives from each side (Allsopp and Wilgenburg 2019: 73).

Following the deal, the YPG started to take control of Kurdish territories on 19 July 2012 in what the PYD-friendly media branded the *Rojava Revolution* (ANF 2018). However, by 2013, the YPG also captured Arab-populated areas in the Hasakah province, which had a large Kurdish population but was very ethnically diverse and not predominantly Kurdish (Allsopp and Wilgenburg 2019: 15). By the end of 2013, the YPG controlled, with the help of the Shammar tribe, Arab-populated areas such as the Yarubiya border crossing in October 2013 and the oil fields around Rmeilan (Drott 2014, Wilgenburg 2014). In July 2013, after a number of fights with Arab Islamist opposition groups, they completely took the mixed city of Ras al-Ain (Serêkaniyê) populated half by Arabs and half by Kurds (Wilgenburg 2014). The YPG also started to recruit Arabs and by 2014 included 300 Arabs in the ranks of a larger YPG force totalling more than 35,000 fighters (Glioti 2014, Lund 2013). The Syriac Military Council also started to cooperate with the YPG (Hurriyet 2013). The YPG created local councils and internal security forces in every town taken (Asayis). Moreover, by 2013, the first plans were announced to create an interim administration (Reuters 2013).

The Supreme Kurdish Council—the intended government of the Kurdish areas—became obsolete because the KNC and PYD failures to share power and overcome ideological differences despite the Erbil Agreement in June 2012 and revised in December 2013 (Allsopp and Wilgenburg 2019: 71). While the PYD followed the Öcalanist ideology, the KNC followed the more traditional Kurdish nationalist approach of the movement led by the KDP's Mullah Mustafa Barzani (Allsopp and Wilgenburg 2019: 82), (Syria Direct 2020). Most, but not all, of the Kurdish political parties within the KNC traced their origins to the first Syrian Kurdish political party established in 1957: the Kurdistan Democratic Party-Syria (*Partiya Demokrat a Kurdistanê li Sûriyê*, KDP-S) (Allsopp and Wilgenburg 2019: 49).

The KNC supported the idea of a geographically defined federal region similar to the Kurdistan Region of Iraq, carrying the name of Kurdistan, while also including other national, ethnic, and religious groups (Allsopp and

Wilgenburg 2019: 82). Therefore, the different ideologies of the Barzanist (KNC) and Öcalanist (PYD) Kurdish movements made it difficult to form a joint PYD-KNC administration. On 22 October 2014, the KNC and PYD signed another agreement. However, this agreement was never implemented due to disagreements, different political alliances, and ideological disputes (Rudaw 2014).

Instead, the Democratic Autonomous Administration formed in January 2014 and followed Abdullah Öcalan's principles of democratic autonomy and the democratic nation. This led to the creation in January 2014 of local canton administrations in the three Kurdish enclaves not connected by land: Jazira (Hasakah province), Afrin, and Kobani (Allsopp and Wilgenburg 2019: 3). The Social Contract of the 'Democratic Self-rule Administration Project' included several references to the administration's multi-ethnic character, including the rights of Kurds, Arabs, and Syriacs (Assyrians) to teach and to be taught their native languages (Çiviroğlu). The Contract also emphasised that the administrations were established in the name of a 'confederation of Kurds, Arabs, Syriacs, Arameans, Turkmen, Armenians, and Chechens.' (Çiviroğlu) Moreover, the Shammar tribal leader Sheikh Hamdi Daham al-Hadi was appointed co-governor for the Hasakah province, where local fighters had helped the YPG capture the Yarubiye border crossing (Allsopp and Wilgenburg 2019: 126). His Sanadid forces later participated in YPG and SDF campaigns in Hasakah province and even Raqqa (Al Jazeera 2017). From the beginning, the YPG had the long-term aim of not just controlling the Kurdish enclaves in northern Syria. The YPG wanted to unite the three Kurdish canton administrations by controlling the ethnic diverse territories on the Syrian-Turkish border from Derik to Afrin (Wilgenburg 2014). This was not possible without the cooperation with local non-Kurdish populations in towns with non-Kurdish majorities, such as Manbij, Bab, Jarabulus and Tal Abyad and cooperation with other armed Sunni groups operating in the area. This also meant more civilians needed to be recruited from these towns for both military and administrative functions. Therefore, the YPG attempted to create more local alliances in provinces such as Hasakah in Aleppo.

However, this ambition led to YPG clashes between 2012 and 2014 with rival armed factions in the provinces of Aleppo and Raqqa. These groups with Islamist and Arab-nationalist tendencies wanted to capture all of Syria's territory and remove Assad from power. The YPG and the YPG-backed Jabhat al-Akrad (Kurdish Front) FSA group had several battles with ISIS, Jabhat al-Nusra, Free Syrian Army (FSA) groups in mixed areas near Aleppo, but also in Tal Abyad in July 2013 (Jadaliyya 2015). However, clashes also took place in the Hasakah province between the YPG and rival rebel groups, with the biggest battle taking place around Serekaniye.

Furthermore, YPG's ambitions raised fears in Turkey that a 'hostile force' would cut 'its (border) ties over land with the rest of Syria and the Middle East' (Daily Sabah 2016). Turkey feared the ultimate goal of the YPG would be to open a corridor to the Mediterranean Sea (Daily Sabah 2018). Turkey therefore heavily supported armed Sunni groups not only against Assad, but especially to prevent territorial success of the YPG. However, because Arab Sunni rivals could not stop the YPG from expanding, Turkey later intervened itself with the Turkish army and started to occupy Syrian territories from 2016.

By January 2014, due to more splits within the Syrian insurgency, the first major clashes started to break out between ISIS and other armed non-state actors in governorates such as Aleppo, Idlib, and Raqqa (BBC 2014). By July 2014, ISIS said it wanted to set up an Islamic state or caliphate in Iraq and Syria, which led to more fighting between ISIS and other groups (BBC 2014). In September 2014, the joint FSA-YPG Euphrates Volcano Operations Room (Burkan al-Firat) was created in Kobani to gain support from the US-led coalition against ISIS that first started to fight ISIS in Iraq (Civiroglu and Wilgenburg 2014; Steele 2015). The Operations Room included FSA groups such as Liwa al-Tawhid (eastern section), Liwa Thuwar al-Raqqa, Kata'ib Shams al-Shamal of the Dawn of Freedom Brigades coalition, Saraya Jarabulus, Jabhat al-Akrad, and Jaysh al-Qasas (ANF 2014; al-Tamimi 2014). Some of these groups such as Jaysh al-Qassas from Deir az-Zour and Liwa Thuwar al-Raqqa, a former al-Qaida affiliate, fled from ISIS and sought refuge with the YPG (al-Tamimi 2014). Groups from the Aleppo countryside such as Jabhat al-Akrad (a YPG proxy group), and Shams Al-Shamal also joined the forces against ISIS.

The group sought to fight in all areas under ISIS control in the governorates of Aleppo and Raqqa, including Karakozak, Sirrin, Jarabulus, Manbij and Raqqa and carried out small operations against ISIS (ANF 2014; Wilgenburg 2014; Steele 2015). Although the YPG initially planned to focus only on the northern Aleppo corridor, they expanded their operations to Raqqa to gain international support. In response, a few days later, ISIS besieged the city of Kobani, seeing this new alliance as a major threat and feared the possibility that it would gain US support (Caksu 2015; Wilgenburg 2014). This attack in fact led the US to back the YPG and its allies with air support on 27 September 2014 and also with ammunition, medical supplies, and weapons on 20 October 2014 (BBC 2015). As a result, the struggle in Kobani lasted from 15 September 2014 until 15 July 2015 (BBC 2015).

The Euphrates Volcano alliance/operations room (in Arabic: *Burkan al-Furat*) preceded the US-backed Syrian Democratic Forces (*Quwwāt Sūriyā al-Dīmuqrāṭiya* – SDF) founded in October 2015 after the victory over the ISIS siege of Kobani (Reuters 2015). The alliance included YPG, groups such as

Jaysh al-Thuwwar (Army of Rebels) (from Idlib and Aleppo), the Arab tribal Jaysh al-Sanadeed militia from the Shammar tribe (Hasakah province), the Christian Syriac Military Council but also other groups previously belonging to the Euphrates Volcano alliance. The US-led coalition labelled the SDF's Arab component as the Syrian Arab Coalition (SAC) (although the SDF or the local Arab SDF forces never used this term) (Reuters 2015). The coalition used this term to assuage Turkish fears that they supported the YPG. As a result, the coalition emphasised that training, advise-and-assist operations, airstrikes, and material support went to the Syrian Arab Coalition and not the YPG (Department of Defense 2016). 'We don't give arms to YPG. Currently we are working with the Sunni Syrian Arabs,' a Department of Defense (DoD) official told a Turkish pro-government news agency in October 2015 (AA 2015). The force had consisted of 3,500 to 5000 fighters (Pentagon Inspector General: 6, 40). According to the DoD, having the 'Syrian Arab Coalition in the lead helps reduce Turkey's sensitivity to the Kurdish YPG' (Pentagon Inspector General: 40). However, in reality, Kurdish commanders continued to lead the SDF, although an increasing number of SDF soldiers had an Arab identity. Many individual fighters enlisted with the SDF, but also independent groups joined the SDF who had previously worked with the YGP, such as al-Sanadid, various small FSA groups from Raqqa (Jaysh Thuwar al-Raqqa), Idlib (Jaysh al-Thuwar), Aleppo, and Deir ar Zour (Elite Forces) (Reuters 2017; Omran 2018; SOHR 2018).

Moreover, in December 2015, a multi-ethnic Syrian Democratic Council (SDC) became the political counterpart to the SDF and started to replace the role of the more Kurdish PYD and TEV-DEM (Allsopp and Wilgenburg 2019: XVI, 128). While the Kurds had completely dominated the PYD and TEV-DEM, the SDC included Syrians in areas with a SDF presence in the Arab-majority provinces. Some fighters even came from areas outside of the northeast of Syria.

From 2014 until 2015, the SDF and YPG took and absorbed significant (mostly Arab-populated) territories from ISIS, including Tal Hamis and Tal Barak (February 2015), Kezwan Mountains and the towns of Tal Tamir, Mabrouka, Suluk, Tal Abyad and Ain Issa (May and June 2015), Sarrin (September 2015), Al-Hol (November 2015), Tishreen Dam (December 2015) (YPG Rojava). Moreover, the YPG continued to expand also towards Deir ar-Zour, by capturing Al-Shaddadi (February 2016) and an area southeast of the Kezwan Mountains (March 2016) (YPG Rojava).

The US-led coalition support for the SDF made it more possible for the SDF and YPG to connect the three cantons as long as ISIS was present in these areas (Allsopp and Wilgenburg 2019: 123). This also resulted in the integration of more Arab territories in the administration territory. The SDF captured the town of Tal Abyad in June 2015 and connected for the first time the cantons of Cizere and Kobani (Reuters 2015). Moreover, in February 2016, the YPG and YPG-aligned FSA rebels captured, allegedly with Russian support, the town of Til Rifaat in Northern Aleppo in north-western Syria (Allsopp and Wilgenburg 2019: 123). The SDF developed an assembly to govern this area called Shahba region alongside the DAAs (Allsopp and Wilgenburg 2019: 123).

Also, SDF-linked forces moved into the northern Aleppo border corridor from the east of the Euphrates. On 4 April 2016, the SDF helped form the Arab-majority Manbij Military Council that included fighters from Sunni Arab factions such as Shams al-Shamal, Jabhat Akrad, Ahrar al-Suriya, (Liwa) Jund al-Haramain, Faruq Brigades, and even Jaish al-Islam (Manbij Military Council).[2] In August 2016, US support helped SDF capture the town of Manbij (Allsopp and Wilgenburg 2019: 124). After SDF conquered Manbij on 14 August 2016, it created the Bab Military Council led by Jamal Abu Juma (Reuters 2016). Furthermore, the SDF created the Jarabulus Military Council on 22 August 2016 (ANHA 2016).[3] These councils were established to besiege the northern Aleppo border strip between Azaz and Jarablus (the so-called Shahba region) and to connect the cantons (Allsopp and Wilgenburg 2019: 123). In response, on 24 August 2016, Turkish-backed groups and the Turkish military launched Operation Euphrates Shield in the northern Aleppo border strip. They intended to capture Al-Rai, Bab, and Jarabulus and prevent the SDF-linked factions from connecting the Kobani and Afrin cantons (Allsopp and Wilgenburg 2019: 123).

From cantons to federalism (2016-2018)

Due to the SDF's expansion into Arab majority areas outside of the traditional Kurdish canton areas, a conference on March 2016 in Rmeilan in northeast Syria planned to establish the self-administered 'Democratic Federation of Rojava - Northern Syria', DFNS (Reuters 2016). An administration only for the Kurdish heartland was no longer feasible. As a result, the internal boundaries of the DFNS were slightly redrawn into three regions: the Afrin region (including Afrin Canton and the Shahba Canton in northern Aleppo, including areas such as Til Rifaat, Ahras, Fafin, Kafr Naya), the Euphrates region (including the newly created Kobani canton and Tal Abyad canton) and the Jazira region (Favier 2018: 7). However, this did not include areas liberated by the SDF in 2016 and 2017 such as Raqqa, Tabqa,

---

[2] Author's interview with with Shervan Derwish, a Manbij Military Council spokesperson, 17 August 2019.
[3] An allegedly Turkish agent assassinated the leader of the Jarabulus Military Council, Abdul Sattar on the same day of the creation of the new council. See: Aranews. 2016. Kurds accuse Turkish intelligence of assassinating military leader in Syria's Jarabulus. http://aranews.net/kurds-accuse-turkish-intelligence-assassinating-military-leader-syrias-jarabulus/ (accessed 20 May).

Manbij or parts of Deir ar Zour. These were expected to possibly join the federation later (Favier 2018: 7). To reflect the ethnic diversity of the regions, the SDF appointed as new co-leaders of the administration an Arab from the Arab-majority border town of Tal Abyad, Mansour Saloum, and a Kurd from the town of Derik (Malikiye) populated by Kurds, and Assyrians, Hediya Yousef (Wilgenburg 2016). However, in December 2016, when the administration removed 'Rojava' (West Kurdistan) from its name to more accurately reflect the ethnic diversity and geography of the new federal region, this led to protests from Kurdish nationalists (Arafat 2016).

The SDF, by 2016, grew to a significant force of 45,000 fighters with 13,000 Arab fighters (ABC News 2016). This starkly contrasted to two years earlier when the YPG only had around 300 Arab fighters (Lund 2013). The SDF also needed to recruit more Arabs in order to capture the so-called ISIS capital of Raqqa. However, despite objections from Turkey, the Trump administration at this time decided to directly arm the Kurdish YPG to take Raqqa, (Reuters 2017). The operations started in November 2016 and in October 2017 led to the capture of Raqqa with the help of heavy air support (BBC 2017).

Moreover, the SDF started to move towards the primarily Arab-populated and oil-rich province of Deir ar Zour and launched the Jazeera Storm campaign on 9 September 2017 to clear ISIS out of the Arab-majority province of Deir ar-Zour (Wilgenburg 2017; Reuters 2017). This led to a race between Russian and Iranian-backed regime forces and the US-backed SDF forces for territory in the Deir ar Zour province (Crisis Group 2020). Just as in Manbij, the operations were supposed to be led by the primarily Arab Deir ar-Zor Military Council developed by the SDF in December 2016 under the command of Abu Khawla (Crisis Group 2020; Awad 2018: 12; Barfi 2017). Also, a civil council was formed for Deir ar Zour, similar to earlier civil councils created for Manbij and Raqqa to rule those territories.

Before 2014, the YPG never planned to capture large parts of Deir ar Zour including its oil and gas fields. The operation resulted from US ambitions in the region to counter ISIS but also to further stop the expansion of territorial control by Iranian-backed militias backing the Syrian government.

Before 2014, the YPG never expressed any ambition to fight in Deir ar Zour nor Raqqa. According to an International Crisis Group (ICG) report from May 2020, the SDF wanted to control the huge oil resources in Deir ar Zour to gain political and economic leverage over Damascus, 'as part of its effort to secure significant autonomy within a decentralised Syria' (Crisis Group 2020). For whatever reason, the SDF decided to capture ISIS territories in Deir ar Zour. This action again increased the SDF-controlled territory far from the traditional Kurdish-populated towns near the border. Although Manbij, Raqqa, and Tal Abyad had small Kurdish populations, Deir ar Zour had none.

Moreover, international support and legitimacy increased for the SDF when it followed coalition interests and fought ISIS in Arab-majority areas. More importantly, this support included airpower, training, and weapons. Due to the coalition support, thousands of Arabs joined the SDF for reasons varying from conscription, the need of salaries, desire to liberate home areas from ISIS, or being allied to one of the most powerful forces backed with US air power (Crisis Group 2017). However, Turkey blocked the political counterpart to the SDF, the Syrian Democratic Council (SDC), from joining negotiations on Syria. This differed from Turkey's acceptance of the KNC that belonged to the Turkish-backed National Coalition of Syrian Revolution and Opposition Forces, also known in Arabic as Etilaf (Kurdistan 24 2019).

The new autonomous administration (2018-2020)

Due to the increase territorial expansion and also opposition to the central regime, an Autonomous Administration in North and East Syria (AANES) was formed to include SDF-controlled areas around Raqqah, Manbij, and Deir al-Zour (Allsopp and Wilgenburg 2019: 89). The administration also moved its administrative capital from the city of Qamishli (traditionally seen as the capital of Syrian Kurdistan) to the town of Ain al Issa located in the Arab-majority Raqqa governorate, which lies between Tal Abyad and Raqqa (Wilgenburg 2019).

According to researchers Harriet Allsop and Wladimir van Wilgenburg, 'these changes in names and organisation reflected various attempts to alter the external appearance of the Administration, de-ethnicise it, widen its appeal and meet pressures and satisfy concerns that inevitably arose from forming alliances, securing external support, and building legitimacy (Allsopp and Wilgenburg 2019: 89).

By March 2019, the SDF also finished its campaign in Deir ar Zour and liberated the last territories held by ISIS. The SDF had sacrificed a total of 11,000 fighters since the beginning of the war (Wilgenburg 2019).

The SDF expanded because of further recruitment during the campaigns in Arab-majority towns. By August 2017, the SDF said it had around 50,000 fighters, with 60 per cent Arab, 30 per cent Kurdish, and 10 per cent Arabic (from other ethnic groups (Reuters 2017). According to a US-led coalition spokesperson, the SDF in 2017 had around 31,000 Kurds and 24,000 Arabs (Reuters 2017). The coalition, by September 2017, had trained around 8,500 troops and delivered weapons, ammunition, and more than 500 vehicles and equipment to more than 40,000 troops (Department of Defense 2017). By

January 2019, the SDF had reportedly 70,000 fighters (Reuters 2019).

This indicates that the SDF was much more effective in recruiting and vetting Arab fighters than did the other Syrian rebel groups. The Pentagon spent $384 million on equipping and training only 180 fighters for Syrian rebel groups: 145 fighters remained in the program, with 95 being in Syria (USATODAY 2015). During this period, the SDF trained thousands inside Syria.

However, Turkey remained uneasy over the SDF successes and the continued US support for the SDF. Therefore, Turkey occupied Afrin during Operation Olive Branch January–March 2018 and caused the SDF and the civil administrations to suffer significant territorial losses (Allsopp and Wilgenburg 2019: 200). After the fall of Afrin, the Afrin canton administration moved to the Shahba area near Til Rifaat.

Although Turkey took control of Afrin, Turkey continued to threaten to attack more areas under SDF control. In June 2019, the SDF started to restructure the SDF and form military councils in order to reorganise border security and to make the SDF more representative (Defense Post 2019). This included around 10 military councils and the already existing councils such as the Manbij, Deir ar Zour, Bab, and Jarabulus councils. From September 2019, the US started to run joint US-Turkish patrols. The YPG began to remove fortifications and units from the border in order to stop further Turkish aggression by trying to make concessions to Turkish security concerns (CNN 2019).

However, the joint patrols did not assuage Turkey's military interests. In October 2019, Turkey launched the Peace Spring operation, which led to Turkey controlling Tal Abyad and Ras al-Ain (Serekaniye) and the US pulling forces away from the border (Allsopp and Wilgenburg 2019: 200; Al Jazeera 2019). Turkey almost pushed through to Ain al Issa, which would have divided that administration (Guardian 2019).

Turkey also carried out demographic changes in Afrin and other territories conquered in the Peace Spring action by settling displaced Syrians in the so-called safe zone under its control (Arafat 2010). As a result, Afrin's ethnic composition changed significantly (Guardian 2018).

Initially, Turkey aimed to control all the border towns between Kobani and Derik to create a so-called safe zone to settle one million Syrians from other areas. This would have also led to significant demographic changes similar to Afrin, but due to a ceasefire negotiated by Russia and US representatives the Turkish expansion was limited to the towns of Serekaniye (Ras al-Ain) and Tal Abyad, which is more than 1,000 km² of territory (Wilgenburg 2019; Haenni and Quesnay 2020: 1). The US decided to keep around 500 to 600 troops in Deir ar Zour and Hasakah, while it pulled out from other areas under SDF control (Wilgenburg 2020).

However, despite the Turkish invasion, the autonomous administration created in 2018 in Ain al Issa stayed intact. The SDF Commander-in-Chief Mazloum Abdi had no major defection of Arab SDF fighters or uprising of Arab citizens in north-eastern Syria to support either Syrian regime forces or Turkey in areas like Raqqa or Deir ar Zour (Wilgenburg 2020).

According to a European-supported think-tank that published a report in February, the autonomous administration and SDF could continue because the 'institutional order has taken root not only in Kurdish-majority areas but in Arab territories as well.' (Haenni and Quesnay 2020: 7). It also confirmed SDF claims of low defection rate among SDF ranks, despite some defections in Tal Abyad and Tabqa Haenni and Quesnay 2020: 8; Wilgenburg 2020).

The stability resulted from the administration and SDF continuing to pay more than 250,000 employees, including 70,000 soldiers, 30,000 police, and 150,000 civil servants (Haenni and Quesnay 2020: 8). The autonomous administration's income stems from mainly oil sales because the SDF controls 80 per cent of the country's oil and gas resources (Hatahet: 2019: 2). Syria's northeast also serves as the country's food basket, producing most of the country's food, including wheat and livestock (Hatahet: 2019: 2). According to the autonomous administration's annual report published in January 2020, their income totalled approximately $115,000,000 of which $72,000,000 comes from oil sales.[4] The administration's annual expenditure of $112,000,000 included $67,000,000 on the SDF and $45,000,000 on civil salaries. Other revenue comes from income taxes, fees, and import duties (Hatahet: 2019: 1). The SDF has also received direct stipends (salaries) from the US military. The Pentagon budget for 2021, includes $400 monthly payments per individual for a total of 10,000 vetted Syrian fighters, mainly SDF fighters but also including rebel fighters in Al-Tanf near the Iraqi border (Detsch 2020; Department of Defense February 2020). In 2017, the Pentagon also paid stipends to the Manbij Military Council, Deir ar Zour Military Council, demining engineers, and Raqqa Internal Security Forces (Pentagon Inspector General 2018: 62).

As a result, despite the Turkish invasion in October 2019, the SDF could easily replace recruits that defected, died, or fled. The AANES also issued an

---

[4] The Syria-based Rojava Information Centre published the translation of the annual report of the Autonomous Administration of North and East Syria on its Twitter account, see: https://twitter.com/RojavaIC/status/1217351447001686023 Full annual report can be found on the official AANES Facebook page: https://www.facebook.com/smensyria/posts/1216247441898524?amp %3B__tn__=-R

amnesty for the forced recruits that defected (Wilgenburg 2020). The SDF and civil employees receive better salaries than civilians and Syrian regime staff, who do not have alternatives for better employment opportunities. Around 20 per cent of the 3.2 million people in the northeast receive their salaries from the autonomous administration (Haenni and Quesnay 2020: 8; Hatahet 2019: 2).

This might explain why, according to United States Army Central Command, most Arab communities in northeast Syria passively support the SDF and associated civil institutions (Pentagon Inspector General 2020: 6). However, the US army command also noted that Arab communities are under pressure from state actors, a reference to attempts by Turkey, Russia, and the Syrian government to compel the local Arab residents to defect (Pentagon Inspector General 2020: 6). So far, they have not been successful because they do not provide better (financial) alternatives. In fact, the economy will probably further deteriorate in the regime areas due to the Caesar act sanctions that will target the Syrian government's leadership (SOHR 2020). Therefore, the regime will not be able to provide alternatives. Unless it launches a new operation to take more territory and destroy the administration system in the northeast, Turkey will have difficulty in providing even limited economic opportunities in its small enclave between Tal Abyad and Ras al-Ain.

Although many Arabs now belong to the administration and the SDF, some Arabs still criticise the SDF and administration because Kurds predominate. Nevertheless, US army analysts said the SDF and SDC have made great strides towards incorporating Arab leaders, including Syriac Christians (Pentagon Inspector General 2020: 56). However, in a different assessment, the US Defense Intelligence Agency noted that the YPG still maintains control over leadership and decision-making, and will not share power with Arabs even in Arab-majority areas (Pentagon Inspector General 2020: 6). Although the top SDF-leadership is still dominated by Kurdish commanders such as Newroz Ahmed (Hawar News Agency 2019), Mazloum Abdi (Hawar New Agency 2019), Cemil Mazlum (Wilgenburg 2019), Ciya Kobani (Firat) (Hawar News Agency 2019), Haqi Kobani (SDF Press 2020), the SDF has recruited many Arabs and placed them in responsible positions. During the meeting of the SDF's General Military Council, it also included non-Kurdish leaders such as Ahmet Mahmoud Sultan (Abu Araj) (Jaysh al-Thuwar leader), Abdul Malik Bard (Jaysh al-Thuwar commander), Jamal Abu Juma (Bab Military Council leader), Abu Khawla (Deir ar Zour Military Council leader), Bandar al-Humaydi (Sanadid forces commander), and Kino Gabriel (SDF spokesperson and Syriac Military Council leader) (Hawar New Agency 2019).

Arabs make up the majority on civilian councils in areas such as Manbij, Raqqa, Tabqa, and Deir ar Zour. According to one source, before the Turkish incursion in October 2019, Arabs made up 65 per cent of all employees of the autonomous administration in northeast Syria. The employees of the Raqqa administration are 90 per cent Arab, while Deir ar Zour is nearly 100 per cent Arab.5

The Autonomous Administration of North and East Syria (AANES) and the SDC include several non-Kurdish leaders such as Abed Hamed Al-Mahbash, co-head of AANES, originally from Raqqa, and Riyad Derrar, an Arab from Deir ar Zour (Hawar 2018; Wilgenburg 2019). This helps explain why the SDF, when negotiating with the Syrian regime, also demands recognition of all the areas under SDF-control as part of the autonomous area, not just the Kurdish areas (Zaman 2019). The SDF refuses Russian demands to negotiate as a Kurdish party instead of as the administration (Rojava Information Centre: 14) and refused to hand over Arab majority areas to the Syrian regime. This assuages fears of the Arab population that the SDF, in order to keep the Kurdish areas on the border, would give up Arab majority areas, such as Raqqa and Deir ar Zour, to the regime.

Concluding remarks

Although the YPG initially controlled only Kurdish territories and initially planned to rule the Kurdish territories through the Supreme Kurdish Committee, the YPG from 2012 to 2014 expanded territorial control not only to Kurdish areas, but also Arab-populated areas. This happened because the Syrian Kurdish areas had been divided into three enclaves. Unlike Iraqi Kurdistan, Syria did not have contiguous ethnically dominant Kurdish territory. To create an autonomous area with connected enclaves, the YPG-led project had to expand and rule in non-Kurdish territories on the Syrian-Turkish border. As a result, the 2014 canton administrations were replaced by a federal administration in 2016, and a general administration for the northeast in 2018. Furthermore, after the battle of Kobani in 2014, the 'YPG brand' needed to change due to its cooperation with the US-led coalition. For this reason, the multi-ethnic SDF and SDC were created in 2015. As a result of the coalition support, the SDF goals expanded beyond connecting the Kurdish enclaves to also fighting ISIS in areas such as Raqqa and Deir ar Zour. In 2018, the new administration integrated these Arab majority territories into the new administration. However, due to the Turkish cross-border operations in 2016, 2018, and 2019, the autonomous administration lost territories such as Afrin, Serekaniye, and Tal Abyad. This also prevented the linking up of the Kurdish enclaves of Kobani and Afrin. Despite the Turkish invasion, the SDF and the autonomous administration stayed intact

---

5 Author's interview with a Syrian who works in the humanitarian sector in north-eastern Syria.

which showed the resilience and success of the political project of the autonomous administration and the SDF. This shows that they had passive support from Arab population due to a lack of better alternatives and the many fighters and employees paid by the administration and the SDF. However, the multi-ethnic character of the SDF not only resulted from the demands of the US-led coalition, because the YPG and administration(s) from the beginning followed Abdullah Öcalan's *Democratic Nation* ideology of granting every ethnicity and religion the right 'to participate'. This differs from a strictly Kurdish ethnic-nationalist ideology such as supporters of the Barzani-movement. Therefore, the SDF could more easily fight in Deir ar Zour or Raqqa, while Barzani's Peshmerga refrained from fighting in Mosul since they did not consider this part of Kurdistan. Therefore, opponents of the YPG have claimed the YPG has no 'Kurdish project' or sacrificed the lives of Kurdish fighters for 'Arab land'.

Although the future of the *Democratic Nation* project in north-eastern Syria remains unclear due to the possibility of a new Turkish invasion and a lack of US willingness to defend the SDF from possible military Turkish threats (since the US argues it cannot fight NATO-ally Turkey), the process of 2012 until 2020 shows that the YPG-SDF and the administrations have shown remarkable ability to build local multi-ethnic administrative and military institutions in areas liberated from ISIS and other militants. They could provide services, create jobs, and recruit many civil servants and fighters from the non-Kurdish population in a relatively short period despite being a non-state actor.

References

ABC News. 2016. Why 200 More US Troops Are Going to Syria https://abcnews. go.com/International/200-us-troops-syria/story?id=44140298 (accessed 20 May 2020).

Akkaya, Ahmet Hamdi and Jongerden, Joost . 2012. Reassembling the Political: The PKK and the project of Radical Democracy, *European Journal of Turkish Studies*, 14 | 2012, http://ejts.revues.org/index4615.html (accessed 12 May 2020).

Anadolu Agency (AA). 2015. US not supplying arms to YPG: defense official. https://www.aa.com.tr/en/world/us-not-supplying-arms-to-ypg-defense-official/438847

ANF (Firat News Agency). 2018. Preparations to mark the beginning of Rojava Revolution underway. https://anfenglishmobile.com/rojava-syria/preparations-to-mark-the-beginning-of-rojava-revolution-underway-28193 (accessed 12 May 2020).

ANF, 2014. Burkan Al Firat Commander: We are alongside the YPG till the victory, https://anfenglishmobile.com/news/burkan-al-firat-commander-we-are-alongside-the-ypg-till-the-victory-10024 (accessed 12 May 2020).

ANF. 2017. 21st Century Epic of Resistance: Kobanê, https://anfenglish.com/features/21st-century-epic-of-resistance-kobane-23006 (accessed 12 May 2020).

Al Jazeera. 2017. What will happen to post-ISIL Raqqa? https://www.aljazeera.com/indepth/features/2017/10/sdf-captures-syria-raqqa-city-isil-171013110014050.html (accessed 12 May 2020).

Al Jazeera. 2019. Turkey's Operation Peace Spring in northern Syria: One month on https://www.aljazeera.com/news/2019/11/turkey-operation-peace-spring-northern-syria-month-191106083300140.html (accessed 12 May 2020).

Allsopp, Harriet & Wilgenburg, Wladimir van. 2019. *The Kurds of Northern Syria. Governance, Diversity and Conflicts*. New York: I.B. Tauris.

Arafat, Hisham. 2016. Rojava' no longer exists, 'Northern Syria' adopted instead, *Kurdistan 24*, http://www.kurdistan24.net/en/news/51940fb9-3aff-4e51-bcf8-b1629af00299/ -rojava--no-longer-exists---northern-syria--adopted-instead- (accessed 19 May 2020).

Arafat, Hisham. 2020. Turkey continues demographic change in northern Syria by resettling hundreds of refugees in Tal Abyad, Ras al-Ain. https://www.kurdistan24. net/ en/news/fec2ad3c-214c-43e6-9cb3-22f096ad4845 (accessed 19 May 2020).

Awad, Ziad. 2018. Deir Al-Zor after Islamic State: Between Kurdish Self Administration and a Return of the Syrian Regime. https://cadmus.eui.eu/bitstream/handle/1814/ 52824/RPR_2018_02_Eng.pdf?sequence=4&isAllowed=y

Barfi, Barak. 2017. Managing Washington's Flawed Partners in Eastern Syria https://www.washingtoninstitute.org/policy-analysis/view/managing-washingtons-flawed-partners-in-eastern-syria (accessed 20 May 2020).

BBC. 2014. Syria rebels capture ISIS headquarters in Aleppo, https://www.bbc.com/ news/world-middle-east-25652381 (accessed 12 May 2020).

BBC. 2014. Isis leader calls on Muslims to 'build Islamic state', https://www.bbc.com/ news/world-middle-east-28116846 (accessed 16 May 2020).

BBC. 2015. Battle for Kobane: Key events. https://www.bbc.com/news/world-middle-east-29688108 (accessed 18 May 2020).

BBC. 2017. Raqqa: IS 'capital' falls to US-backed Syrian forces https://www.bbc.com/ news/world-middle-east-41646802 (accessed 16 May 2020).

Çaksu, Ersin, Interview With Burkan al-Firat Commander: We Are Fighting To Rebuild A Democratic And Inclusive Revolution, *Ozgur Gundem,* https://rojavareport. wordpress.com/2015/07/08/interview-with-burkan-al-firat-commander-we-are-fighting-to-rebuild-a-democratic-and-inclusive-revolution/ (accessed 16 May 2020).

Çiviroğlu, Mutlu. 2014. The Constitution of the Rojava Cantons' https://civiroglu.net/ the-constitution-of-the-rojava-cantons/ (accessed 12 May 2020).

Çiviroğlu, Mutlu and Wilgenburg, Wladimir van. 2014. Kurdish-Arab Rebel Alliance May be Key to Obama's Syrian Strategy, Atlantic Council https://www.atlanticcouncil.org /blogs/menasource/kurdish-arab-rebel-alliance-may-be-key-to-obama-s-syrian-strategy/ (accessed 12 May 2020).

Crisis Group. 2017. Fighting ISIS: The Road to and beyond Raqqa. https://www. crisisgroup.org/middle-east-north-africa/eastern-mediterranean/syria/b053-fighting-isis-road-and-beyond-raqqa (accessed 20 May 2020).

Crisis Group. 2020. Middle Euphrates River Valley, Syria. https://www.crisisgroup. org/trigger-list/iran-us-trigger-list/flashpoints/middle-euphrates-river-valley (accessed 19 May 2020).

CNN. 2019. US and Turkish troops conduct first joint ground patrol of Syrian 'safe zone'. https://edition.cnn.com/2019/09/08/middleeast/us-turkish-troops-joint-syria-ground-patrol-intl/index.html (accessed 19 May 2020).

Daily Sabah. 2016. YPG-dominated SDF crosses west of Euphrates, raises Turkey's concerns https://www.dailysabah.com/mideast/2016/06/02/ypg-dominated-sdf-crosses-west-of-euphrates-raises-turkeys-concerns (accessed 15 May 2020).

Daily Sabah. 2018. YPG-dominated SDF crosses west of Euphrates, raises Turkey's concerns. https://www.dailysabah.com/mideast/2016/06/02/ypg-dominated-sdf-crosses-west-of-euphrates-raises-turkeys-concerns (accessed 15 May 2020).

Defense Post. 2019. New Syrian military councils are the SDF's latest push for decentralisation https://www.thedefensepost.com/2019/06/23/syria-sdf-military-councils/

Department of Defense. 2016. Syrian Democratic Forces Initiate Next Phase of Raqqa Isolation, https://www.defense.gov/Explore/News/Article/Article/1026910/syrian-democratic-forces-initiate-next-phase-of-raqqa-isolation/ (accessed 17 May 2020).

Department of Defense. 2017. Collaboration Fuels Fight Against ISIS, Official Says. https://www.defense.gov/Explore/News/Article/Article/1239452/collaboration-fuels-fight-against-isis-official-says/ (accessed 17 May 2020).

Department of Defense. February 2020. Justification for FY 2021 Overseas Contingency Operations (OCO), https://comptroller.defense.gov/Portals/45/Documents/defbudget/fy2021/fy2021_CTEF_J-Book.pdf (accessed 20 May 2020). Detsch, Jack. SDF avoids fight with Trump over budget cut. *Al Monitor* https://www.al-monitor.com/pulse/originals/2020/02/sdf-syria-avoid-fight-budget-trump.html (accessed 20 May 2020).

Drott, Carl. 2014. Arab Tribes Split Between Kurds And Jihadists. *Carnegie Middle East Centre.* 2014, https://carnegie-mec.org/syriaincrisis/?fa=55607 (accessed 12 May 2020).

Favier, Agnes. 2018. Syria After Islamic State: 'Everything Needs to Change, So Everything Can Stay the Same'? *Middle East Directions.* https://cadmus.eui.eu/bitstream/ handle/1814/51925/ResearchReport_2018_01.pdf?sequence =1&isAllowed=y (accessed 18 May 2020).

Glotti, Andrea. 2014. Syrian Kurds recruit regime loyalists to fight jihadists', Al Monitor, https://www.al-monitor.com/pulse/originals/2014/02/pyd-kurds-syria-regime-assad-autonomy.html (accessed 15 May 2020).

Guardian. 2018. 'Nothing is ours anymore': Kurds forced out of Afrin after Turkish assault. https://www.theguardian.com/world/2018/jun/07/too-many-strange-faces-kurds-fear-forced-demographic-shift-in-afrin (accessed 20 May 2020).

Guardian. 2019. At least 750 Isis affiliates escape Syria camp after Turkish shelling https://www.theguardian.com/world/2019/oct/13/kurds-say-785-isis-affiliates-have-escaped-camp-after-turkish-shelling (accessed 20 May 2020).

Haenni, Patrick and Quesnay, Arthur. 2020. Surviving the Aftermath of Islamic State: The Syrian Kurdish Movement's Resilience Strategy. Middle East Directions. https://cadmus.eui.eu/bitstream/handle/1814/66224/MED_WPCS_2020_3.pdf?sequence=1&isAllowed=y

Hatahet, Sinan. 2019. The Political Economy of the Autonomous Administration of North and East Syria. Middle East Directions. https://cadmus.eui.eu/bitstream/handle/1814/65364/MED_WPCS_2019_16.pdf?sequence=1&isAllowed=y

Hawar News Agency. 2018. Who are co-chairs of Autonomous Administration in North, East Syria's Executive Council http://www.hawarnews.com/en/haber/who-are-co-chairs-of-autonomous-administration-in-north-east-syrias-executive-council-h4215.html (accessed 20 May 2020).

Hawar News Agency. 2019. Newroz Ahmed: YPJ are committed to continue struggle and fulfilling their responsibilities http://www.hawarnews.com/en/haber/newroz-ahmed-ypj-are-committed-to-continue-struggle-and-fulfilling-their-responsibilities-h11041.html (accessed 20 May 2020).

Hawar News Agency. 2019. SDF General Military Council meeting started in presence of prominent commanders http://www.hawarnews.com/en/haber/sdf-general-military-council-meeting-started-in-presence-of-prominent-commanders-h6979.html (accessed 20 May 2020).

Hawar News Agency. 2019. SDF liberated al-Bagouz from IS http://www.hawarnews.com/ en/haber/sdf-liberated-al-bagouz-from-is-h7808.html (accessed 20 May 2020).

Hawar News Agency. 2020. 'Mazloum Abdi: We are ready to negotiate with Turkey if the latter is sincere' http://www.hawarnews.com/en/haber/mazloum-abdi-we-are-ready-to-negotiate-with-turkey-if-the-latter-is-sincere-h14014.html

Jadaliyya. 2015. The Reality of Ethnic Cleansing and Kurdish State in Syria. https://www.jadaliyya.com/Details/32395 (accessed 12 May 2020).

Hurriyet. 2013. Syriacs establish military council in Syria. https://www.hurriyetdailynews.com/syriacs-establish-military-council-in-syria-40329 (accessed 12 May 2020).

Knapp, M., Flach, A., & Ayboga, E. 2016. *Revolution in Rojava: Democratic autonomy and women's liberation in Syrian Kurdistan*. London: Pluto Press

Komun. 2018. Democratic Nation. https://komun-academy.com/2018/06/27/democratic-nation/ (accessed 12 May 2020).

Kurdistan 24. 2019. Syrian opposition reelects Kurd as vice-president https://www.kurdistan24.net/en/news/bd60c855-425c-44c6-8158-25d5f4f3fe02. (accessed 20 May 2020).

Lund, Aron. 2013. Syria's Kurdish Army: An Interview With Redur Khalil. https://carnegie-mec.org/diwan/54016?lang=en (accessed 15 May 2020).

Manbij Military Council. 2018. Manbij Military Council announces the withdrawal of the last batch of the People's Protection Units advisers from Manbij (Arabic). http://manbijmc.org/archives/3648 (accessed 15 May 2020).

Öcalan, Abdullah. 2016. Democratic Nation. Cologne: International Initiative/Neuss. http://Öcalanbooks.com/downloads/democratic-nation.pdf (accessed 13 May 2020). Omran (For Strategic Studies. 2018. Military and Security Structures of the Autonomous Administration in Syria https://omranstudies.org/publications/reports/military-and-security-structures-of-the-autonomous-administration-in-syria.html (accessed 18 May 2020).

Pentagon Inspector General. 2016. Operation Inherent Resolve. Quarterly Report to the United States Congress | April 1, 2016 – June 30, 2016. https://media.defense.gov/2017/Apr/13/2001732248/-1/-1/1/FY2016_LIG_OCO_OIR_Q3_REPORT_JUN 20161.PDF (accessed 17 May 2020).

Pentagon Inspector General. 2018. Inherent Resolve and Operation Pacific Eagle- Philippines I Quarterly Report to the United States Congress I April 1, 2018 - June 30, 2018 https://oig.usaid.gov/sites/default/files/2018-10/quarterly_oir_063018.pdf (accessed 17 May 2020).

Pentagon Inspector General. 2020. Lead Inspector General for Operation Inherent Resolve I Quarterly Report to the United States Congress I January 1, 2020 – March 31, 2020, http://www.dodig.mil/reports.html/Article/2185122/lead-inspector-general-for-operation-inherent-resolve-i-quarterly-report-to-the/ (accessed 20 May 2020).

Reuters. 2012. After quiet revolt, power struggle looms for Syria's Kurds. https://www.reuters.com/article/us-syria-crisis-kurds/after-quiet-revolt-power-struggle-looms-for-syrias-kurds-idUSBRE8A619520121107 (accessed 12 May 2020).

Reuters. 2013. Kurds declare an interim administration in Syria. https://www.reuters.com/ article/us-syria-crisis-kurds/kurds-declare-an-interim-administration-in-syria-idUSBRE9AB17E20131112 (accessed 12 May 2020).

Reuters. 2015. New Syrian rebel alliance formed, says weapons on the way. https://www.reuters.com/article/us-mideast-crisis-syria-kurds/new-syrian-rebel-alliance-formed-says-weapons-on-the-way-idUSKCN0S60BD20151012 (accessed 17 May 2020).

Reuters. 2015. Syria Kurds seize town from Islamic State near its 'capital'. https://uk.reuters.com/article/uk-mideast-crisis-syria/syria-kurds-seize-town-from-islamic-state-near-its-capital-idUKKBN0P316H20150623 (accessed 20 May 2020).

Reuters. 2016. U.S. to arm Syrian Kurds fighting Islamic State, despite Turkey's ire. https://www.reuters.com/article/us-mideast-crisis-usa-kurds-idUSKBN18525V

(accessed 18 May 2020).

Reuters. 2016. Syria's Kurds rebuked for seeking autonomous region. https://www.reuters.com/article/us-mideast-crisis-syria-federalism/syrias-kurds-rebuked-for-seeking-autonomous-region-idUSKCN0WJ1EP (accessed 20 May 2020).

Reuters. 2016. Islamic State pulls families out of towns in Syrian north. https://www.reuters.com/article/us-mideast-crisis-syria-islamic-state-idUSKCN10U1L1 (accessed 20 May 2020).

Reuters. 2017. U.S.-backed forces, Syrian army advance separately on Islamic State in Deir al-Zor, https://www.reuters.com/article/us-mideast-crisis-syria-sdf/u-s-backed-forces-syrian-army-advance-separately-on-islamic-state-in-deir-al-zor-idUSKCN1BJ2J3 (accessed 12 May 2020).

Reuters. 2017. Exclusive: U.S.-backed Raqqa battle should end in two months, says senior SDF commander https://ca.reuters.com/article/topNews/idCAKCN1B81SN-OCATP (accessed 19 May 2020).

Reuters. 2018. Kurdish-led council deepens authority across Syrian north and east. https://www.reuters.com/article/us-mideast-crisis-syria-council/kurdish-led-council-deepens-authority-across-syrian-north-and-east-idUSKCN1LM25I (accessed 12 May 2020).

Reuters 2019. Explainer: Where do the Kurds fit into Syria's war? https://www.reuters.com/article/us-mideast-crisis-syria-kurds-explainer-idUSKCN1P81JF (accessed 12 May 2020).

Rojava Information Centre. 2020. Six months on: political, security and humanitarian outcomes of Turkey's 2019 invasion of North and East Syria https://rojava informationcenter.com/2020/05/six-months-on-political-security-and-humanitarian-outcomes-of-turkeys-2019-invasion-of-north-and-east-syria/ (accessed 20 May 2020).

Rudaw 2014. Divided Syrian Kurds reach deal in face of ISIS threat. *Rudaw,* URL: http://www.rudaw.net/english/kurdistan/221020141 (accessed 12 May 2020).

SDF Press. 2020. Commandos Graduate Its 6th Session In Euphrates Territory http://sdf-press.com/en/2020/04/commandos-graduate-its-6th-session-in-euphrates-territory/ (accessed 20 May 2020).

Syria Direct. 2020. The rivaling philosophies of Barzani and Öcalan weigh over Syria's Kurds, https://syriadirect.org/news/the-rivaling-philosophies-of-barzani-and-Öcalan-weigh-over-syrias-kurds-timeline/ (accessed 12 May 2020).

SOHR (Syrian Observatory for Human Rights). 2018. 15 rebel factions are ready to fight under SDF banner in Aleppo and Idlib. https://www.syriahr.com/en/?p=38102 https://syriadirect.org/news/the-rivaling-philosophies-of-barzani-and-Öcalan-weigh-over-syrias-kurds-timeline/ (accessed 18 May 2020).

SOHR. 2020. U.S. sanctions on Syrian regime | With economy in freefall, will 'Caesar Act' topple Al-Assad? https://www.syriahr.com/en/?p=165445 (accessed 18 May 2020).

Steele, Jonathan, 2015. Syrian Kurdish leader hails 'Euphrates Volcano' fight against IS', Middle East Eye, https://www.middleeasteye.net/news/syrian-kurdish-leader-hails-euphrates-volcano-fight-against (accessed 12 May 2020).

Al-Tamimi, Aymenn Jawad, 2014. The Factions of Kobani (Ayn al-Arab), http://www.aymennjawad.org/15689/the-factions-of-kobani-ayn-al-arab (accessed 12 May 2020). YPG ROJAVA. Date unknown. About us. https://www.ypgrojava.org/About-Us (accessed 12 May 2020).

USATODAY. 2015. Pentagon's failed Syria program cost $2 million per trainee https://eu.usatoday.com/story/news/world/2015/11/05/pentagon-isil-syria-train-and-equip/75227774/ (accessed 20 May 2020).

Wilgenburg, Wladimir van. 2014. Kurdish Enclaves in Syria Battle Islamist Militant

Groups. *Jamestown Foundation*, Terrorism Monitor, https://jamestown.org/program/kurdish- strategy-towards-ethnically-mixed-areas-in-the-syrian-conflict/ (accessed 12 May 2020).

Wilgenburg, Wladimir van. 2014. Syrian Kurds blame Iran, Turkey for ISIS attacks https://www.al-monitor.com/pulse/originals/2014/03/redur-xelil-pyd-kurds-pkk-isis-syria-regime-kobani.html#ixzz6NZ4XwoFB (accessed 12 May 2020).

Wilgenburg, Wladimir van. 2017. Formation of Euphrates Volcano Sep 9, 2014. http://vvanwilgenburg.blogspot.com/2017/03/formation-of-euphrates-volcano-sep-9.html (accessed 12 May 2020).

Wilgenburg, Wladimir van. 2017. Meet Dr Liwla Abdullah, spokeswoman for SDF operation to take Deir ar-Zour from ISIS. *The Region.* https://theregion.org/article/11652-meet-dr-liwla-abdullah-spokeswoman-for-sdf-operation-to-take-deir-ar-zour-from-isis (accessed 16 May 2020).

Wladimir van Wilgenburg, 2016. Kurdish National Council in Syria condemns federalism declaration by Kurdish rival. *ARA News* http://aranews.net/2016/03/kurdish-national-council-syria-condemns-federalism-declaration-kurdish-rival/ (accessed 16 May 2020).

Wilgenburg, Wladimir van. 2018. New administration formed for northeastern Syria, Kurdistan 24, https://www.kurdistan24.net/en/news/c9e03dab-6265-4a9a-91ee-ea8d2a93c657 (accessed 12 May 2020).

Wilgenburg, Wladimir van. 2019. Turkish-backed groups launch attack near strategic Syrian town of Ain Issa, https://www.kurdistan24.net/en/news/8c7251b9-f237-472a-a1f5-47cc24a12e7c (accessed 20 May 2020).

Wilgenburg, Wladimir van. 2019. Thousands of civilians flee Turkish attacks despite ceasefire deal https://www.kurdistan24.net/en/news/a1170589-1682-49e8-8274-018fa0972e1d (accessed 20 May).

Wilgenburg, Wladimir van. 2019. Syrian Kurds say Turkey's plan for refugee resettlement unacceptable. https://www.kurdistan24.net/en/news/13d8d64c-bd74- 4658-ae58-c13b1c2af2aa (accessed 20 May).

Wilgenburg, Wladimir van. 2019. SDF says over 11,000 of its forces killed in fight against the Islamic State. https://www.kurdistan24.net/en/news/0dafe596-6536-49d7-8e23-e52821742ae9 (accessed 20 May 2020).

Wilgenburg, Wladimir van. 2019. Kurdish-backed council says EU should not obstruct prosecution, repatriation of ISIS fighters https://www.kurdistan24.net/en/news/79a889a0-f258-4b4a-aedb-34cd30c0a16f (accessed 20 May 2020).

Wilgenburg, Wladimir van. 2020. US forces block Russian military patrol in northern Syria.https://www.kurdistan24.net/en/news/a69d17b5-2f27-4cd3-8dbb-fdc5e4cd7 170 (accessed 20 May 2020).

Wilgenburg, Wladimir van. 2020. The Future of Northeastern Syria: In Conversation with SDF Commander-in-Chief Mazloum Abdi https://www.washingtoninstitute.org/fikraforum/view/The-Future-of-Northeastern-Syria-In-Conversation-with-SDF-Commander-in-Chi (accessed 20 May 2020).

Wilgenburg, Wladimir van. 2020. General pardon for those who deserted their positions. http://vvanwilgenburg.blogspot.com/2020/02/general-pardon-for-those-who-deserted.html (accessed 20 May 2020).

Zaman, Amberin. 2019. Turkish intervention could trigger Syria's 'second great war' https://www.al-monitor.com/pulse/originals/2019/03/syria-kurdish-mazlum-kobane-damascus-talks-assad-russia.html (accessed 25 May 2020).

CHAPTER 7

TURKEY'S WAR IN SYRIA: PREVENTION OR EXPANSION

Arzu Yilmaz

Introduction

The international community have mostly perceived Turkish military interventions in north of Syria as the "legitimate right [of Turkey] to protect its borders", since the Syrian crisis that later deteriorated into a proxy war has revealed a dramatic decline in Middle Eastern states' capacities to politically and militarily control their territorial peripheries.

This article, however, argues that Turkey's war in Syria has fundamentally been driven by its expansionist aspirations rather than a desire to prevent threats caused by multiple insecurities on Turkey-Syria border. Nevertheless, a specific focus on Turkey's diametrically opposite approaches towards the Kurds in the Middle East in last decade, first as "strategic partners" and then as "existential threats", reveals that from the early days of the Syrian crisis onwards, Turkey has been pursuing territorial expansion in the Middle East.

In this context, this article first examines the Kurdish Question as a concept which basically explains the international community's indifference, at best, to Turkish military interventions in Syria; and then, it traces the transformation of Ankara's approach towards the Kurdish question in the context of the political turmoil in the Middle East. Finally, through a particular focus on Turkey's invasion of Afrin in 2018, it discusses how Turkey has instrumentalised the Kurdish question to mould and legitimise its expansion in the region.

Kurdish question within the context of status quo in the Middle East

Conventionally, the Kurdish question has been perceived as a domestic issue of national concern for the Middle Eastern states with Kurdish populations, i.e., Turkey, Iraq, Iran, and Syria. This perception was basically shaped in the Cold War era when domestic and foreign policies were distinctly separate. The Kurdish question was, then, regarded as a 'threat' to the constituent states' territorial integrity to be countered both inside and outside of the borders by the central authorities.[1]

In this context, an absolute control over the national borders separated the Kurds socially, economically, and culturally from each other in the Middle East, whereas the Kurdish identity was basically reshaped and differentiated by the nationalist projects of Turkey, Iraq, Iran, and Syria.[2] Furthermore, Kurdish national movements that emerged as a reaction to these nationalist projects were formed by the geopolitical fragmentation of Kurdistan.[3]

Given the linguistic and religious differences, fragmentation has been interpreted to constitute the nature of the Kurdish society. These fragmentations have been used to emphasise the political differences among Kurds and to legitimise the conceptualisation of the Kurdish question as a merely domestic issue. In this sense, Kurds were at best understood as vulnerable minority groups within their respective nation-states rather than a nation itself. Kurdistan thereby became a geo-cultural term without any political reference to Kurds. Therefore, until today, containment of Kurds within national boundaries has been possible.

This state of affairs remained constant even in the 1990s when the Soviet Union collapsed. However, in accordance with the international community's intervention in domestic politics, the Kurds' struggle became internationally visible and they were encouraged to support the democratization process in Turkey and/or the decentralization of Iraq. The Kurds in Iraq joined the reconstruction of the state in the post-Saddam era in order to maximize their autonomous gains. Also, the Kurdistan Workers' Party (PKK) that aimed, until the early 1990s, to achieve an independent Kurdish state, changed to demanding equal rights within the territorial boundaries of Turkey.[4]

One can argue that Turkey has been the primary beneficiary of this status quo posture towards the Kurdish question in the Middle East. Hence, the most challenging issue for Turkey in the 1990s was the rise of the Kurdish movement while micro-nationalism movements arose in the Balkans and the post-Soviet territory. The European Union membership process firmly

---

[1] In this article the arguments about the Kurdish question are cited from my previous articles. For further reading: Arzu Yilmaz, 'The Changing Dynamics of the Kurdish Question', *SWP Comment*, 2018/C(45), 2018. Available at: https://www.swp-berlin.org/en/publication/kurdish-question-changing-dynamics/ (Accessed on 9 October 2017); Arzu Yilmaz , 'Kürt Milliyetçiliğine Eleştirel Bir Bakış: Kürt Mülteciler ve Kurdistan Milliyetçiliği', *Mülkiye Dergisi*, Cilt 39(1), pp:37-56, Ankara, 2015.

[2] For further reading: Denise Natali, *Kürtler ve Devlet: Irak, Türkiye ve Iran'da Ulusal Kimliğin Gelişmesi*, Avesta, İstanbul, 2009; Abbas Vali (ed.), *Kürt Milliyetçiliğinin Kökenleri*, Avesta, İstanbul, 2005

[3] For further reading: Cengiz Güneş, *Türkiye'de Kürt Ulusal Hareketi: Direnişin Söylemi*, Dipnot, Ankara, 2013; David Romano, *The Kurdish Nationalist Movement: Opportunity, Mobilization and Identity*, Cambridge, New York, 2006; Edward O' Ballance, *The Kurdish Struggle: 1920-1994*, ST Martin Press, New York, 1996.

[4] For further reading: David Romano, Cengiz Güneş (ed.), *Conflict, Democratization and the Kurds in the Middle East*, Palgrave, New York, 2014.

confined the framework for the solution to Kurdish question to Turkey's territorial unity.[5] Moreover, its NATO membership strengthened Turkey's position in the Middle East because of the dual containment policy against Iraq and Iran. In the 1990s, Turkey has exercised cross-border military operations in Iraqi territory with the support of both NATO and the European countries. These military operations, in the end, paved the way for Turkey to dampen the PKK insurgency and to dominate the Kurdistan Region of Iraq through political and economic measures.[6] In time, Turkey's role in the Middle East as a whole was enhanced further by the West as Turkey has become the poster child for a democratic transformation in the Arab World particularly when the US military power was about to decline in the region.[7]

A relative change in Turkey's policies towards the Kurdish Question, however, came to the surface in the aftermath of the Syrian civil war when Turkey urged a new political order in the Middle East. In this context, the Kurds who were perceived as a 'threat' to national security for a hundred years, turned into a 'strategic partner' in the Middle East. Yet, Turkey's primary objective was to develop a Sunni axis in the Middle East as the successor of the Ottoman Empire.[8] According to this new goal, Kurds were expected to play their role just like far in the past, in the 16th century when their ancestors cooperated with the Ottomans against the Safavids.[9]

Turkey's expansion in the Middle East via Turkish-Kurdish "strategic partnership"

The Turkish-Kurdish 'strategic partnership' surfaced within the context of a peace process (the İmralı Process) in early 2013 when the Arab Spring transformed regimes in the region. The so-called peace process first proposed to end the long-lasting Kurdish conflict in Turkey by amending the constitution and granting Kurdish collective rights within a presidential

[5] For further reading: Ayşe Betül Çelik, Bahar Rumelili, 'Necessary But Not Sufficient: The Role of the EU in Resolving Turkey's Kurdish Question and the Greek-Turkish Conflicts', *European Foreign Affairs Review*,11:2003-222, 2006.

[6] For further reading: Bill Park, 'Turkey-Kurdish Regional Government Relations After the US Withdrawal from Iraq', *US Army War College Strategic Studies*, https://www.peacepalacelibrary.nl/ebooks/files/378166689.pdf (Accessed on 13 December 2018)

[7] For further reading: Melina Benli Altunisik, 'The Turkish Model and Democratization in the Middle East', *Arab Studies Quarterly*, 27,1:45-63, 2005.

[8] For further reading; Alessia Chriatti, 'Neo-Ottomanist Diplomacy: the Turkish Geopolitics in Syria', *XXVI Convegno SISP*, 2012, https://www.sisp.it/files/papers/2012/alessia-chiriatti-1385.pdf (Accessed on 12 April 2017); Emre Öktem, 'Turkey: Successor or Continuing State of the Ottoman Empire?', *Leiden Journal of International Law*, Vol. 24, No. 3, 2011, pp: 561-583.

[9] For further reading: Arzu Yilmaz, "Bölgesel Gelişmelerin Çözüm Sürecine Etkileri", *Barış Açısını Savunmak*, Necmiye Alpay, Hakan Tahmaz (ed.), Metis, Istanbul, 2015.

system.10 However, the key objective was to establish a Turkish-Kurdish alliance in the rapidly-changing regional equilibrium in the Middle East. Nevertheless, the motto of the process was 'Kurds will not divide Turkey, but Turkey will get bigger with the Kurds'[11.]

Abdullah Öcalan, the imprisoned leader of the PKK, noted in his speech at Newroz of 2013:

> The Peace Process is the framework of a new political order in the Middle East...For the past two hundred years, conquests, Western imperialists' interventions and oppressive mentalities have pushed Arabic, Turkish, Persian and Kurdish entities to form artificial states, borderlines, problems [...]The peoples of the Middle East and Central Asia are waking up. They are returning to their own.[12]

Öcalan's emphasis on the past two hundred years was apparently reflecting the rising neo-Ottoman discourse. In this perspective, the Middle East's ill-fated status quo was a result of Western interference in the region that ended the Ottoman rule. According to Öcalan, the Kurdish question that derived from such a status quo would eventually be resolved through a liberation from Western dominance. Within the context of the peace process, which was defined as a "historical agreement of fraternity and solidarity under the flag of Islam", the Kurds not only in Turkey but also in Iraq and Syria would be the "strategic partners of Turkey" in Ankara's efforts to build a new political order in the Middle East.[13]

In fact, Iraqi Kurds were already ready for such a partnership with Turkey. Besides boosting economic relations, Turkey opened a consulate in Erbil, the capital of Kurdistan Regional Government (KRG) in 2010. Given the constant denial for decades of Kurdish rule in Iraq, this was a signal of recognition of the legitimacy of the KRG.[14] Following the US decision to withdraw its troops from Iraq in late 2011, Turkey-KRG relations shifted to a new type of economic engagement. Turkey soon after in 2012 began accepting oil transferred directly from Iraqi Kurdistan, in defiance of

[10] Sedat Ergin, 'Başkanlık planları ile İmralı Süreci ayrışmalı', Hürriyet ,19 March 2013, http://www.hurriyet.com.tr/baskanlik-planlari-ile-imrali-sureci-ayrismali-22846005 (Accessed on 9 October 2017).

[11] Eyüp Can, 'Kürtler Türkiye'yi Bölecek mi?', Radikal, 23 January 2013, http://www.radikal.com.tr/ radikal.aspx?atype=haberyazdir&articleid=1118129 (Accessed on 9 October 2017).

[12] 'Full transcript of Abdullah Ocalan's ceasefire call', Euronews, 22 March 2013, http://www.euronews.com/2013/03/22/web-full-transcript-of-abdullah-ocalans-ceasefire-call-kurdish-pkk (Accessed on 28 September 2017).

[13] Ibid.

[14] Aydın Selcen, 'Erbil Başkonsolosluğu nasıl açıldı?', Gazete Duvar, 26 March 2017, https://www.gazeteduvar.com.tr/yazarlar/2017/03/26/erbil-baskonsoloslugu-nasil-acildi/ (Accessed on 9 October 2017).

Baghdad.[15]

The essence of Turkey-KRG relations became clear when the president of the KRG, Masoud Barzani, attended Turkey's Justice and Development Party's (AKP) Congress in September 2012. In his speech at the event, Barzani called Kurds "to support the AKP and its leader, the prime minister of Turkey, Recep Tayyip Erdoğan".16 In exchange, he not only received the Turkish government's approval as the leader of the Kurdish people but also aligned himself with the newly emerging Sunni axis in the Middle East. Important to note here is that the AKP Congress also hosted the president of Egypt, Mohamed Morsi; the vice president of Iraq Tariq al-Hashimi; and the Hamas leader, Khaled Mashal wherein the prime minister of Turkey vowed to build a 'New Turkey and the Middle East'[17.]

Against this backdrop, the peace process served as the culmination of such ongoing efforts. From the Kurdish perspective, the Kurds would gain either an autonomous or independent status under Turkey's patronage while the conditions in the Middle East were about to change. From Iraqi Kurds' perspective, as the prime minister of the KRG, Nechirvan Barzani, noted: 'To become independent, we [The Iraqi Kurds] have to receive the approval of at least one of our [KRG's] neighbours'.[18] Within the context of the peace process, then, the KRG appeared to have already received Turkey's approval when the AKP spokesperson Hüseyin Çelik stated that 'Kurds have the right to decide their future' in Iraq.19 Meanwhile, in May 2014, the oil flow continued at the daily rate of over 500,000 barrels to Turkey through a new pipeline connecting the Kurdish oil fields with the existing Kirkuk-Ceyhan pipeline.[20]

Moreover, the KRG also provided a safe space for the PKK fighters who withdrew from Turkey upon the ceasefire brokered between the PKK and Turkey in the wake of the peace process. The prime minister of the KRG, Nechirvan Barzani, declared that the KRG would do whatever was required

---

[15] Craig Shaw, Zeynep Sentek and Efe Kerem Sozeri, 'Turkey energy deals helped open door to Kurdish independence', *The Black Sea*, 10 October 2017, https://m.theblacksea.eu/stories/article/en/erdogan-and-the-kurds (Accessed on 20 October 2017).

[16] 'İşte Barzani'nin açıklamaları', *Hürriyet*, 30 September 2012, http://www.hurriyet.com.tr/iste-barzaninin-aciklamalari-21590668 (Accessed on 9 October 2017).

[17] Zeynep Gürcanlı, 'Ak Parti Kongresi'nde ağır konuklar', Hürriyet, 30 September 2012, http://www.hurriyet.com.tr/ak-parti-kongresinde-agir-konuklar-21588818 (Accessed on9 October 2017).

[18] Jay Newton-Small, 'An Interview with Nechirvan Barzani: Will There Be an Independent Kurdistan?', Time, 21 December 2012, http://world.time.com/2012/12/21/an-interview-with-nechirvan-barzani-will-there-be-an-independent-kurdistan/ (Accessed on 9 October 2017).

[19] 'Turkey's AKP Spokesman: Iraq's Kurds Have Right to Decide Their Future', Rudaw, 13 June 2014, http://www.rudaw.net/english/kurdistan/130620142 (Accessed on 20 October 2017).

[20] Aram Ekin Duran, 'Ankara-Erbil hattı petrolle güçleniyor', Deutsche Welle, 25 June 2014, http://www.dw.com/tr/ankara-erbil-hatt%C4%B1-petrolle-g%C3%BC%C3%A7leniyor/a-17734883 (Accessed on 9 October 2017).

to support the peace efforts between Turkey and the PKK.21 The details of such a support has never been revealed. The facts on the ground, however, indicated that the PKK commanders, in particular, would engage in civil life in the KRG when the PKK finally laid down its arms. In those days, for example, the PKK fighters showed up in media outlets in civilian clothes meeting with the KRG's prominent political leaders.[22]

At the same time, the newly emerging Kurdish rule in Syria would ultimately provide a framework for the PKK's transformation into a legitimate political actor, while the KRG was closely cooperating with Turkey to balance the PKK's dominance in Syria. The Supreme Kurdish Committee (SKC), was formed in July 2012 to serve as a common platform for all Syrian Kurdish parties including both the KRG-backed Kurdish National Council (ENKS) and the PKK-affiliated Democratic Union Party (PYD).[23]

From the PYD's perspective, the peace process would , at the worst case, pave the way for better relations with Turkey, according to which stated "an autonomous administration in the north of Syria is unacceptable". Nonetheless, after starting the peace process, regarding the Kurdish rule in Syria the Turkish Foreign Ministry noted that "Provisional governments to meet daily needs, such as education and health, are understandable"[24]. Meanwhile, PYD members occasionally visited Turkey to meet with Turkish military officers. The most important outcome of these initial relations between the PYD and Turkey was, for sure, the decline of the radical Islamic groups' attacks from Turkey on the Kurdish ruled areas.[25]

However, the Kurdish-Turkish relations in Syria remained tense, at first, because of the PYD's reluctance to side with Turkey against the Assad regime. Yet, due to the "third way" strategy declared after the eruption of the civil war in Syria, in 2012, the PYD's goal was "to secure Kurdish majority areas, to keep the cantons alive, and to achieve recognition". [26] In this regard, the PYD would not fully commit to any side of the conflict in Syria other than partnerships that served primarily its purpose. Therefore, as Damascus didn't attack the Kurdish ruled areas and continued, for instance, to appoint civil servants and to pay their salaries in some parts of the Jazira canton, the

---

[21]'Barzani'den Çözüm Sürecine Destek', Habertürk, 2 May 2013, https://www.haberturk.com/dunya/haber/840825-barzaniden-cozum-surecine-destek (Accessed on 9 October 2017).

[22] 'PKK'den bir ilk', *Haberler*, 6 May 2013, https://www.haberler.com/pkk-dan-bir-ilk-4595630-haberi/ (Accessed on 9 October 2017).

[23] Hazal Ates, 'Barzani Unites Syrian Kurds Against Assad', *Al-Monitor*, 16 July 2012, http://www.al-monitor.com/pulse/politics/2012/07/barzani-grabs-assads-kurdish-car.html (Accessed on 25 October 2017).

[24] 'Rojava özerkliğe doğru mu gidiyor?', *BBC Türkçe*, 12 November 2013, http://www.bbc.com/turkce/haberler/2013/11/131112_rojava_kurucu_meclis (Accessed on 20 October 2017).

[25] Ibid.

[26] Arzu Yılmaz, 'Üçüncü Yol', *Birikim*, 23 October 2015, http://www.birikimdergisi.com/haftalik/7284/ucuncu-yol#.WeoVEROCxE4 (Accessed on 20 October 2017).

PYD stayed indifferent to the Assad regime.[27]

Turkey's response to such a position was first to restrain the PYD from participating in the Geneva II Conference initiated by the United Nations in February 2014. Turkey accused the PYD of aligning with the Assad regime.[28] The PYD's position vis-a-vis the Assad regime also increased tensions with the Syrian National Council (SNC) and the ENKS. Moreover, the SNC has fundamentally refused to accept any Kurdish rule in northern Syria.[29] On the other hand, the ENKS repeatedly accused the PYD of violating the power-sharing agreement in 2012 as the PYD resisted the deployment of the Syrian Kurdish fighters (Roj Peshmerga) trained in Iraqi Kurdistan. The escalation of the tension finally resulted in the KRG's closure of the Semalka border crossing on the Iraq-Syria border. And, the KRG started to dig trenches to block the access to Syria from Iraqi Kurdistan while the ENKS joined the ranks of the SNC.[30]

The first crack in the peace process deepened, however, when the so-called Islamic State of Iraq and the Levant (ISIS) surfaced in 2014. The emergence of the ISIS eased the tension among the Kurdish parties, but sent Turkey on an irreversible direction against all the Kurds.

The new political setting in the Middle East resulting from the emergence of ISIS

The emergence of ISIS in 2014 disrupted the Middle East's political equilibrium. Turkey had sought international intervention against the Assad regime in Syria. However, once ISIS captured Mosul in Iraq in June 2014, the newly formed international coalition merely targeted ISIS but not the Assad regime. The coalition did not want to weaken the Assad regime's effective fighting against ISIS. Turkey responded this international and regional political orientation with a clear reluctance to join the fight against ISIS and increasingly pursued its goal of toppling Bashar al-Assad. Moreover, Turkey strengthened its support for jihadist groups in Syria despite the blurring

---

[27] For further reading, see: Fabrice Balance, 'The United States in Northern Syria', *Hoover Institution*, 2018, https://www.hoover.org/sites/default/files/research/docs/383981576-the-united-states-in-north eastern-syria-geopolitical-strategy-cannot-ignore-local-reality_1.pdf (Accessed on 7 December 2018).

[28] Cengiz Çandar, 'Under pressure from Turkey, UN excludes PYD from Syria talks', *Al-Monitor*, 29 January 2016, http://www.al-monitor.com/pulse/originals/2016/01/turkey-usa-syria-talks-ankara-won-batlle-against-pyd.html (Accessed on 20 October 2017).

[29] Harriet Allsopp, 'Kurdish Political Parties and the Syrian Uprising', *The Kurdish Question Revisited*, (ed.) Gareth Stansfield and Mohammed Shareef, C. Hurst &Co., 2017, p. 302.

[30] FehimTastekin, 'KRG trench divides Syrian, Iraqi Kurds', *Al-Monitor*, 21 April 2014, http://www.al-monitor.com/pulse/originals/2014/04/krg-trench-divides-syrian-iraqi-kurds.html (Accessed on 25 October 2017); 'Kurdish National Council to join the Syrian Coalition', *ARA News*, 8 September 2013, http://aranews.net/2013/09/kurdish-national-council-joins-the-syrian-coalition/ (Accessed on 9 October 2017).

relations between ISIS and the jihadist groups.[31]

The emergence of ISIS had also a significant impact on Turkey-Kurdish relations. In August 2014, ISIS unexpectedly attacked Shingal, a district on Iraq-Syria border controlled by the KRG. The ISIS soon headed towards Erbil, the capital city of the KRG. The KRG, then, asked for emergency support first from Turkey. But Turkey did not respond to this call.[32] Turkey's excuse was the ISIS' occupation of Turkey's Mosul consulate wherein the ISIS held Turkish diplomats and employees as hostages.[33] Deeply disappointed with Turkey's refusal, the KRG chief of staff stated that Turkey had in fact guaranteed to protect the KRG in case of any assault.[34] In the end, the USA military's prompt air attacks and the PKK fighters' and Iran's support on the ground helped the KRG to save both Erbil and some parts of the disputed areas in Iraq.[35]

Turkey's reluctance to help the KRG against the ISIS was actually not an exceptional attitude resulted from the ISIS' occupation of Turkey's Mosul consulate. When the ISIS escalated violence against the Kurdish-ruled city Kobane in Syria in September 2014, Turkey again remained inactive.[36] Moreover, Turkey's President Erdoğan stated as if giving a good news that 'Kobane is just about to fall'.[37] But Kobane did not fall as the USA unexpectedly provided air support to the PYD's armed forces, the People's Protection Units (YPG). Furthermore, despite Turkey's objections, the USA also helped the KRG military forces pass through Turkey to support the YPG forces in Kobane;38 and then, initiated meetings to redress the imbalance of power in Kurdish political forces in Syria and Iraq by brokering

---

[31] Tulin Daloglu, 'Turkey finally designates Jabhat al-Nusra a terrorist group', *Al-Monitor*, 6 June 2014, http://www.al-monitor.com/pulse/originals/2014/06/turkey-al-nusra-terrorist-organization-syria-al-qaeda.html (Accessed on 9 October 2017).

[32] Hevidar Ahmed, 'Senior Kurdish Official:IS was at Erbil's Gate, Turkey did not help', *Rudaw*, 16 September 2014, http://www.rudaw.net/english/interview/16092014 (Accessed on 9 October 2017).

[33] 'İŞİD Türk Konsolosluğuna Saldırıp Çalışanları Kaçırdı', *Hürriyet*, 11 June 2014, http://www.hurriyet.com.tr/dunya/isid-turk-konsolosluguna-saldirip-calisanlari-kacirdi-26591687 (Accessed on 9 October 2017).

[34] 'Senior Kurdish Official', Rudaw, 16 September 2014, http://www.rudaw.net/english/interview/16092014 (Accessed on 9 October 2017).

[35] Spencer Ackerman, Kim Willsher and Haroon Siddique, 'US air strikes hit Isis again as efforts intensify to evacuate Yazidi refugees', *The Guardian*, 11 August 2014, https://www.theguardian.com/world/2014/aug/10/us-air-strikes-isis-iraq-yazidi-refugees (Accessed on 9 October 2017).

[36] 'İŞİD Kobane'ye Saldırdı', *Aljazeera*, 7 October 2014, http://www.aljazeera.com.tr/haber/isid-kobaniye-saldirdi (Accessed on 9 October 2017).

[37] 'Erdoğan: Şuan Kobani düştü düşüyor', *Cumhuriyet*, 7 October 2014, http://www.cumhuriyet.com.tr/ haber/siyaset/127825/Erdogan__Su_an_Kobani_dustu_dusuyor.html (Accessed on 9 October 2017).

[38] 'Erdoğan: Türkiye'ye ragmen ABD, PYD'ye silah yardımı yapmıştır', *Cumhuriyet*, 7 October 2014, http://www.cumhuriyet.com.tr/video/video/133431/Erdogan__Turkiye_ye_ragmen_ABD__PYD_ye_silah_yardimi_yapmistir.html (Accessed on 9 October 2017).

the Duhok Agreement in October 2014.[39]

Consequently, Turkey's attempt to partner with the Kurds in the Middle East within the context of the Peace Process resulted in the emergence of the Kurds as a significant military and political actors in the fight against ISIS under the leadership of the US. Even worse, while the Kurds gradually became a 'strategic ally of the West' in the region, Turkey was left outside the political equilibrium in both Iraq and Syria.[40]

Turkey was entirely excluded from the Syrian theatre when a Turkish F-16 plane shot down a Russian Su-24 plane on the Turkey-Syria border in November 2015.[41] Turkey lost even its limited access in Syria because of Russian military blockade.[42] Moreover, Turkish-Russian relations erupted into an economic and political crisis while Turkey suddenly found itself in a 'dangerous loneliness'.[43]

In this context, Turkey had to admit the failure of its policy towards Syria.[44] Such an acknowledgement actually indicated the failure of the Turkish foreign policy in a broader context with both regional and international actors. Then, the newly formed Turkish goal became 'more friends, fewer enemies'.[45] In doing so, Turkey signaled a return to its status quo ante posture with a greater emphasis on border security, which in practice designated the Kurds as an 'existential threat'.

Setting the clocks back to the "Kurdish Threat"

In fact, the Turkish National Assembly recognized the ISIS in October 2014, as a terrorist organization and authorized cross-border military actions in Syria and Iraq.[46] The authorization bill, however, clearly focused on the

---

[39] 'Divided Syrian Kurds reach deal in face of ISIS threat', *Rudaw*, 22 October 2014, http://www.rudaw.net/english/kurdistan/221020141 (Accessed on: 25 October 2017).

[40] Murat Özçelik, 'Turkish Foreign Policy in the Middle East', *Turkish Policy Quarterly*, September 2014, http://turkishpolicy.com/article/705/turkish-foreign-policy-in-the-middle-east-fall-2014 (Accessed on: 25 October 2017).

[41] 'Turkey's Downing Russian Warplane:What We Know', BBC,1 December 2015, https://www.bbc.com/news/world-middle-east-34912581 (Accessed on 29 October 2017).

[42] Nick Penzenstadler, 'Turkey, NATO call on Russia to stop airspace violations', USA Today, 30 January 2016, https://www.usatoday.com/story/news/world/2016/01/30/turkey-says-another-russian-jet-violated-turkeys-airspace/79563500/, (Accessed on 29 October 2017).

[43] Kadri Gürsel, 'Tehlikeli Yalnızlık', *Milliyet*, 20 October 2014, http://www.milliyet.com.tr/tehlikeli-yalnizlik/dunya/ydetay/1956985/default.htm (Accessed on 29 October 2017).

[44] Murat Yetkin, 'Başımıza gelen birçok şey Suriye politikası sonucu', *Hürriyet*, 18 August 2016, http://www.hurriyet.com.tr/numan-kurtulmus-basimiza-gelen-bircok-sey-suriye-politikasi-sonucu-40200349 (Accessed on 28 August 2017).

[45] Serkan Demirtaş, 'A retreat in Turkey's More Friends, Fewer Enemies Policy', *Hürriyet*, 2 August 2017, http://www.hurriyetdailynews.com/opinion/serkan-demirtas/a-retreat-in-turkeys-more-friends--fewer-enemies-policy-116213 (Accessed on 29 October 2017).

46 Liz Sly, 'Turkish parliament authorises potential military action in Syria and Iraq', *The Washington*

PKK as the primary threat to be addressed. Nevertheless, instead of becoming an active ally in the fight against ISIS, Turkey soon deployed harsh security measures in the Kurdish-populated provinces including Diyarbakir, where massive demonstrations took place in support of Kobane.[47] These developments were in fact demonstrating that the peace process and the rapprochement policies between Turks and the Kurds were about to end. The breakdown, however, became evident when Turkey launched military operations against the PKK bases in Iraq in July 2015.[48]

The military operations against the PKK bases in Iraq were remarkable as the timing coincided with Turkey's decision to open its Incirlik base to the International Coalition against ISIS.[49] Yet, Turkey got the opportunity to step into Iraq to attack the PKK bases exactly when the USA and Turkey reached out an agreement on Incirlik base. However, Turkey could not extend its military operations throughout Syria as the USA refused Turkey's claims that "The PKK and the YPG are the same terrorist organisation".[50] and clearly regraded the YPG different from the PKK.[51]

Meanwhile, as a response to Turkish airstrikes in Iraq, the PKK called for resistance against the Turkish government, which resulted in the escalation of violence in Kurdish provinces.[52] The PKK-affiliated urban militias attempted to set up check points in some cities while the Democratic People's Congress (DTK), the largest political forum that gathered Kurdish non-governmental organisations in Turkey, adopted a 14-article declaration laying out the main principles of their demand for self-rule.[53] In turn, Turkey launched an intensive military offensive and declared 'Special Security Zones' particularly in Kurdish provinces. Finally, the "Kurdish threat" was again back on the national agenda.[54]

Post, 2 October 2014, https://www.washingtonpost.com/world/middle_east/turkish-parliament-authorises-military-action-in-syria-iraq/2014/10/02/cca5dba8-7d0c-4e70-88bb-c84abbdca6d2_story.html?utm_term=.96c8826b43e7 (Accessed on 29 October 2017).

[47] 'Diyarbakır'da OHAL Manzaraları', *Sabah*, 8 October 2014, https://www.sabah.com.tr/gundem/2014/10/08/diyarbakirda-ohal-manzaralari (Accessed on 29 October 2017).

[48] 'Türkiye Füzelerle PKK Kampını Vurdu', *Hürriyet*, 24 July 2015, http://www.hurriyet.com.tr/gundem/turkiye-fuzelerle-pkk-kamplarini-vurdu-29804076 (Accessed on 29 October 2017).

[49] 'ABD: Türkiye izin verdi IŞİD İncirlikten vurulacak', *BBC*, 24 July 2015, https://www.bbc.com/turkce/haberler/2015/07/150724_incirlik_turkiye_abd (Accessed on 29 October 2017).

[50] 'Erdoğan DAİŞ PKK ve uzantısı YPGnın farkı yok', *BBC*, 14 October 2015, https://www.bbc.com/turkce/haberler/2015/10/151014_erdogan_konusma (Accessed on 29 October 2017).

[51] 'ABD Israrcı YPG Terör Örgütü Değil', *Milliyet*, 28 May 2016, http://www.milliyet.com.tr/abd-israrci-ypg-teror-orgutu-degil/dunya/detay/2253131/default.htm (Accessed on 29 October 2017).

[52] 'Cemil Bayık: Silahlanın Tünel Kazın', *Sabah*, 20 July 2015, https://www.sabah.com.tr/gundem/2015/07/20/cemil-bayik-silahlanin-tunel-kazin (Accessed on 29 October 2017).

[53] 'Turkey's Kurds Call for Self-rule', *Deutche Welle*, 28 December 2015, https://www.dw.com/en/turkeys-kurds-call-for-self-rule/a-18946432 (Accessed on 29 October 2017).

[54] 'Türkiye'nin Yeni OHAL'i', Agos, 8 August 2015, http://www.agos.com.tr/tr/yazi/12422/turkiyenin-yeni-ohali-37-gecici-guvenlik-bolgesi (Accessed on: 29 October 2017).

A selective emphasis on security as well as brutal political and military measures revealed that Turkey was in search for status quo ante regarding the Kurdish Question. Such a shift was consolidated when a deadly military coup attempt against the Turkish government marked a monumental turning point in Turkish political affairs.[55] Upon increased public sentiments about the survival of the Republic of Turkey, Erdoğan's government addressed not only the Kurds, recently designated "strategic partners" in the Middle East, but also its long-lasting ally within the NATO as "existential threats" for Turkey. According to the ruling party AKP, the Western countries, the USA who supported the "Gülenist Terror Organisation (FETÖ)" in particular, was the actual actors behind the coup attempt in Turkey.[56]

As a consequence, Turkey-USA relations were disrupted by a set of crises which resulted in statements such as, 'The White House has decided to give up on Turkey as an ally.'[57] However, not the "FETÖ", but the USA-YPG cooperation in Syria soon came to the forefront as the main reason of tense relations between the USA and Turkey. In such circumstances, it was Russia who opened the doors of Syrian theater to Turkey.

The "Red Apple": Afrin Operation 2018

In the newly formed status quoist posture, Turkey redefined its interest in the Middle East with a particular emphasis on the security of its borders and territorial integrity. The 'Rabia' sign embraced by the AKP party as a symbol of solidarity with the demonstrators at Tahrir Square in Egypt turned into a symbol of 'One nation, one flag, one homeland, one state' in Turkey.[58] In this context, Turkey claimed a legitimate right to launch military operations throughout the Middle East for its security interests. Given this, prevention of the emerging "Kurdish terror corridor" on Turkey's southern borders extending from Iraqi Kurdistan to the Mediterranean was "Turkey's primary strategic priority in the region".[59]

This change in Turkey's priority in Syria paved the way for closer relations

---

[55] 'Darbe Girişimi Gecesi Türkiye'de ne oldu', BBC, 16 July 2016, https://www.bbc.com/turkce/haberler-turkiye-36813808 (Accessed on: 29 October 2017).

[56] 'Erdoğandan Batı'ya Suçlama', *VOA*, 2 August 2016, https://www.mynet.com/erdogandan-batiya-suclama-110102569719 (Accessed on 29 October 2017).

[57] Steven Cook, 'We wanted Turkey to be a partner. It was never going to work', *Washington Institute*, https://www.washingtonpost.com/outlook/turkey-is-an-overrated-american-ally/2018/08/17/652ce464-a18a-11e8-93e3-24d1703d2a7a_story.html?utm_term=.5016d8434cd6 (Accessed on 7 December 2018)

[58] Ahmet Murat Aytaç, 'Rabia: Siyasal Bir Simgenin Başarısızlığı', *Gazete Duvar*, 5 December 2018, https://www.gazeteduvar.com.tr/yazarlar/2018/12/05/rabia-siyasal-bir-simgenin-basarisizligi/ (Accessed on 7 December 2018)

[59] Merve Çalhan, 'Afrin: Response to PYD's fait accompli', *Daily Sabah*, 30 August 2017, https://www.dailysabah.com/op-ed/2017/08/30/afrin-response-to-pyds-fait-accompli (Accessed on 29 October 2017).

with Russia while Turkey-USA relations faced a dangerous unravelling.[60] This newly emerging Turkish-Russian rapprochement first resulted in the Operation Euphrates Shield in August 2016. Russia finally consented to Turkey entering Syrian territory and blocking the connection between Kobane and Afrin cantons ruled by the PYD.[61] In fact, promptly after the Operation Euphrates Shield, Turkey wanted to move into the Afrin canton as well. But Russia did not let this happen and deployed its observers in Afrin to prevent Turkish assaults.[62] Both Russia and the USA rolled back Turkey's military attempts to capture Manbij, a city under the YPG control on the western bank of the Euphrates River.[63]

In fact, Russian's and the US' relations with the Kurds in Syria were not so different. Similar to the USA, Russia also conducted joint operations with the YPG, for instance, in the Kurdish-ruled city of Afrin. In fact, one could argue that it was Russian support which ensured the Kurds' survival on the western bank of the Euphrates river.[64] In addition, Russia was the only international actor opposed to the Turkish blocking of the PYD's participation in the Geneva peace process and stated clearly that the PYD should also be involved.[65] Last, but not least, unlike the Western countries, Russia has never recognized the PKK as a terrorist organization.[66]

Such apparent hard-line issues, however, became less significant as Turkish-Russian relations deepened through the energy ties of the Turkstream natural gas pipeline and Akkuyu Nuclear Power Plant Agreement.[67] And, then the Turkish-Russian partnership peaked with Turkey's purchase of Russian S-400 missiles. By partnering with NATO member Turkey in Syria, Moscow could finally strengthen its position vis-a-

---

[60] Philip Gordon, Amanda Sloat, 'The Dangerous Unraveling of the US-Turkish Alliance', Foreign Policy, https://www.foreignaffairs.com/articles/turkey/2020-01-10/dangerous-unraveling-us-turkish-alliance (Accessed on 10 January 2020)

[61] Serhat Erkmen, 'What's Turkey's military goal in Syria?', *Deutsche Welle*, 1 December 2016, http://www.dw.com/en/whats-turkeys-military-goal-in-syria/a-36600491 (Accessed on 29 October 2017).

[62] Semih Idiz, 'Ankara must go through US, Russia to get to YPG', *Al-Monitor*, 6 September 2017, https://www.al-monitor.com/pulse/originals/2017/09/turkey-russia-ankara-prepares-new-syria-operation.html (Accessed on 29 October 2017).

[63] 'Syrian state to be buffer between Manbij and Turkish forces', *Rudaw*, 2 March 2017, http://www.rudaw.net/english/middleeast/syria/02032017 (Accessed on 29 October 2017).

[64] 'Russia to 'maintain security' in Afrin in deal with Kurdish force: YPG', *Rudaw*, 29 August 2017, http://www.rudaw.net/english/middleeast/syria/29082017 (Accessed on 29 October 2017).

[65] Syria Peace Talks Should Be Direct, Include Kurds - Russian Envoy to UN, Spuntik, 09. February 2017,https://sputniknews.com/politics/201702091050499124-talks-syria-kirds-improvements/ (Accessed on 29 October 2017)

[66] Yerevan Saeed, 'Russian ambassador in Turkey says PKK not a terrorist organization', *Rudaw* 19 October 2015, http://www.rudaw.net/english/middleeast/turkey/19102015 (Accessed on 29 October 2017).

[67] Gareth Windrow, 'The Importance of Energy Ties', Insight Turkey (Winter 2017), Vol.19, No.1, pp.17-32.

vis the USA, in particular.[68] Nevertheless, Russia initiated Astana process in cooperation with Iran and Turkey gradually replaced the Geneva process for a political solution in Syria. Meanwhile, the Astana process opened the doors for the Turkish government to the Syrian city of Idlib, a hub for jihadist groups. During the Astana talks held in September 2017, Russia, Iran, and Turkey agreed to establish four de-confliction zones, which paved the way for Turkish military expansion in Syria. A month later, in October, Turkey deployed its troops in Idlib, a city next to Afrin. According to many observers, Turkey's ultimate goal in Idlib was to intervene in Afrin.[69] Ultimately, Turkey achieved this goal in early 2018 with the consent of Russia, while the Western countries were indifferent.

Indeed, there has been a kind of modus vivendi between Washington and Moscow on a sphere of influence partition plan in Syria, with the east of the Euphrates river being under the USA control and the west of the Euphrates river under Russian.[70] Therefore, it was primarily Russia who let Turkey to launch the Operation Olive Branch operation in Afrin.[71] However, by justifying "Turkey's legitimate security concerns about its borders", the USA as well as the European countries were also supportive of Turkey's military action.[72]

In the end, not 'toppling Assad' but the "Kurdish threat" provided Turkey with the international legitimacy to seize the control of more than 4000 square kilometres in Syria.[73] Moreover, Turkey has built its own rule in the city of Jerablus, al-Bab and Afrin by backing the Syrian opposition groups.[74] The facts on the ground have simply indicated that Turkey has almost annexed these cities while the demography of the Turkey-controlled

---

[68] Jonathan Marcus, 'What Turkey's S400 missile deal means for NATO?', https://www.bbc.com/news/world-europe-48620087, (Accessed on 13 June 2019)

[69] Soli Özel, 'What are Turkey's Ultimate Aims in Syria?', *Carniege*, 19 October 2017, http://carnegie-mec.org/diwan/73459?lang=en (Accessed on 29 October 2017).

[70] David Ignatius, 'Working with Russia might be the best path to peace in Syria', *The Washington Post*, 4 July 2017, https://www.washingtonpost.com/opinions/global-opinions/working-with-russia-might-be-the-best-path-to-peace-in-syria/2017/07/04/c2589c9e-6029-11e7-a4f7-af34fc1d9d39_story.html?utm_term=.f49c8f887398 (Accessed on 29 October 2017).

[71] Leonid Issaev, 'Why is Russia helping Turkey in Afrin?', *Aljazeera*, 29 January 2018, https://www.aljazeera.com/indepth/opinion/russia-helping-turkey-afrin-180125122718953.html (Accessed on 29 November 2018).

[72] David Graeber, 'Why are world leaders backing this brutal attack against Kurdish Afrin?', *The Guardian*, 23 February 2018, https://www.theguardian.com/commentisfree/2018/feb/23/world-leaders-brutal-attack-kurdish-afrin-turkish-army (Accessed on 29 November 2018).

[73] Ece Toksabay, Mehmet Emin Caliskan, 'Erdogan says Turkey may extend Afrin campaign along whole Syrian border', *Reuters*, 19 March 2018, https://www.reuters.com/article/us-mideast-crisis-syria-afrin-turkey/erdogan-says-turkey-may-extend-afrin-campaign-along-whole-syrian-border-idUSKBN1GV14U?feedType=RSS&feedName=worldNews (Accessed on 29 November 2018).

[74] 'Türkiyeden Kaymakam Atanacak', *Yeni Akit*, 4 April 2018, https://www.yeniakit.com.tr/haber/turkiyeden-kaymakam-atanacak-afrin-antakyaya-ait-olacak-443668.html (Accessed on 3 December 2018).

provinces has dramatically changed.[75]

One can argue that Syrian opposition groups, particularly the Free Syrian Army (FSA) has fulfilled the role that Ankara had expected the Kurds to play within the context of the peace process. In fact, Turkey has supported the FSA since the Syrian crisis erupted. However, it was soon evident that the FSA was not competent to combat the Assad regime forces even though toppling the Assad regime was no longer a priority. The FSA's performance against the ISIS and other jihadist groups also did not meet with the expectations. Nevertheless, the 'train and equip' program developed for the FSA by the USA and Turkey stumbled when the Jabhat al-Nusra captured a group from the FSA.[76] The USA then acknowledged the failure of the 'train and equip' program in Syria.[77] The FSA, however, have kept operating in Syria under the command of Turkish forces during the Operation Euphrates Shield and Operation Olive Branch.[78] Furthermore, the FSA members who lost their lives have been adopted as martyrs while President Erdoğan named them as 'Kuvayı Milliye' forces of Turkish survival.[79]

Against this backdrop, apparently, "fighting against the Kurds" served more than "partnering with the Kurds" to Turkey's goal in the Middle East. It is fair to claim that Turkey's seemingly shift to a status quoist posture to prevent the emergence of a Kurdish corridor was in fact a tactical deception. Nevertheless, the Turkish strategy, as clearly stated, has been to "maintain effective influence in shaping what comes next" in Syria, in particular.[80] Hence, the President of Turkey rallied the Turkish public to support the invasion of Afrin by referring to the pan-Turkic cause of 'Red Apple'.[81] As President Erdoğan has repeatedly declared that Turkey also wanted presence

---

[75] Paul Iddon, 'Turkey slowly implementing demographic change in Afrin', *Rudaw*, 3 May 2018, http://www.rudaw.net/english/analysis/03052018 (Accessed on 29 November 2018).

[76] 'US-trained Syria fighters gave equipment to Nusra Front', *Al Jazeera*, 26 September 2015, http://www.aljazeera.com/news/2015/09/trained-syria-fighters-gave-equipment-nusra-front-150926011820488.html (Accessed on 29 October 2017).

[77] Michael D. Shear, Helene Cooper and Eric Schmitt, 'Obama Administration Ends Effort to Train Syrians to Combat ISIS', *The New York Times*, 9 October 2015, https://www.nytimes.com/2015/10/10/world/middleeast/pentagon-program-islamic-state-syria.html (Accessed on 29 October 2017).

[78] David Enders, 'Under Turkish tutelage FSA becomes better organised, but its mission shifts', 25 March 2018, https://www.thenational.ae/world/mena/under-turkish-tutelage-fsa-becomes-better-organised-but-its-mission-shifts-1.716057 (Accessed on 29 November 2018).

[79] 'Erdoğan: ÖSO Kuvayı Milliye gibi Sivil Oluşumdur', *Deutche Welle*, https://www.dw.com/tr/erdoğan-öso-kuvayı-milliye-güçleri-gibi-sivil-oluşumdur/a-42364790 (Accessed on 7 December 2018).

[80] Ziya Meral, 'What are Turkey's Ultimate Aims in Syria', *Carniege*, http://carnegie-mec.org/diwan/73459 (Accessed on 29 October 2017).

[81] The cause of 'Red Apple' refers to the far-Turkish nationalists aspirations to conquer new lands and bring all Turkic peoples under one flag. 'Erdogan Invokes Pan-Turkic myth of conquest as army attacks Kurdish Afrin', Kurdistan 24, https://www.kurdistan24.net/en/news/029927e2-e1ba-4c91-a41e-813bdccb9565 (Accessed on 22 January 2018)

in Anbar, Mosul, Telafer, and Shingal.[82]

Conclusion

The international system has radically moved away from its promises to protect liberal universal values. Moreover,, reconstructing the nation-states has become a common goal in name of building stability in the Middle East, in particular . It is doubtful, however, whether such efforts would help to maintain a stable and sustainable political order in the region. Nevertheless, the power vacuum derived mainly from the absence of the USA power as well as shifting alliances in the region trigger the ambitions of regional powers who are in pursuit of expansion in the region such as Turkey and Iran.

In this regard, Turkey has already to a certain extent realized its goal by instrumentalising the Kurdish Question. Yet Ankara could step in Syria once it raised the 'Kurdish threat' as a cause for its military invention. By doing so, Ankara has not only legitimized the seeming annexation of parts of Syria in the eyes of international community, but also consolidated its authoritarian regime and ill-fated Syrian policy in the eye of Turkish public.

Overall, Afrin Operation 2018 took place within the context of an evident international and regional consensus on rolling back the Kurds within national boundaries after the defeat of ISIS. Following the Kurdish independence referendum in 2017, first the KRG forces were pushed back from the disputed areas in Iraq. The occupation of Gri Spi and Serekaniye by Turkey in the eastern coast of Euphrates River in 2019 was the last attempt to contain the Kurdish rule in name of safe-guarding the territorial integrity of the constituent states. As of 2020, however, Turkey's war in Idlib and Turkey's rule in Jerablus, Al-Bab and Afrin, has demonstrated that the 'prevention of the Kurdish corridor" is paving the way for a hub of radical Islamist groups under the patronage of Turkey.

Given this, the Turkish invasion in Syria requires asking the question of to what extent the international community will turn blind eye on Turkish territorial expansion in Syria. If this question is not addressed soon, the Turkish invasion would then not be a problem of just the Kurds and/or the Assad regime, but of all those who would inevitably suffer from the instability in the Middle East.

References

Alpay, Necmiye & Tahmaz, Hakan (ed.) 2015: Barış Açısını Savunmak, Istanbul: Metis.
Altunisik, Melina Benli 2005: The Turkish Model and Democratization in the Middle East, Arab Studies Quarterly, 27,1, pp. 45-63

---

[82] 'Erdoğan'dan Rakka mesajı', *DeutscheWelle*, 29 April 2017, http://www.dw.com/tr/erdoğandan-rakka-mesajı/a-38637610 (Accessed on 29 October 2017).

Çelik, Ayşe Betül & Rumelili, Bahar 2006: Necessary But Not Sufficient: The Role of the EU in Resolving Turkey's Kurdish Question and the Greek-Turkish Conflicts', European Foreign Affairs Review, 11, pp. 203-222

Güneş, Cengiz 2013: Türkiye'de Kürt Ulusal Hareketi: Direnişjn Söylemi, Ankara: Dipnot.

Natali, Denise 2005: Kürtler ve Devlet: Irak, Türkiye ve İran'da Ulusal Kimliğin Gelişmesi, Istanbul: Avesta.

O' Ballance, Edward 1996: The Kurdish Struggle: 1920-1994, New York: ST Martin Press.

Öktem, Emre 2011: Turkey: Successor or Continuing State of the Ottoman Empire?, Leiden Journal of International Law, Vol. 24, No. 3, pp. 561-583

Romano, David 2006: The Kurdish Nationalist Movement: Opportunity, Mobilization and Identity, New York: Cambridge.

Romano, David & Güneş, Cengiz (ed.) 2014: Conflict, Democratization and the Kurds in the Middle East, New York: Palgrave.

Stansfield, Gareth & Shareef, Mohammed (ed.) 2017: The Kurdish Question Revisited, London: C. Hurst &Co.

Vali, Abbas (ed.) 2005: Kürt Milliyetçiliğinin Kökenleri, Istanbul: Avesta.

Yilmaz, Arzu 2018: The Changing Dynamics of the Kurdish Question, SWP Comment, 2018/C(45).

Yilmaz, Arzu 2015: Kürt Milliyetçiliğine Eleştirel Bir Bakış: Kürt Mülteciler ve Kurdistan Milliyetçiliği, Ankara: Mülkiye Dergisi, Cilt 39(1), pp. 37-56

CHAPTER 8

THE IMPACT OF TURKEY'S 2019 INVASION ON NORTH AND EAST SYRIA

Thomas McClure & Nina Steinhardt

Throughout the Turkish invasion of North and East Syria, the Rojava Information Center (RIC) collected information from a network of sources across the region as well as RIC field teams, documenting the impact of the invasion on civilian populations and infrastructure. The RIC has found that the Turkish Armed Forces and its proxy militias are responsible for widespread attacks on non-combatants, systematic looting and destruction of private property and public infrastructure, and mass displacement of civilians. The RIC documented a clear trend of Turkish forces targeting health workers, vehicles and infrastructure, as well as destruction of water and electricity facilities, bakeries, roads, grain storage facilities, and so on. A number of high-profile human rights violations, such as the field execution of female Syrian politician Hevrin Khalef and the strike on a civilian convoy which left thirteen civilians dead, take place against a background of a systematic attempt to make life unliveable for civilians in the zones Turkey aims to occupy. The forcible displacement of the civilian population in general and the Kurdish, Yazidi, and Christian populations in particular, to facilitate the installation of Turkmen and Arab militiamen and their families, ought to be seen as a process of demographic engineering for which the Turkish government is ultimately responsible.

Preface

On 9 October 2019, Turkey started their long-threatened invasion of North and East Syria following US President Donald Trump's much-criticised decision to withdraw US military support for the Syrian Democratic Forces. Widespread and indiscriminate shelling and air strikes targeting most of the cities and villages along the border caused civilian deaths, injuries, damage to infrastructure, and mass population movements away from the conflict. Turkey has met with near-global condemnation for its 2019 offensive into North and East Syria. More than the figures – 200,000 displaced within a week, hundreds killed[1, 2]– high-profile rights violations have provoked an international response. Chief among these were the field executions of leading female Syrian politician Hevrin Khalef and other civilians by Turkish-backed faction Ahrar al-Sharqiya on 12 October, along with the 13 October strike on a civilian convoy heading into Sere Kaniye which left thirteen civilians dead.

These crimes, graphically documented on video and broadcast around the world, should not be considered as isolated incidents conducted by rogue individuals. Throughout the invasion of 2019, the Rojava Information Center documented systematic crimes against civilians committed by both the Turkish Armed Forces (TAF) and its proxy militias organised under the banner of the 'Syrian National Army', henceforth referred to as the 'Turkish-backed National Army' (TNA).[3] These attacks included the obstruction of information-gathering and the targeting of press, civilians and civilian neighbourhoods, civilian and humanitarian infrastructure, and medical staff and health infrastructure. Looting and property crimes, such as seizure of private homes and business, were also documented.

Taken together, these testimonies paint a picture of what can be termed 'Turkey's war on civilians' – a systematic attempt to make life unliveable for civilians in the zones Turkey aims to occupy. The ultimate aim is forcibly displacing the civilian population in general and the Kurdish, Yazidi and Christian populations in particular, facilitating the installation of Turkmen and Arab militiamen and their families and the de facto expansion of Turkey's territorial control.

In addition to being a humanitarian crisis in its own terms, Turkish attacks are compounding the effects of the Syrian Civil War that the region was already experiencing. North and East Syria alone currently hosts 1.9 million people in need of humanitarian assistance, many of them internally displaced people (IDPs) who have fled the Turkish invasion or conflict elsewhere in Syria.[4] With current estimates placing the number of displaced civilians at 200,000 – 300,000, the number of Syrians who have been displaced or become refugees has exceeded 12 million. Directly following the commencement of the Turkish invasion, 15 international aid agencies released a statement saying that 'the aid response in Syria is already stretched

---

[1] Refugees International. 2019. Displacement and despair: The Turkish invasion of North and East Syria. https://reliefweb.int/report/syrian-arab-republic/displacement-and-despair-turkish-invasion-northeast-syria.

[2] United Nations. 2019. Hundreds of thousands of civilians at risk in Syria amid ongoing violence in northeast and northwest. https://news.un.org/en/story/2019/11/1050961.

[3] Rojava Information Center. 2019. 'Factions in the Turkish-backed 'Free Syrian *Army*."

[4] UN chief urges new transit point for aid to Syria. 2020. https://www.france24.com/en/20200222-un-chief-urges-new-transit-point-for-aid-to-syria.

to breaking point' and additional refugees would require 'humanitarian assistance that the international community is not in a position to provide.'⁵

The Turkish invasion and occupation of the Afrin region of North and East Syria in 2018, which displaced 300,000 people, must be considered as part of their human rights record. The region is now occupied and controlled by Turkish proxy forces, including jihadist groups such as the Sultan Murad Brigade and Ahrar Al-Sharqiya, who engage in looting, confiscation of property, abduction for ransom, forced displacement, extrajudicial killing, and sexual violence against women and girls. The UN has reported that since the invasion, 'areas in northern Syria, such as Afrin, al-Bab, Jarablus, and Azaz that were already under the control of Turkish forces and/or affiliated armed groups, are continuing to face lawlessness and rampant criminality and violence'.⁶ The regions newly occupied by Turkey are now facing a similar fate.

Press and information-gathering in the conflict

Rojava Information Center (RIC) is an independent, volunteer-staffed organization based in North and East Syria. The RIC is made up international journalists and media activists working alongside local volunteer staff, providing journalists, researchers and the general public with information about North and East Syria. In order to do this, we work in partnership with civil and political institutions, journalists, and media activists across the region.

Throughout the Turkish invasion of North and East Syria, the RIC collected information from a network of sources across the region as well as sending field teams to the front line and displacement camps to conduct interviews with those affected by the violence. Even as most foreign journalists evacuated the region following the arrival of Syrian government forces, the RIC continued to collect information and produce research and documentation on the situation. Through this work, the RIC aimed to overcome the obstructions to carrying out media work caused by Turkey and its proxy forces deliberate targeting of press to prevent information-gathering.

In order to assess the impact of the Turkish invasion, the RIC compiled a cross-referenced database of rights violations for which there is either reliable photographic or video evidence or eyewitness testimony collected by our field teams. While by no means comprehensive, this database of over 150

---

⁵ 15 aid agencies warn of humanitarian crisis in North-East Syria. 2019. https://reliefweb.int/report/syrian-arab-republic/15-aid-agencies-warn-humanitarian-crisis-north-east-syria-civilians-risk
⁶ 11 October OHCHR Press Briefing on Syria. 2019. https://www.ohchr.org/EN/NewsEvents/Pages/DisplayNews.aspx?NewsID=25129&LangID=E.

incidents gives a broad picture of rights violations throughout the conflict.[7]

At least three journalists have been killed in Turkish airstrikes since the start of the invasion, while many international press have fled the region as the humanitarian and security situation deteriorated.[8] Several journalists have been injured, such as Zozan Berkele, a local journalist working for all-female station Jin TV. Ms Berkele was shot in the hand by Turkish forces while attempting to cover a joint Turkish-Russian patrol on 11 November in the Kobane countryside.

Significant difficulties face any journalist or researcher attempting to gather information on rights violations committed by Turkey and the TNA. Journalists or researchers cannot enter areas under Turkish occupation, which are 'closed to the media except for those licensed by Turkey, and closed to local and international human rights organizations… Journalists and activists in these areas are also subjected to restrictions and abuses that amount to killing, kidnapping and torture,' according to the Index On Censorship.[9]

War against civilians – health, infrastructure, civilians

Our field teams have been able to speak to a wide range of civilians directly affected by the invasion, including civilians targeted by airstrikes and heavy weapons; medical staff targeted in the same way; those who have lost their homes, property and livelihood to looters; those who have returned into the zone of occupation and secretly observed and filmed the destruction of their own homes; those who have been asked to pay ransoms for the return of the bodies of family members killed by Turkish-backed factions; IDPs affected by damage to humanitarian infrastructure; and NGO staff, civil officials and civilian activists working to assist civilians and IDPs affected by the issues outlined above.

Monitoring group Airwars recorded between 172 and 225 civilian casualties and between 419 and 553 serious civilian injuries, the real figure is possibly much higher.[10] The Health Authority of North and East Syria has issued 478 death certificates for civilians confirmed or assumed to have

---

[7] Rojava Information Center. 2019. Rights violations during the Turkish invasion of NE Syria. https://rojavainformationcenter.com/2019/12/database-documenting-war-crimes.

[8] CPJ Safety Advisory: Covering Rojava and northern Syria. 2019. https://cpj.org/2019/11/cpj-safety-advisory-covering-rojava-and-northern-s.php.

[9] Zouhir Al-Shimale. 2019. Journalists in northern Syria face intimidation and insecurity every day. https://www.indexoncensorship.org/2019/04/journalists-in-northern-syria-face-intimidation-and-insecurity-every-day.

[10] Airwars. 2019. Turkish military in Iraq and Syria. https://airwars.org/conflict/turkish-military-in-iraq-and-syria/.

died.[11] The Kurdish Red Crescent, a local NGO which is the primary humanitarian actor in the region, has recorded over 2400 injuries to civilians, principally shrapnel from artillery shelling and airstrikes but also gunshot wounds, burns, and injuries from mines.[12] These disparities give some indication of the gap between empirically verifiable data and the reality on the ground.

There have been several documented incidents of civilians being targeted while attempting to return to homes and property in Sere Kaniye. RIC interviewed Abdulrezaq Sino, the only survivor of a shooting on 16 October which killed three people: Resho Mehmud Berkel, Mustafa Ehmed Sino, and Rezan Khelil Cholo.

Mr Sino left Sere Kaniye as an IDP on the 11 October but decided to return to Sere Kaniye to check on the private park he owned there. He and his nephew Mustafa, plus Mr Berkel and Mr Cholo, were driving north on the 716 road when they came under a 'hail of bullets' fired by Turkish-backed forces. Mr Sino was struck by one bullet.

He threw himself out of the car, which stopped 15 to 20 meters ahead, and crawled into a nearby carwash shop. While hidden inside, he heard gunmen calling to one another in Arabic, enabling him to identify them as members of Turkish-backed factions. As night fell he moved to another building nearby and was eventually found by SDF fighters, recognizing them by the sound of women's voices: 'I could hear the voice of a female fighter, and so I thought, they must be [the YPJ],' he told RIC.

A conclusive autopsy has not been possible because the Turkish-backed forces hold the bodies of the three men. Mr Sino called the telephone of Mustafa Sino, his nephew, and it was answered by a fighter in the Turkish-backed forces: 'One answered and said, "you must come now, bring money and you can bring back the bodies." They wanted money for the bodies.'

Mr Cholo's mother received photos showing an unidentified member of the Turkish-backed faction Sultan Murad Division posing with the victims' bloodied corpses along with a fighter identified as Heytham of Sultan Murad Division demanding payment for its return. Kurdish journalist Vedat Erdemci was similarly killed by Turkish fire during the offensive. When Erdemci's mother called his phone to try and trace him, TNA fighters then sent a photo of Erdemci's decapitated corpse to his mother, kicking the head around to expose his face. This treatment of corpses, including demanding

---

[11] Humanitarian Affairs Committee of North and East Syria. Statement provided to RIC, 20 November 2019.
[12] Kurdish Red Crescent. 2019. Turkish military and Islamic groups invasion in Northeast Syria. http://hskurd.org/wp-content/uploads/2019/11/9th-october-to-14th-of-november-doc.pdf.

ransom, could be considered a war-crime.

Our team was also present in Tel Tamer hospital on 22 October during the arrival of Mahir Abdo Sadon and Ednan Abdulaziz Juma, two civilians who tried to return to their shop in Sere Kaniye only to be targeted by Turkish-backed fighters near Mishrafa.

Mahir told RIC: 'At Mishrafa, we took the non-paved road. We were driving as normal on the motorbike when there was a blow on my face. Something exploded and the world fell apart.' He and Ednan became conscious while lying on the ground with the motorbike destroyed. They crawled back to the main road where they were able to flag down another car to bring them to Tel Tamer hospital.

In another similar incident in Tel Abyad, on 20 October, two elderly villagers from Eriyada village, Mehmud Alseyad and Mustafa al Hesen, who had been sleeping in the desert tried to return to their homes to collect blankets. They were both shot dead. These accounts indicate that Turkish-backed forces have been targeting civilians in circumstances where they could not be mistaken for combatants.

It is important to note that Turkish shelling against civilian neighbourhoods has not been limited to the supposed field of operations between Sere Kaniye and Tel Abyad. In Ayn Diwar, a village near Derik on the Turkish border, Abdullah Shero described random shelling which destroyed his family home on 11 October: 'all our four buildings and two homes were burned. We haven't got anything left. Now, we have got together nylon to set up tents. We are civilian people.'

In nearby Perrik, a Christian village, Bave Dani Hannah described to RIC researchers a similar incident on 12 October: 'My son Dani and the shepherd were struck while they were tending the sheep. Salah [the shepherd] was killed, and my son's leg was broken. There were five or six families left in the village, but there's no one left now.'

The city of Qamishlo had the highest rate of civilian casualties in the opening days of the war despite being outside the planned sphere of invasion. Victims include Mohammed Yousef Hussein (12), who was killed, and his sister Sara Yousef Hussein (8), who lost her leg when a shell struck their home in Qidurbek neighborhood on 10 October.

Villagers in the west Kobane countryside described similar attacks to a RIC field team. Speaking in Siftek village, Qahraman Devan Shekho told RIC: 'We fled due to the shelling. A week later I returned to the village, and I couldn't open my door. When I forced it open, I realised that the inside was full of mud and stones. A shell damaged the whole wall, a tank struck our home. If we had been here, we would have been killed. I don't understand why they would do this. I am a civilian; I have never worked as a soldier.'

These accounts are indicative of a wider trend. RIC researchers were present in Sere Kaniye as shelling started. IDPs who fled the city described indiscriminate shelling and airstrikes provoking mass panic, with many IDPs fleeing on foot, leaving personal possessions and family members behind.

A strike on a humanitarian convoy in Sere Kaniye on 13 October, graphically captured on video, was the biggest single civilian loss of life, with thirteen civilians killed.[13] In this incident, a shell believed to have been fired from a Bayraktar strike drone struck a caravan of civilian activists driving into the city to deliver aid and evacuate wounded.

Throughout the conflict, random shelling along the border and away from military targets has caused mass civilian death and displacement without incurring any military gain for Turkey, while Turkish-backed forces have intentionally opened fire on civilians on multiple occasions. These targeted attacks on civilians attempting to return to their homes and property constitute a violation of their right to return following their involuntary displacement. The indiscriminate shelling described to RIC by multiple interviewees, primarily from Sere Kaniye but also from settlements along the border from Derik through to Kobane, may also constitute a war crime.

Targeting health infrastructure

One trend which clearly emerges from the database is Turkey's targeting of health workers, vehicles, and infrastructure – primarily belonging to the Kurdish Red Crescent and the local health authority, but also to international NGOs. Five health workers have been killed by Turkish forces thus far, as well as at least seven wounded.

Kurdish Red Crescent worker Kawa told RIC: 'We had a medical base in the village Salihiye. We were waiting there for the arrival of wounded civilians [on 12 October]. Early in the morning there was an airstrike, and some of us were injured.' On 9 November, an ambulance owned by German NGO Cadus, but operated by local staff, came under fire while moving toward the frontline near Sere Kaniye.

In another notable incident, on 13 October, three health workers were executed by Turkish-backed factions near the Suluk roundabout near Tel Abyad. The Kurdish Red Crescent and RIC confirmed many other instances in which shelling and drone strikes targeted medical staff and facilities.

---

[13] Rojava Information Center. 2019. 13 October daily summary. https://rojavainformationcenter.com/daily-summary/.

Targeting civilian and humanitarian infrastructure

The indiscriminate shelling which has claimed civilian lives also destroyed private property and civilian and humanitarian infrastructure – water and electricity facilities, bakeries, roads, grain storage facilities, and so on.

An incident which has had significant humanitarian impact is the 9 October targeting of Allouk water station in a Turkish airstrike. According to UN figures, the strike on the Allouk pumping station left 450,000 people without access to water, with 22 out of 34 pumps put out of service. Four out of ten attempts by the Syrian Arab Red Crescent to reach the station for repairs were unsuccessful.[14] On 9 November, following two weeks' negotiations, a team could finally reach the station to start carrying out repairs – only for the power lines to be struck and the water-station put out of service for a third time in the following days.[15] These attacks have continued even as the frontlines have stabilised. At the time of writing on 24 February, gunmen from Turkish-backed militias entered Allouk station and forced it to cease operations, once again leaving up to a million civilians and IDPs without any access to water.[16]

Further targeting of civil infrastructure includes the 12 October bombing of the high-tension power line linking the Mabrouka station with the Tishreen dam, cutting off electricity to most cities west of Qamishlo. Later that same day, an electrical substation was targeted, causing electricity blackouts across the city. Throughout February 2020, power lines continued to be targeted south of Sere Kaniye and power lines and telecommunications facilities have been targeted around Tel Abyad and Sere Kaniye.

Omar Issa, from the Electrical Emergency Center in Qamishlo told RIC: 'Turkey targeted these utilities deliberately, to force people to abandon their homes and their land. When the Mabrouka station was struck, Sere Kaniye, Hasakah and Tel Tamer were left without electricity.' Similar strikes targeted the oil fields at Saida near Tirbespiye on 11 October, igniting fast-spreading fires which took out the electricity network throughout this region.

The principal bakery in Qamishlo was targeted on 12 October, while grain silos have come under fire around Tel Abyad, Sere Kaniye and Tel Tamer. At least one silo, in Sakhirat in Tel Abyad, was reportedly destroyed in Turkish shelling. It held more than 11,700 tons of wheat ready for processing and distribution as subsidised bread by the Autonomous Administration.[17] The bakery was also shelled in Tel Abyad, contributing to widespread bread

---

[14] OCHA situation report, 19 November 2019.
[15] OCHA HNAP flash update, provided to RIC, 14 November 2019.
[16] Rojava Information Center. Unpublished interview with Sozda Ahmed, Autonomous Administration Water Bureau, 24 February 2020.
[17] Qamishlo Economic Committee, forthcoming research paper provided to RIC November 2019.

shortages across the city and enabling Turkish-backed factions to profit from the sale of looted grain.

Eyewitnesses also confirmed to RIC the shelling of churches in Qamishlo and Tirbespiye and schools across Sere Kaniye and Tel Abyad, in addition to the already mentioned targeting of hospitals.[18] Though it is difficult to get an accurate picture of the scale of destruction within the zones of occupation, the UN has documented the targeting and partial or complete destruction of 20 of 150 schools in Sere Kaniye district.[19]

The impact on local agriculture and economy is worsened by the loss of 475,000 hectares of agricultural land around Tel Abyad, and 144,000 around Sere Kaniye. These fields primarily grew the local staples of wheat and barley, as well as cotton. An estimated 275,000 head of sheep, goat and cattle were also lost.[20]

As noted above, roads in civilian use have been targeted by artillery and airstrikes, sometimes specifically targeting civilian vehicles, rendering these roads unusable. Throughout the conflict, Turkish-backed factions seized key stretches of road within and bordering the zone of conflict, preventing safe passage of civilians.[21] [22]

These attacks have had a significant logistical impact, decreasing access both for humanitarian actors and for ordinary farmers and traders, with a subsequent 20% increase in food prices across markets and shortages of fresh produce.[23]

Targeting internal security infrastructure

Beyond the immediate humanitarian consequences of the Turkish invasion, the attacks are having a longer-term destabilizing effect. At the time of invasion, the Administration's security forces were still actively fighting ISIS sleeper cells, and the invasion opened the door to a resurgence of ISIS and other jihadist groups as local authorities have had to reduce counter-terror operations. Since the start of the invasion a sharp increase in sleeper-cell attacks throughout North and East Syria indicates that the SDF's reallocation of forces to defend against the Turkish forces has opened the way for ISIS sleeper cells to carry out attacks.[24]

---

[18] Rojava Information Center. Unpublished field interviews conducted 9 October - 19 October 2019.

[19] OCHA HNAP update provided to RIC, 14 November 2019.

[20] Qamishlo Economic Committee, forthcoming research paper provided to RIC November 2019.

[21] RIC field team observations from start of invasion to present.

[22] OCHA HNAP update, 14 November 219.

[23] RIC field team, Qamishlo, 20 November 2019.

[24] Database: November sleeper-cell attacks and raids, https://rojavainformationcenter.com/2019/ 12/database-november-sleeper-cell-attacks-and-raids/.

Rojava Information Center documents sleeper-cell attacks by ISIS and Turkish-backed groups throughout North and East Syria on a month-by-month basis. Our 2019 review found that following the Turkish invasion, ISIS sleeper-cell attacks rose 63%, with 83 documented attacks in November compared to 51 in September – 85% of which were claimed by ISIS. The ISIS forces were able to assassinate Christian religious leaders and community leaders working with the Autonomous Administration, while SDF anti-ISIS raids plummeted to record lows as the military force was forced to focus on resisting the Turkish invasion.[25]

Facilities holding ISIS-linked detainees have been targeted by Turkish forces during the invasion. The camps al Hol, Ayn Issa and Roj all hosted ISIS-linked women and their children, from Syria and Iraq as well as foreign nationals who had travelled to join the ISIS caliphate. The Turkish invasion triggered outbreaks of violence due to decreased security in the camps and internal agitation from ISIS adherents. ISIS communications aimed at ISIS-linked women in camps urge them to prepare to break out.

Prior to the start of the conflict, the Autonomous Administration warned that it would not be able to both effectively guard ISIS detainees in prisons and camps and defend itself against Turkish invasion. On 13 October, this warning became reality, as 785 ISIS-linked foreigners escaped from Ayn Issa camp. The escapees, of which only a fraction was recaptured, were all from the camp's high-security section dedicated to foreign ISIS-linked women and their children. Escaped detainees were later captured attempting to cross into Turkey or Iraq. Several ISIS-affiliated Ayn Issa escapees were later identified seeking shelter in Turkish-held regions of Syria.

Al Hol Camp has a long history of violence and tension due to high numbers of ISIS-linked women and their children in the camp, including 11,200 foreign nationals. As war broke out, the situation rapidly degenerated as camp residents took advantage of the unstable security situation to riot and stage breakouts in order to rejoin the remnants of ISIS.

In the first month following invasion, significant violent activity broke out in Al Hol camp on 9, 11, 13, 15, 18, 20 and 23 October. These incidents have included attacks on the camp security forces, arson, attempted murders, and breakout attempts. One camp staff member reported that camp residents were preparing to assassinate the staff while awaiting outside support from ISIS to facilitate breakouts. The women – from Syria and Iraq – claim that they wanted to 'join the war against the Kurds' or 'return to Baghouz'.

---

[25] Rojava Information Center. 2019. 2019 review of sleeper cell attacks and anti-ISIS raids in North and East Syria. https://rojavainformationcenter.com/2020/01/good-work-undone-2019-review-of-sleeper-cell-attacks-and-anti-isis-raids-in-north-and-east-syria/.

Strikes and shelling on or near facilities holding ISIS fighters in Derik, Kobane, Qamishlo, and Ayn Issa also drew international attention, indicating a systematic attempt to break open prisons and facilitate escape. These strikes were successful in several instances, with hundreds of ISIS-linked individuals escaping in Ayn Issa and Qamishlo following these strikes. There was ongoing shelling of Navkur and Jirkin prisons in Qamishlo, and two prisons near Mashtenur in Kobane.

Displacements, IDP camps, and humanitarian aid

Turkish shelling, air strikes, and ground incursions created massive waves of displacements, with 191,069 people displaced from border areas in just the first two days of the Turkish invasion per the figures from the UN's Humanitarian Needs Assessment Program, seen by RIC.[26] Displacement figures reached 250,000 to 300,000 throughout the conflict, with several waves of displacement occurring as ceasefires were negotiated and then expired, and Turkish-backed forces advanced towards population centres. UNICEF calculated that the invasion displaced at least 70,000 children.[27]

Most displaced people fled to the cities and surroundings of Raqqa, Tel Tamer, and Hasakah, with smaller numbers spread throughout North and East Syria. Tens of thousands settled in temporary accommodation in Tel Tamer and Hasakah, with local organizations and the Administration providing the bulk of support.[28] Within a week, an estimated 100,000 displaced people crowded into schools, mosques, gardens, and family homes in Tel Tamer and Hasakah without adequate food, water, or blankets. By 1 November, 63 schools in Hasakah housed displaced people, including 433 women who were pregnant or breastfeeding, and 813 infants. In addition to the displaced families in schools, 66,000 were temporarily accommodated in houses in Hasakah. At the time of writing this essay in February 2020, most of the displaced population had found housing in temporary accommodation in Tel Tamer and Hasakah.

Thousands of displaced residents have ended up in camps. This includes already existing camps such as Mahmoudli camp near Raqqa, the newly reopened Newroz Camp near Derik, and new camps such as Washokani near Hasakah for IDPs from Sere Kaniye and Tal Saiman near Ayn Issa for IDPs from Tel Abyad. In December 2019, an estimated 4,120 people resided in

---

[26] Violations Documentation Center Northeast Syria. 2019. https://twitter.com/vdcnsy/status/1182
701814870876161.

[27] UNICEF. 2019. Nearly 70,000 children displaced as violence escalates in northeast Syria. https://www.unicef.org/turkey/en/press-releases/nearly-70000-children-displaced-violence-escalates-northeast-syria.

[28] RIC field team interview with Hasakah NGO Coordination Committee. 28 October 2019.

Washokani, 29,410 in Newroz, and 2,304 in Tel Saiman.[30] Camp populations are increasing as infrastructure develops and more families arrive.

Over 13,000 refugees fled to Iraq via the Semalka border crossing, where the Kurdish Regional Government of Iraq (KRG) expanded and reopened two refugee camps. At the Bardarash camp in KRG, 75% of the refugees were women and children, including unaccompanied children and disabled adults.

The Turkish invasion had a significant impact on the existing refugee and IDP population of North and East Syria. Two camps within the zone of conflict were evacuated, and the situation in other camps degenerated due to waves of new arrivals, evacuation of international NGOs, and disruption to aid.

From the start of the invasion, Turkish forces targeted the city of Ayn Issa, the headquarters of the Autonomous Administration of North and East Syria, with air strikes and shelling. In Ayn Issa camp, sited at the edge of the city, sleeper-cell attacks in and around the camp compounded Turkish bombing, triggering widespread panic and mass breakout attempts. Humanitarian actors withdrew as the situation descended into chaos. The camp, which housed 950 foreign ISIS affiliates (many of whom successfully escaped), as well as over 12,000 IDPs from Raqqa and Deir ez Zor, was evacuated between 14-16 October to Arisha camp, Mahmoudli camp, and other ad-hoc encampments. With additional strain resulting from an influx of residents and the severe disruption of the flow of humanitarian aid to the region,[31] the situation of existing camps approached the breaking point, with shortages of tents and food at Mahmoudli and Hol camps. On 11 October, Mabruka refugee camp, housing approximately 4,000 people (63% children) was evacuated and relocated to Arisha and Mahmoudli camps further from the border.[32] Invading forces soon overran the former camp.

The situation at Hol camp, already overcrowded and volatile due to the large number of evacuees from the former ISIS stronghold Deir ez Zor, severely deteriorated. Virtually no NGOs remained active in Hol camp by 10 October and international food aid stopped reaching the camp. The camp experienced a string of break-out attempts[33] and internal chaos including at least 20 tent-burning incidents in the camp throughout November, compared

---

[29] OCHA. 2019. Syrian Arab Republic: North East Syria Displacement.
https://reliefweb.int/map/syrian-arab-republic/syrian-arab-republic-north-east-syria-displacement-18-december-2019.
[30] RIC field team visits and contact with camp administration. 2020.
[31] RIC field team interviews, Kobane. 19-23 November 2019.
[32] OCHA HNAP update. 14 November 2019.
[33] RIC interviews with camp staff, 11 October to 24 November 2019.

to 9 the month before.[34]

Due to the strain caused by the invasion, crucial support was withdrawn from the camps. As of 15 October, all international staff working for NGOs such as the International Committee of the Red Cross (ICRC), Doctors without Borders, and Mercy Corps were evacuated. At the commencement of the conflict, Kurdish Red Crescent withdrew medical teams from several camps – including Al Hol, Roj, Arisha and Ayn Issa – in order to respond to emergencies at the border. The Administration, local NGOs, the ICRC, and the UN continued to run very reduced and limited services at the remaining camps.

From the end of November, some residents have been able to return to areas which remained largely calm following the initial wave of shelling in the first week of the invasion, such as Qamishlo, Amude, Dirbesiye, and Derik. However, Tel Abyad, Sere Kaniye and the surrounding countryside are now occupied by Turkish proxies. Shelling and ground clashes continue around the perimeter of the occupied zone with the establishment of the new status quo of low-level warfare. Hundreds of houses have been seized and occupied by Turkish-backed militias and the volatile security situation deters displaced residents from returning.

Civilians who remain in areas under Turkish control are under extreme pressure. In newly occupied Sere Kaniye and Tel Abyad, as in Afrin, TNA fighters seize civilians' phones at checkpoints, looking for 'YPG flags, photos of martyrs, or Kurdish songs'.[35] Any of these are enough to result in arrest. The small number of civilians who remain in Sere Kaniye – mostly women with young children and the very old – only use their telephones at night and in their own homes, when they are less likely to be detected by the occupying forces. Interviewees have told RIC that those attempting travel back into the zone of occupation must pay bribes at checkpoints ranging from 2,000SYP to 5,000SYP (c. €4 to €10, or roughly a day's wages, at the time of writing).[36]

Khalte Akash from Sere Kaniye told RIC: 'When someone returns to Sere Kaniye, his ID card is taken. They falsely accuse them of being criminals. Many of those who return are arrested, and their location is not known.' Internal security briefings circulated by an international NGO (INGO) and seen by RIC confirm reports of people accused of links to the SDF being abducted at checkpoints.[37]

In such circumstances, it is difficult to give a full picture of the impact of

---

[34] Hol camp snapshot, UN, 21 November 2019.

[35] RIC field interview with former Sere Kaniye resident, 29 October 2019.

[36] RIC field interviews with former Sere Kaniye residents, 24 October to 23 November 2019.

[37] Security briefing from INGO (anonymity protected), seen by RIC, 24 November 2019.

Turkey's invasion. For example, journalists and researchers have told RIC they believe that the figures provided by United Nations Office for the Coordination of Humanitarian Affairs (OCHA) for IDP returns to regions now under Turkish control are far too high to be accurate – giving figures of 22,050 returns to Sere Kaniye and 39,000 to Tel Abyad by 28 October, just a week after SDF withdrew from Sere Kaniye. These figures are contradicted by interviews and observations on the ground, as well as footage of an empty city centre populated primarily by men in military fatigues, with houses marked out as the new property of various factions.

Echoing the comments of multiple IDPs interviewed by RIC, Mohammed Baaqi of the NGO Hevi Association told RIC:

> The [OCHA] numbers aren't accurate. Some of those who went back were arrested immediately, others after a couple of days. There are some people who went and came back because they saw that they can't stay there – there is no food, no water, no electricity. The majority of IDPs are still in Tel Tamer, Hasakah and Qamishlo...[38]

The Humanitarian Affairs Committee of North and East Syria has likewise disputed OCHA figures showing around 130,000 total IDP returns, saying they have documented around 60,000 returns to areas still outside of Turkish control but very little movement back to Sere Kaniye or Tel Abyad, in contrast to OCHA figures.[39]

OCHA normally receives displacement figures via local humanitarian partners. However, with international and local humanitarian actors unable to safely access the zone of Turkish occupation, except those linked to the Turkish state apparatus, it is neither clear where the OCHA figure is derived from nor possible to put forward empirical evidence disproving it.[40]

Looting, theft, and property crimes

The large-scale expulsion of the civilian population – particularly Kurds and Christian minorities such as Armenians – has provided occasion for widespread looting and property crimes, committed both by individual members of Turkish-backed factions and on a more systematic basis. A fatwa issued by the Syrian Islamic Council, the Turkish-linked religious authority tied to the Syrian National Council, declares it permissible to wage jihad against the SDF, with the SDF's guns, belongings, and property considered

---

[38] RIC Interview with Mihammed Baaqi. Local NGO Hevi. 19 November 2019.

[39] Humanitarian Affairs Committee statement provided to RIC. 14 November 2019.

[40] Will Christou. 2019. How many civilians are returning to the Turkish 'safe zone'? https://syriadirect.org/news/how-many-civilians-are-returning-to-the-turkish-%e2%80%98safe-zone%e2%80%99/.

as legitimate war spoils.[41]

Though the fatwa does not grant permission to loot the property of private civilians, the reality on the ground is that Turkish-backed forces have been given free rein. Every family must have at least one person in mandatory military service in the SDF; thus, every family de facto becomes a 'legitimate' target. It is a pattern documented in Afrin since its seizure in March 2018, with Turkish-backed factions looting everything from ancient archaeological heritage sites through private homes to the region's olive groves – where crops and oil presses were seized, and ancient trees grubbed up and sold as firewood.[42]

The same processes that took place in Afrin are now underway in Sere Kaniye and Tel Abyad, with public property, businesses, and cooperatives seized by Turkish-backed forces. Wheat silos have been among the most prominent targets. Under the Autonomous Administration, wheat was purchased, processed into the local staple bread, and then distributed via neighbourhood associations at subsidised cost. Several silos have now been seized by Turkish-backed factions, with some plundered and resold by Turkish factions.[43] This has led to widespread bread shortages in both Sere Kaniye and Tel Abyad.[44] [45]

Looting of copper wire from electrical infrastructure by Turkish-backed faction Jabhat al-Shammiya in the Tel Abyad countryside has left the surrounding villages and settlements without power.[46] At the border crossing from Sere Kaniye into Turkey, factions illegally transferred the city's 400,000 litre reserves of diesel fuel into Turkey,[47] while the Bedlo gas station in Ayn Arus near Tel Abyad has also been looted – contributing to fuel shortages in both cities. All of these incidents underscore that looting does not only have an impact on the private individuals robbed of property, but also creates a wider impact on the local community and economy.

Prior to the invasion, cooperatives were being introduced across North and East Syria as a third branch of the local economy, ultimately intended to become the foundation of a new 'social economy.' These cooperatives, which

---

[41] Syrian Islamic Council. 2019. https://sy-sic.com/?p=6465&fbclid=IwAR07pknOEcL8-Z6JxhPJJ HRTDxlJzluT2qwaqkj2Rcf6edRfUD8mGYpUw0w.

[42] Robert Schuman Centre for Advanced Studies. 2019. Afrin Under Turkish Control: Political, Economic and Social Transformations. https://cadmus.eui.eu/bitstream/handle/1814/63745/MED_2019_10.pdf?sequence=3&isAllowed=y.

[43] Forthcoming research paper from Qamishlo Economic Committee provided to RIC; interviews conducted by RIC field team in Hasekah and Tel Tamer 29 Oct to 6 November; Syrian Observatory of Human Rights

[44] RIC field interview, 26 November

[45] http://www.syriahr.com/?p=346669

[46] Footage provided to RIC field researchers

[47] http://www.syriahr.com/en/?p=147302

were particularly prominent in both Tel Abyad and Sere Kaniye, have been a natural target for looters. In Sere Kaniye, the cooperative Mesopotamia Bakery was seized by Turkish-backed factions, resulting in the loss of machinery and reserves. Co-operative agricultural associations have also been plundered, with a total loss of 800 tons of wheat and 1500 tons of fertilizer from six co-operatives in the Sere Kaniye countryside.[48]

RIC has also been able to document the looting of specific homes and businesses in Sere Kaniye by interviewing small business owners and private individuals who have lost their homes and livelihoods.

Business owner Riad[49], who trades in household goods, told RIC that he had spoken directly with the militia members who seized his warehouse:

[They] wanted me to pay them $500,000 for my own property. I told them no, of course. I don't have the money to pay them. I have nothing left. I left in a car with only what I could carry, some small personal possessions. [In any case] I cannot safely travel back into the city: I am sure they would kidnap me. They are kidnapping many people who go back. I cannot trust them.

Another prominent local property-owner, Fuad Pasha, told RIC:

I worked as a farmer, but I was also one of the most prominent citizens in Sere Kaniye, and for this reason I, like everybody who was connected to the Autonomous Administration, became a target. My home was burned, this is proof. Turkish-backed fighters got into the fields that I owned and looted everything: my horses, my agricultural equipment and tractors, electrical generators and pumps, in particular my cotton fields. I owned seven to eight buildings, all of which have been seized and burned. The financial losses I incurred amounted to at least 100,000,000SYP [At least $133,000 at the exchange rate at the time]. I owned 2000 dunum [200 hectares] of cotton. They are also digging up and stealing my cotton; my tractors, oil, water tankers.

The same fate has befallen many private homes. RIC researchers have interviewed at least five IDPs from Tel Abyad and seven from Sere Kaniye who reported seizure or destruction of their property, as well as prevention of return in some instances. Fatma*, an Arabic woman from Sere Kaniye, told RIC: 'I saw on Facebook that my home had been looted. My husband is Kurdish, and he isn't especially close to the Autonomous Administration: he just plays in a football team. And yet we have lost everything. We are living in a park. We didn't do anything to deserve this.' She provided footage from

---

[48] Forthcoming research paper from Qamishlo economic committee; RIC field interviews
[49] Name changed to protect identity.

the inside of her home to RIC, showing ransacked rooms stripped of everything of value.

While it is sometimes difficult for locals to identify exactly which of the Turkish-backed factions has seized their homes, factions often write their names on private property which they claim as their own. Clandestine footage included in the RIC database shows almost every property on main streets marked up with the names of factions including Sultan Murad and Liwa Mutasim, as well as individual fighters.[50] In another high-profile incident, homes belonging to Armenian Christian families in Tel Abyad were marked out as the new property of Jabhat-al-Shammiya.[51]

Likewise, a house in Sere Kaniye was marked as the property of Abu Mohammed al-Janoudi of TNA faction Liwa-al-Mutasim, with the graffiti declaring the owners 'forbidden to return'. RIC researchers found the home's owner Saleh Ahmed in Hasakah.

He told RIC: 'Our home has been looted by Turkish proxies; we cannot go back. In Sere Kaniye, civilians have been killed for their minivans, which were then stolen. Now there are no Kurds or Christians, including Armenians, in Sere Kaniye.'

Similar incidents are reported in Tel Abyad, where the vegetable oil factory, chicken farms, factories and workshops producing pipes, bricks, ice, potato chips, cleaning products and confectionary; and grain and cotton processing stations have all been reported as looted.[52]

The implicit and explicit denial of the right of return described both here and earlier in this report, especially to Kurds and Christians, works to facilitate the expropriation of civilian property and livelihood.

Widespread petty looting by individual faction members or small groups is also commonplace. Many interviewees reported phones being seized and their owners being detained following a search of the contents, as well as the seizure of phones from anyone seen to be filming the actions of Turkish-backed groups in the city. Other civilians report mobile checkpoints controlled by factions within the Turkish-backed forces demanding payments of up to 5000SYP to move within the city, as well as to enter the city itself.[53] Internal security briefings circulated by an INGO and seen by RIC confirm these reports.

Elizabeth Tsurkov, a researcher who speaks directly with members of

---

[50] Footage provided to Syria Independent Media Team, 15 November 2019.
[51] Syrian Observatory for Human Rights. 2019. In Ras al-Ayn, factions of the 'National Army' continue their violations. http://www.syriahr.com/en/?p=146432.
[52] Qamishlo Economic Committee, forthcoming research paper provided to RIC November 2019.
[53] RIC field interviews, 24 October to 23 November 2019.

Turkish-backed factions, told RIC that looting was 'so widespread I don't think they would remember any one incident in particular...' TNA members speaking to Ms Tsurkov painted an overall picture of lawlessness, with it 'impossible' for the military police to control factions' criminality, and frequent infighting over the control of checkpoints as a way to extort cash from passers-by.[54]

Such thefts are compounded by kidnap for ransom. In Raqqa, RIC researchers spoke to Mohammed Brahim Bin Mohammed, 70, whose family paid a ransom of 400,000SYP (around $500) to secure his release following ten days of imprisonment and torture.

This looting, seizure of property, and kidnapping are difficult to monitor and confirm due to the region in question being unsafe to enter. However, many witnesses interviewed by RIC corroborate accounts of these abuses. The scale and frequency of these crimes indicate that they occur systematically, rather than one-off incidents.

Conclusions

Mass displacements, damage to local infrastructure, and the disruption of the local economy have had a devastating impact on civilian populations. Systematic attacks on internal security infrastructure has led to widespread escape of detained ISIS fighters and ISIS-linked women. The range of attacks compound and build upon one another to constitute a multifaceted assault on all civilians' right to a free, safe, and peaceful existence. Medical teams cannot reach civilians targeted by shelling because Turkish forces deny safe access for ambulances, and looting of civil infrastructure denies civilians access to bread, electricity, and other staples.

The Turkish Armed Forces (TAF) bear clear responsibility for some of the incidents detailed previously. Air strikes targeting civilians, clearly marked medical and humanitarian convoys, and civilian infrastructure are the most obvious examples of war crimes which could only be committed by the TAF, since only their forces operate warplanes and strike drones. However, a cursory investigation of the command and control structure of jihadist factions like Ahrar-al-Sharqiya, Jaysh-al-Islam and Sultan Murad shows that responsibility flows directly to the Turkish Armed Forces.

The Kurdish population, who have borne the brunt of the invasion, should be understood as a regional minority group being subjected to forcible demographic engineering. The violence targeting civilians identified throughout this report should be contextualised as part of an intentional

---

[54] Tsurkov, Elizabeth. 2019. Who Are Turkey's Proxy Fighters in Syria? https://www.nybooks.com/
daily/2019/11/27/who-are-turkeys-proxy-fighters-in-syria/.

effort by Ankara to drive the Kurdish population from the border regions, in order to facilitate a program of forced demographic change which some experts say 'shows the hallmarks of ethnic cleansing'.[55]

Turkey has proven itself neither capable of nor willing to control the actions of its proxy militias under the banner of the TNA, while members of its own armed forces are directly culpable for some of the incidents outlined previously. The responsibility now lies with international news organizations to document these offenses, with international humanitarian organizations to move to mitigate the human cost of the Turkish invasion, and with both state and non-state international actors to follow up on this evidence and through legal and political channels to hold Turkey accountable for its actions.

The international community's failure to effectively respond to the occupation of Afrin should not be repeated. However, although local and international bodies have documented rampant human rights abuses and inability to access humanitarian aid, this has yet to make an impact on international actors' attitudes towards Turkish President Erdoğan's government.[56] In fact, the UN is considering funnelling all humanitarian aid through Turkish-controlled Tel Abyad following the closure of the sole UN aid crossing into North and East Syria, shut down in January 2020 by UN Security Council decree. Not only would this move legitimise the invasion and occupation, it would essentially cut off humanitarian aid from reaching any areas of North and East Syria under the governance of the Autonomous Administration.[57] International actors must work to re-open the flow of aid to North and East Syria.

As outlined above, Turkey does not allow independent journalists, human rights monitors, or humanitarian observers into the zones it occupies in Syria, while violently crushing civilian journalism and activism within these zones. International actors should insist that Turkey allows an independent fact-finding mission to enter both Afrin and the newly occupied zone between Sere Kaniye and Tel Abyad, comprising UN observers as well as independent journalists, and to conduct a thorough assessment of the rights violations being conducted there. This needs to happen as soon as possible to prevent both the loss of evidence, and the entrenchment of systematic rights abuses in the newly occupied areas of Tel Abyad and Sere Kaniye, as has previously been observed in Afrin. With Turkey now threatening to expand its zone of

[55] Richard Hall, 'When they come, they will kill you': Ethnic cleansing is already a reality in Turkey's Syrian safe zone. 2019. https://www.independent.co.uk/news/world/middle-east/turkey-syria-safe-zone-ethnic-cleansing-death-toll-sna-a9225896.html.

[56] Rojava Information Center. 2019. Turkey's track record: The occupation of Afrin. https://rojavainformationcenter.com/2019/11/turkeys-track-record-the-occupation-of-afrin.

[57] Orient News. 2020. UN chief urges new transit point for aid to Syria. https://orient-news.net/en/news_show/177479/0/UN-chief-urges-new-transit-point-for-aid-to-Syria.

occupation into Kobane, it could also prevent a third, equally catastrophic, invasion from taking place.

Due to its non-state status, the Autonomous Administration of North and East Syria is consistently denied political recognition. This results in exclusion from international negotiations, such as peace accords and constitutional committees, and has a significant impact on their ability to access and coordinate aid. The UN should insist on the inclusion of the Autonomous Administration in the constitutional process in order to work towards a long-term political solution.

CHAPTER 9

UNITED STATES-KURDISH RELATIONS OVER NORTH-EASTERN SYRIA: FROM INSTRUMENTALISM TO DOCTRINISM?

Nazan Bedirhanoğlu

October 31, 2014 was not an ordinary day for the Rhode Island College community. Barack Obama was about to give a speech on their campus and a large crowd enthusiastically filled a hall waiting to see him. Some in the crowd, however, were even more interested in this public spectacle: it was almost one and a half month after the siege of Kobane by the so-called Islamic State of Iraq and Levant (ISIS). Members of the New England Kurdish Association (NEKA), a non-profit cultural organisation of Kurdish Americans, were ready at the hall, wearing 'Save Kobane' and Kurdistan-map t-shirts, even though the event's organisers strictly prohibited the use of any political symbols during the event. While the crowd gathered, two officials asked the group about their leadership and Mehmet Akbas stepped forward thinking that they would be warned about the 'no signs' rule.

Without any explanation, the officials took him to a room where Akbas anxiously awaited before he noticed the presidential seal on the desk in the middle of the room. After a moment of intense surprise, he began to work on his lines because he was about to meet the President of the United States. After all, the group went to the event to appeal for US support for the Kurds fighting against the ISIS in Kobane. In what Akbas described as a friendly conversation, Obama reassured him that the Global Coalition, the anti-ISIS military force recently established under the leadership of the United States, was actively helping the Kurds in the region and would continue to do so. ISIS was, however, a lesser concern for Akbas. Instead, he wanted to make sure that the United States was wary of the plans of Kurds' strongest enemy, Turkey, in the region (Akbas 2018). Just two weeks before this conversation, the Turkish President Erdoğan, with unconcealable satisfaction, stated that 'Kobane [was] about to fall!' in a public address to the Syrian refugees in Turkey, even though Turkey formally belonged to the Global Coalition (Haberturk 2014). Akbas's conversation with Obama was not publicised, but it reassured the Kurdish communities in the United States, who saw Obama's messages as a promise for continued support at the highest level.

In fact, all the evidence at that moment nurtured this sort of optimism. The US support after 2014 had been a game changer for the Kurds' fight against ISIS in north-eastern Syria. This partnership also helped the Kurds to appear in the headlines in international media and contributed to their worldwide recognition. However, the history of their relationship with the United States also caused the Kurds to be leery of their strong ally's fickle politics. They were proven right: President Donald Trump's declarations in December 2018 and his decision on 6 October 2019 to withdraw the US troops led to the ensuing Turkish incursion into north-eastern Syria. This surprised policy analysts in the United States but not the Kurdish forces in Syria. Bipartisan voices immediately argued that this move would both cripple the fight against the ISIS and open space for the Russian and Iranian influence in the region. Ironically, Russia agreed with the respectable political commentators in the United States, who labelled the withdrawal decision as a 'betrayal' of the Kurds (Galbraith 2019; Ignatius 2019; Rodionov 2019) and another moment of repeated abandonment of the Kurds by the United States since the 1920s (Gibson 2019).

Was President Trump's decision to withdraw also an abandonment of the recent US foreign policy of alliance with the Kurds? Why do President Trump's declarations and actions about the Kurdish presence in north-eastern Syria seem erratic and inconsistent? Will the United States leave north-eastern Syria, stop supporting the Kurdish-led forces, and, thereby, create a political gap in the region for Turkey to fill? To address these questions, I discuss the historical significance of the US policy on north-eastern Syria in the broader US-Kurdish relations and I make three arguments that, I believe, will help us to make sense of the contradictory moves by the United States in its relationship with the Kurdish-led coalition in Syria.

First, the Kurds in north-eastern Syria have not been, until recently, a high priority in the US Middle East policy. In fact, the United States engages with the Kurdish forces in north-eastern Syria not as a result of an independent policy concern but to advance its strategies concerning other actors in the region such as the ISIS, Turkey, and the Syrian regime. Relationships with these other actors determine US policy on Kurdish issues.

Second, this instrumental approach towards the Kurds in policymaking makes the US-Kurdish relations highly susceptible to the domestic political considerations of the executive branch of the United States. This has been particularly the case during the Trump administration. On the one hand, Trump's fickle moves are, in fact, in alignment with the instrumentalism of the US official foreign policy concerning the Kurds in the Middle East. On the other hand, Trump's instrumentalism does not reflect the US national interests but his personal political agenda.

Third, Kurds' success in both defeating ISIS on the ground and setting the socio-political context for a peaceful society in north-eastern Syria now convince a growing segment of the US foreign policy community that the United States should reconsider its long-held pragmatic attitude about the Kurds and develop a coherent policy on the Kurds. Especially with the formation of the Autonomous Administration of North and East Syria (AANES), Kurds were able to diversify the ethnic composition of SDF (Syrian Democratic Forces), initiate talks between PYD (Democratic Union Party) and Kurdistan National Congress (KNC), and take several diplomatic initiatives to be included in international negotiations about the future of Syria.

These endeavours currently push the United States to a more doctrine-based idealism and away from its long-standing realism that resulted in the United States abandoning the Kurds several times in their recent history. Thus, the policymaking and executive circles critical of Trump's withdrawal decision frequently refer to the need to be trustworthy and send a message to the future allies and partners (Brice, Heavey, and Chiacu 2019; Dent 2019).

In order to support these arguments, I first focus on the history of US policymaking related to the Kurds. Then, I move on to the alliance formed between the Kurds and the United States after the US troops withdrew from the region and consider the similarities and differences between Obama and Trump administrations in their relationship with the Kurds of north-eastern Syria. In the third section, I discuss the recent US-Turkish relations with regard to north-eastern Syria to illustrate the instrumental character of the US policy concerning the Kurds. In the fourth section, I look at institutional policymaking in the United States and elucidate the delicate balance between realism and idealism that shapes the Kurdish policy. In this regard, I revisit the institutional reactions of US policymakers concerning their Kurdish policy and identify a growing call for a Kurdish policy based on principles and values in order to highlight the reliability of the United States within international institutions and not to deter future partners and allies from cooperating with the USA. In the final section before the concluding remarks, I depict the current Kurdish policy of the United States as a by-product of its approach towards Syria, ISIS, and Turkey. I conclude with some predictions on the future of US-Kurdish relations with respect to north-eastern Syria.

Continuity or rupture in the Kurdish policy of the United States?

The United States does not have a coherent Kurdish doctrine and approaches the Kurdish movements as an instrument in its relationship with the nation states that colonised the Kurds, namely Turkey, Iraq, Iran, and

Syria. After the Second World War, the United States gradually replaced the United Kingdom as the rising hegemonic power in the region. American interests in the Middle East were guided ideologically by Cold War antagonisms and theoretically by Modernisation Theory (Latham 2011; Gilman 2004). This intellectual baggage prioritised containing the Soviet Union, controlling oil reserves, and forming new security alliances through NATO. Between the early 1960s and the end of the Cold War, this framework shaped the covert and short-lived contacts with the Kurds as an extension of the US efforts to give a new direction to the regional geopolitical dynamics.

Given that US policy on Kurdish issues has historically aligned with the US relationship with the coloniser states, Kurds divided into different states did not enjoy the same attention by the United States. Kurds in Iran were and are ignored. Kurds in Syria were not even recognised as a distinct geopolitical player until their fight against ISIS after 2014. Because of Turkey's NATO membership, the United States has turned a blind eye to the human rights violations against Kurds in Turkey for many decades. Only Kurds in Iraq had regular contacts, albeit limited and clandestine, with the United States. After the first Gulf War, these contacts took a new turn with the establishment of Kurdistan Regional Government in Iraq.

In fact, this differential treatment signifies a normative distinction in the US foreign policy that identifies the Iraqi Kurds, most specifically KDP (Kurdistan Democratic Party), as 'the good Kurds' and those of Turkey, most specifically PKK (Kurdistan Workers' Party), as 'the bad Kurds' (Gunter 2016). Therefore, the US foreign policymakers must understand the diversity of the Kurds and specify 'which Kurds' when it comes to the US foreign policy. In parts of the region, Kurds simply do not exist in the mental map of the US foreign policymakers, while others are seen as mere pawns to be occasionally supported and eventually abandoned. In short, the United States had denied political agency to the Kurds as a nation well until the 1990s.

The consistent indifference of the United States towards the Kurds in Iran provides a striking example to support this point. Following the Second World War, the United States followed the situation in Iran closely but Kurds received no support either from the British (Roosevelt 1947) or the Americans. Following the short-lived Mahabad Republic, the US diplomats in the region became concerned that the pressures upon the Kurds in Iran could open the door to Soviet influence. Nevertheless, the Shah brutally oppressed the remnants of the Mahabad Republic without facing any reaction by the United States (Voller 2014; Little 2010). Not much changed after the Islamic regime came to power in Iran and continued to use the old violent and repressive policies it inherited from the Shah regime. Nonetheless, to this day, Iranian Kurds have not been noticed by the United States policymakers despite the deep animosity between Iran and the United States since 1979 (Entessar 2019).

A surprising contrast exist between Iranian Kurds' political experiences and the history of the Kurds in Iraq. During the Cold War, the United States favoured the Iraqi Kurds over the Kurds in other countries in the region. The support of the United States proved to be a lifeline for the Iraqi Kurds facing hostility by various governments in the region including its own. From the vantage point of the United States, Kurdish nationalism in Iraq could be instrumental to curtail the Soviet influence (Little 2010). In this context, Mulla Mustafa Barzani's insurgency against Iraqi prime minister Abdul Karim Qassim and later against the Ba'ath regime eventually gave way to a promise of Kurdish autonomy in Iraq in 1970, as Barzani's KDP received support from Iran, Israel, and the Nixon administration in order to destabilise the Iraqi regime between 1972 and 1975. However, the support was eventually cut off (Gibson 2015) after Iran, Iraq, and the United States agreed to pacify the Iraqi Kurds with the Algiers Agreement in 1975 (Khalidi 2009). In short, even the Iraqi Kurds had an inconsistent relationship with the United States.

Furthermore, these states' abandonment of the Iraqi Kurds in the late 1970s would indirectly facilitate the massacres by Saddam Hussein's dictatorship in the ensuing decade. In fact, the United States approached even these severe humanitarian crises that periodically hit the Kurds with an instrumentalist perspective. Successive administrations turned a blind eye to the most violent attacks such as the Anfal ethnic cleansing campaign and the Halabja massacre in the 1980s due to the policy of pitting Iraq against Iran at that time. Iraq's use of chemical weapons on its Kurdish population clearly violated the Geneva Protocol on chemical weapons but the United States and the international community chose to ignore these crimes. Evidence revealed later confirmed that the United States knew about Iraq's use of chemical agents (Hiro 2002). After fourteen years had passed, the George W. Bush administration finally cited the chemical attacks on Kurds to justify the US invasion of Iraq (Burns 2002).

Even when the Cold War ended, the United Nations Security Council passed the Resolution 688 that condemned the repression of Kurdish people only after one and a half million Kurds fled their homelands in 1991 with the fear of another Anfal-like campaign (UNSCR 1991). This resolution became the basis of a no-fly zone maintained by the Global Coalition forces after the first Gulf War. The no-fly zone formed the nucleus of what later became Kurdistan Regional Government (KRG).

The KRG proved to be a salient actor from the vantage point of the United States once the United States shifted its policy on Iraq from dual containment to regime change (Charountaki 2011). Operation Iraqi Freedom and the invasion of Iraq by the United States in 2003 created an unprecedented lacuna for the KRG to operate as a quasi- or de facto state. The KRG proved itself to be a reliable partner to the United States, exported oil and gas, and served a safe region for US troops unlike the rampant violence in the rest of Iraq. Although the United States government still does not consider recognising an independent Kurdish state, the KRG now exists as a legitimate political entity with formal representation in Washington, D.C.

Local partnership with the Kurds in north-eastern Syria

Like their compatriots in Iraq, the Kurds in Syria found that weakening of the central regime and the ensuing civil war became necessary but not sufficient conditions for forming a reliable alliance with the United States. Similarly, the political stability and the peaceful coexistence of multiple ethnic and religious groups in Rojava's cantons were also not enough for the United States to see the Kurdish leadership as a credible actor. US policymakers began to take seriously the YPG (People's Protection Units), YPJ (Women's Protection Units), and later the SDF when they proved their usefulness in the fight against ISIS. In March 2019, after liberating the last territory held by ISIS, the SDF declared that they lost 11,000 fighters in the war with ISIS in addition to 21,000 injured (Wilgenburg 2019). Only in March 2014 did the United States start aiding Kurds fighting the Islamic State in Kobane by initially airdropping weapons and supplies (Barnes 2014). The United States announced a broad international coalition to defeat the ISIS on 10 September 2014 and the Combined Joint Task Force (CJTF) initiated the Operation Inherent Resolve (OIR) on 17 October 2014 (Department of Defense 2017). Under the OIR, coalition forces led by the United States assisted the combat forces on the ground with targeted air strikes and gave training and support to both Iraqi security forces and the SDF.

This policy change clearly indicated the Obama Doctrine's new direction in the Middle East (Goldberg 2016). This doctrine's main feature was not its policy coherence but its goal to externalise 'the strategic and operational burden of war to human and technological surrogates' (Krieg 2016). Obama's main policy objective was withdrawing US soldiers from Iraq. Since 2009, the troops located in big cities in Iraq had already been reduced in number. When the US military left Iraq by the end of 2011, the country was nowhere near political stability. Al-Qaida quickly began to terrorise the cities with explosions once the US troops left. The Islamic State also increased violent attacks and took advantage of the lack of political authority. Many analysts described the Islamic State's filling this lacuna in the absence of the United States as a major failure of Obama's foreign policy; they said his premature withdrawal caused the advent of ISIS.

Although Obama pledged to minimise the US military presence in the Middle East, the ISIS expansion into Syria and the siege of Kobane in 2014 changed his intentions. With tacit support by Turkey, the Islamic State attacked Kobane and surrounded the Kurdish forces in the city. The US-led coalition carried out air attacks on the Islamic State fighters and created a lifeline for the Kurdish forces (BBC News 2014). The official US support to the Kurdish forces fighting ISIS marked a turning point in Kurdish-US relations. This decision fits well with the externalizing aspect of the Obama doctrine that envisaged delegating the fighting to local forces and provide a minimal US presence on the ground. The establishment of OIR through Camp Arifjan in Kuwait was the first operational headquarters to be back in the region since US troops left the region in 2011 (Landler 2011).

In contrast to Obama, President Trump has been a much more controversial figure since his very first day in office. Some of the controversies resulted from his foreign policy choices on a variety of issues ranging from trade to immigration. In his first month in office, he froze migration of Syrian refugees to the USA. Trump's other new Middle East policies, such as withdrawing from the Iran deal, reversed the former administration's work. However, there are also some continuities, especially concerning the Kurdish policy. In terms of his Middle East or, more specifically, his Syrian and Kurdish policy, Trump pledged in his inaugural speech to 'reinforce old alliances and form new ones—and unite the civilised world against radical Islamic terrorism, which we will eradicate completely from the face of the Earth' (Trump 2017). He signalled that he would keep targeting the ISIS because the strengthening of this group and the destabilisation in the Middle East would create new threats to the US national security.

More importantly, the 2017 National Security Strategy of the Trump administration announced that ISIS was crushed on the battlefield of Iraq and Syria and praised the allies' contributions (United States 2017). This document identifies the jihadist organisations as the most important threat to the US homeland even after their territorial defeat and notes that the United States 'will retain the necessary American military presence in the region to protect the United States and our allies from terrorist attacks and preserve a favorable regional balance of power. We will assist regional partners in strengthening their institutions and capabilities, including in law enforcement, to conduct counterterrorism and counterinsurgency efforts.' Despite the strong statement, vague expressions such as 'necessary American military presence' open up ample space for multiple interpretations of the Trump administration's real intentions as well as its reluctance to clearly name and identify its allies. The Kurds, however, did not have much room for speculation. This document's opaque language clearly signalled that the US offered conditional support and the Kurds could receive it only when in battle.

The withdrawal of the US troops

In line with his 'America First' policy, President Trump initially announced the plans to withdraw the approximately 2,200 US troops from Syria in December 2018, declaring that ISIS was defeated. Republicans and Democrats alike criticised this abrupt decision and expressed their suspicions about the defeat of ISIS (Landler, Cooper, and Schmitt 2018). A day after President Trump's plans of withdrawal became public, Defense Secretary James Mattis resigned from his position (CNN 2018). The following day, Brett McGurk, the US envoy to the Global Coalition fighting the Islamic State, declared that he could neither defend nor implement this kind of withdrawal and resigned in protest over this decision (Labott 2018).

These two resignations signal a disruption in power politics inside the United States. After all, foreign policy had been a special terrain of the US politics relatively isolated from daily political brawls. Although Trump, as an antagonizing president, has a very high and unprecedented turnover record in his administration and senior staff (Dunn Tenpas 2020), resignations of Mattis and McGurk in protest of the removal decision strongly indicate the Trump administration's internal division over its Kurdish policy.

Regardless of the unravelling developments on the battleground, both the Obama and Trump administrations planned to reduce the number of US troops in the Middle East. Therefore, this impetuous decision was *not a change from the written policy orientation*. However, the visible rift between the Defense and State Departments and the White House reflects a serious *change from the usual policymaking processes* in the United States. Modern US history has not had instances such as the resignation of Mattis alongside other top Pentagon officials. Broadly speaking, the Pentagon aimed to counterbalance the new policy actions towards the Syrian Kurds that Trump announced on Twitter. The Pentagon defined the Kurdish military cooperation as its assistance to the Kurdish-led Syrian Democratic Forces (SDF) and other fighters as 'a crucial part' of the US strategy to 'support the lasting defeat of ISIS' (United States Department of Defense 2019). In fact, the resistance to Trump's withdrawal decision reveals the presence of a strong faction in the Defense and State Departments that seek a more stable policy towards the local partnership with the Kurds.

This much contested and controversial decision certainly created deep shockwaves in the Middle East. In less than a month following Trump's announcement, Ilham Ahmed, the head of the Executive Committee of the Syrian Democratic Council, travelled to the United States for damage control and to advocate for a coordinated withdrawal. In an arranged dinner,

President Trump told Ahmed that he loved the Kurds and reassured her that Kurds would not be abandoned. Ahmed expressed the Kurds' concern that they could face a massacre if Turkey invaded the Kurdish regions (Atwood 2019).

Beyond Ahmed's concerns, the threat by ISIS was not completely over. The defeat on the ground of ISIS in March 2019 marked its transition from a 'territory-holding force to an insurgency in Syria and solidified insurgent capabilities in Iraq' (Lead Inspector General 2019). Thus, only continual pressure on ISIS could prevent its resurgence in the Middle Euphrates Valley (Lead Inspector General 2019a). This warning convinced Trump to delay the withdrawal of the US soldiers in face of the possible re-emergence of ISIS in the region.

However, almost a year after Ahmed's visit and following a phone conversation with Erdoğan, Trump nevertheless announced the withdrawal of US troops from Syria on 6 October 2019. This gave, in effect, the green light for the Turkish incursion. Without further ado, Turkey started Operation Peace Spring on 9 October. Erdoğan claimed that the incursion into north-eastern Syria would 'neutralise terror threats against Turkey and lead to the establishment of a safe zone' between Turkey and the territory controlled by the People's Protection Units (YPG), a group he labelled as a 'terrorist organisation' (Erdoğan 2019). Despite Turkey's declaration of perceived security threats coming from the Syrian side of the border, Kurds in Syria had not engaged in any cross-border action towards Turkey.

Vice President Mike Pence's visit to Turkey on 17 October 2019 resulted in a ceasefire which Turkey insisted on calling 'a pause' to the Operation Peace Spring. With Pence's visit and the Sochi Memorandum of Agreement between Russia and Turkey on 22 October, Turkey managed to create a safe zone between Turkey and Syria. On 27 October, the Syrian Democratic Forces announced that, in agreement with Russia, they would 'reposition' their units and accept the deployment of Syrian central government troops on the border. Kurds were left with no choice but to side with the Syrian central government and Russia.

One reason why Kurds hastily sought Russian protection was that Operation Peace Spring was not the first Turkish offense in the region. Turkey has conducted military operations in north-eastern Syria since 2016. Most notably, Turkish forces, in collaboration with the Free Syrian Army, initiated the Operation Olive Branch invasion into the Kurdish-administered Efrîn in January 2018. Although other Global Coalition forces harshly criticised this operation against the YPG, Trump kept his warnings on the soft side and simply asked Erdoğan to scale-down the incursion (Neuman 2018). In return, the Turkish foreign minister published an article in the US journal *Foreign Policy* to generally justify Turkey's incursion and specifically the operations in Efrîn. Repeating the hackneyed official narrative of Turkey, he claimed that PKK, YPG, and ISIS were terrorist organisations posing similar threats to the Turkish security in the region (Cavusoglu 2018). Although the capture of illegally dispatched arms to Syria through Turkey's National Intelligence Agency revealed Turkey's covert relations with the jihadist groups (Agence France Press 2015), the United States condoned these actions in order to appease its NATO ally.

Because the United States did not strongly react to these earlier operations, Erdoğan had the impression that as long as Turkey did not confront the US forces directly, the United States would overlook Turkey's military involvement in the region, be it hand-in-hand with the jihadists or against the Kurdish forces. However, immediately after the start of Operation Peace Spring, multiple initiatives attempted to introduce sanctions on Turkey. Although sanctions were not imposed, it was the first time the Kurdish question in Syria was cited to justify these steps taken against Turkey.

US sanctions towards Turkey and aftermath of the US withdrawal

Against this backdrop, US policy analysts began to question Turkey's status as an ally and formed several proposals to impose sanctions on Turkey in the wake of Turkey's invasion of north-eastern Syria. NATO-ally Turkey's purchase of S-400 missiles from Russia over the summer of 2019 worsened the already unstable US-Turkey relationship.

Since Turkey's incursion in Syria in October 2019, several attempts to impose sanctions on Turkey reaffirmed the US support to Syria's Kurdish forces fighting against ISIS. Right after Turkey's incursion into north-eastern Syria to contain Kurdish forces, Trump called Erdoğan to ask him to stop the invasion. Following this futile attempt, White House declared sanctions against individuals, entities, or associates of the Turkish government involved in 'actions that endanger civilians or lead to the further deterioration of peace, security and stability in northeast Syria' (Middle East Monitor 2019). However, these sanctions similarly proved useless, as they were lifted when Turkey agreed to a cease-fire after Pence's visit to Turkey.

On 29 October 2019, the US House of Representatives passed the 'Protect Against Conflict by Turkey Act' (PACT Act) by an overwhelmingly 403-16 vote that introduced targeted sanctions against Turkey. The legislation called Turkey's military invasion of north-eastern Syria on 9 October 2019, 'an unacceptable and unnecessary escalation of tensions with the potential to cause a severe humanitarian crisis and undo the collective gains made in the fight against the Islamic State of Iraq and Syria (ISIS)'. The act reaffirms that 'the SDF have been critical partners to United States and allied counter-ISIS and broader counterterrorism efforts in Syria, and the United States should continue this partnership with the SDF' (Engel 2019). It also cited Turkey's purchase of S-400 air and missile defence system from Russia as a significant transaction proscribed in the Countering America's Adversaries Through Sanctions Act which included sanctions against Russia, North Korea, and Iran. The bill introduced sanctions against senior Turkish officials, namely, the Minister of National Defence, the Chief of the General Staff of the Turkish Armed Forces, the Commander of the 2nd Army of the Turkish Armed Forces, and the Minister of Treasury and Finance of Turkey. In addition, the bill prohibited arms transfers to the Turkish military units in Syria and targeted foreign financial sanctions on Halkbank, a major public bank in Turkey. The bill also targeted Erdoğan personally by asking for a 'report on the estimated net worth and known sources of income of Turkish President Recep Tayyip Erdoğan and his family members (including spouse, children, parents, and siblings), including assets, investments, other business interests, and relevant beneficial ownership information' (Engel 2019). Senator Lindsay Graham also initiated a sanctions bill to be discussed at the Senate, which is still on the Senate's legislative calendar. This bill calls to 'continue to support the Syrian Kurdish communities, who have been key partners of the United States in the ongoing fight the Islamic State of Iraq and Syria' (Graham 2019).

These initiatives and Trump's reversal of the sanctions indicate that Congress has a different perspective on Trump's policy towards Kurds as well as his appeasement policy towards Erdoğan. Erdoğan's acts over the last couple of years had severely undermined the historical Turkish-US partnership and raised questions about Turkey's status as an ally as well as NATO member. However, the vote for sanctions demonstrates bipartisan opposition to Trump's policy of withdrawal. Although President Trump maintained a relationship with the Kurdish forces in Syria, his Kurdish policy was mainly a by-product of his Turkey policy.

In other words, if the United States advanced in its struggle against the ISIS, that was because of the Kurdish-led forces. If the ISIS offshoots still survive in Syria and if Russia filled the gap left behind by the United States, that was because of Turkey. Nonetheless, Trump chose to work with Turkey. However, so that the Kurds' continued efforts for international recognition finally pay off, the *Pax Kurdistana* in north-eastern Syria and the military successes of the Kurdish-led forces against the ISIS still should have been contrasted with Turkey's erratic foreign policy manoeuvres that proved its unreliability as a partner for the United States and the international community. Thus, a Kurdish doctrine requires revising the United States' existing Turkish doctrine.

Main drivers of US Kurdish policy: Syria, ISIS, and Turkey

As reflected in the concatenation of events covered in this section, the conflict in Syria, the threat of ISIS, and the relationships with Turkey shape the contemporary US policy towards the Kurds of north-eastern Syria. First, the United States did not have clear policy objectives in Syria at the outset of the civil war. The US government's main concern in the Middle East was simply removing the US troops from Iraq. As the war in Syria continued and humanitarian cost of the war became unavoidable, the international community and regional actors pressured the United States to intervene. More importantly, Iran and Russia involvement in the Syrian war had consequences for the already trembling balance of power in the region.

Refugees are another major concern related to the war in Syria. Although most Syrian refugees went to neighbouring countries, the refugee crisis alarms Europe and the United States because they do not want to open their doors to the displaced people of Syria and place a high priority on stopping the influx of refugees. A more stable Syria is the obvious solution to keep refugees away from these states. The Western powers see a secondary solution as keeping the displaced people where they are. Therefore, countries hosting refugees, such as Turkey, use this issue as a threat in their relations with the West. This eventually leads to appeasement of Turkey on other issues such as the Turkish military operations in Syria.

Against this backdrop, almost reluctantly, the United States supported a solution to the Syrian conflict 'through the nationwide cease fire and political process outlined in United Nations Security Council Resolution 2254' (Pompeo 2020). Given that Trump administration explicitly doubts the legitimacy of international institutions, the use of the United Nations reflects the unwillingness of the United States to directly lead in Syria. Under this Security Council resolution adopted in December 2018, the United States promotes the ongoing Syrian Constitutional talks in Geneva despite Russia and Turkey backing these negotiations and including Iran as a key player.

As a by-product of this policy, the United States tacitly supports the Kurdish demands to be included in these negotiations. Kurds have advocated for their inclusion in international negotiations since 2012. Mostly due to Turkey's opposition, the Kurdish representatives were excluded from the talks in Geneva brokered by the United Nations that started in 2012 and the Astana talks brokered by Russia, Turkey, and Iran in 2017. The most recent round of constitutional talks initiated in 2019 also does not include Kurds. Although the United States does not push other parties to include Kurds to these negotiations, it provides an implicit support. To this aim, the deputy special envoy to the Global Coalition, William Roebuck, mediates the unity talks between the PYD and the KNC with the hope that a united Kurdish front will have more legitimacy to be involved in diplomatic efforts to negotiate Syria's future.

Economic sanctions also affect the Kurds in the general framework of the US policy on Syria. The United States has imposed different types of sanctions on Syria since 2004. However, since 2011, the United States introduced more targeted sanctions. Most notably, the Caesar Act of 2019 against the Assad regime contributed to the devastation of the Syrian economy (Department of State 2020). Because the economic deterioration and the tremendous depreciation of the Syrian pound also has an impact on the SDF governed areas, the United States spared the AANES from these sanctions.

The United States' main objective concerning ISIS and the jihadist groups in general is to prevent attacks on American soil, Americans elsewhere, and the US allies. The global war on terror since 9/11 remains one of the main tenets of US foreign policy. Unsurprisingly, the United States' invasion of Iraq in 2003 initiated protracted instability and rampant violence in the region. The subsequent withdrawal of US forces from Iraq in 2011 aggravated the situation and eventually led to the rise of ISIS. Even before the advent of ISIS, US foreign policy continually focused on the perceived threat of global terrorism. This justified the military deployment in Afghanistan, drone attacks in Pakistan, and the invasion of Iraq. US military presence in these countries disrupted socio-economic conditions, dismantled political organisations, and prolonged the conflicts causing an unprecedented death toll and displacement. A major failure for the United States is that despite the humanitarian and monetary costs of these wars since 2001, none of these places have achieved stability (Costs of War 2019). When ISIS emerged, US public opinion clearly opposed deploying US military in battles in the Middle East in the United States. However, because ISIS is considered a direct danger to the US interests home and abroad, both Obama and Trump administrations had to find a way to prevent the proliferation of ISIS with minimal involvement of the US troops.

To this aim, the United States worked with partners and allies to 'create conditions for an enduring defeat' of ISIS and other jihadist groups (Global Coalition 2020). Partnership with the Kurdish-led forces proved to be effective and fitting into the foreign policies of both Obama and Trump administrations. Both administrations pledged to replace direct military engagement with proxies in the Middle East conflicts.

US Defense Department officials refer to the partnership with YPG and later with the SDF as a model partnership that proved to be effective due to the 'capability and willingness' of the forces on the ground (Mulroy 2020). The support given to the SDF fits into the framework outlined by the

National Defense Strategy of 2018, which James Mattis developed. Despite his resignation, his framework remains in use (Mattis 2018). Although the territorial caliphate of ISIS was destroyed in March 2019, this US strategy document defines the organisation as an ongoing threat to stability. In a survey conducted by Amy Austin Holmes, most SDF fighters share this concern and argue that US-led coalition forces should stay in the region until stability is reached (Holmes 2019).

Finally, relations with Turkey is a main determinant of the United States' Kurdish policy. Turkey has pursued a Western-oriented policy since the Second World War and maintains close ties with the United States as a NATO ally. Since the early 2010s, Turkey has moved away from its traditional foreign policy of sustaining the status quo and Westernism. Conservation of the status quo meant minimal relations with the rest of the Middle East to avoid involvement in regional conflicts other than the Kurdish issue, which Turkey defines as a red line for its national security.

Erdoğan's first decade in power was marked with a newly branded 'zero problems with neighbours' policy that centred around Erdoğan key's aspirations to be a regional power. During this time, Turkey maintained good relations with the European Union and showed progress in the accession process. The Turkish government even initiated peace talks with the PKK. In this framework, Erdoğan's government had good relations with the Assad government until 2011.

Turkey's proactive involvement in the Syrian crisis in 2011 against the Assad regime marked the end of the zero-problems policy. Questions arise over Erdoğan's motivation to be so deeply involved in the Syrian conflict. Religious concerns played a role, yet Erdoğan (a fundamentalist Sunni) and Assad (an Alawite) were good friends for the most of the 2000s. Thus, political and economic factors probably also played a role in Turkey's turn against Assad as well. Turkey's economic growth in the early 2000s significantly profited from the devastation of Iraq after the invasion and subsequent civil war. Turkish enterprises were deeply involved in rebuilding the infrastructure of the Kurdistan Regional Government (KRG) in Iraq. Turkey's economic investments in KRG helped develop close ties with the Kurdish administration. Turkey needed a new Iraq after the 2008 crisis, which was to be Syria. Also, negotiations with Kurds began to benefit Kurdish politics rather than Erdoğan's party, the AKP, at the ballot box. Last but not least, Kurds gained a stronghold in Syria that would also have an impact on Turkish domestic politics in the coming years.

Thus, Erdoğan and his political party, AKP, had no other option but to have its 'nationalistic turn' in domestic and foreign politics. Once they delved in the depths of the Syrian conflict, progress on all other fronts came to a halt. The government abandoned the Kurdish peace process in 2015 resulting in a strong backlash for its imprisonment of Kurdish politicians, destruction of Kurdish cities, and even killing Kurdish civilians.

Collapse of the earlier zero-problems policy also had repercussions for the relations with the United States. Issues such as Turkey's purchase of the S-400 missiles, the imprisonment of an American pastor in Turkey, and Turkey's assault on US partner YPG in Syria complicated the US-Turkish relations. The previously mentioned US sanctions were introduced in this environment.

Although these sanctions refer to Turkey's actions against the Kurds in Syria, the Kurdish question does not constitute the main axis of US-Turkish relations. In fact, Turkey's erratic foreign policy in the Middle East has not collided with the main tenets of the US policy in the Middle East. Turkey's attack on the Kurdish forces in Syria triggered the sanctions but they resulted from the accumulating tension between Turkey and the United States over the last couple of years. Despite the recent tumultuous relationships between these two countries and Turkey's close contacts with Russia since 2016, Turkey's strategic orientation remains with the Western powers and the NATO alliance. Although Mr. Erdoğan's ambitious foreign policy raises questions over Turkey's Western orientation and its membership in NATO, the United States ultimately sees most of these distractions as part of Erdoğan's domestic policy interests (Zanotti and Clayton 2020).

The United States seeks to balance its relations between the Kurds of Syria and Turkey. To reduce Turkey's concerns, the United States identifies YPG as mostly separate from PKK. Nonetheless, the United States does not have direct relations with the PKK, listed as a terrorist organisation since 1997 by the United States due to Turkey's requests. Moreover, partnership with SDF can be justified by its ethnic diversification to include more Arab fighters than Kurds (Holmes 2019) so the Kurdish forces in the region can be relabelled as multi-ethnic or even Arab-majority forces. In order not to alienate Turkey, the United States did not directly intervene when Turkey assaulted the SDF-controlled areas in Syria. The United States mostly allows Turkey's safe zone. The OIR mission statement indicates that the Global Coalition targets 'designated areas in Iraq and Syria' (CJTF-OIR 2017) and the designated areas excludes areas west of the Euphrates River. Therefore, the OIR mandate legitimises non-involvement in Turkey's actions in this region.

Although the United States does not militarily confront Turkey's actions in the region, bipartisan commissions in the United States Congress challenge the repression of ethnic and religious rights under the Free Syrian Army and Turkish forces. Reports by the United States Commission on International

Religious Freedom point out that Turkey's invasion of Efrîn had alarming consequences on religious freedom and human rights. These reports praise AANES dedication to uphold its commitment to religious freedom and civil rights (USCIRF 2020).

In general, the United States does not intervene in Turkey's domestic Kurdish question despite the increasing human rights violations; that policy is extended to not constraining Turkey's actions in Syria. At the same time, the United States seeks to maintain a balance in its policy towards Turkey and Kurds of Syria by not alienating Turkey while supporting the SDF. Although Trump announced a withdrawal of US forces and gave a green light for Turkey's incursions, eventually the United States did not remove all of its forces from the region. Instead, some troops were repositioned around the oilfields controlled by the Kurdish-led forces. This protection brought about a deal between Syrian National Council and a US-based oil company Delta Crescent Energy.

Concluding remarks: Expectations on the future of US-Kurdish relations

For decades, Kurds have been struggling for their rights in their homelands. However, because of their victory in an existential fight against ISIS, only recently have Kurds emerged in the global public view as a pivotal actor in their region. Fear of ISIS as a global threat galvanised the Western powers into forming a Global Coalition directed by the US that assisted the Kurdish-led SDF. Nevertheless, the recent, erratic US policies—including the abrupt decision to withdraw—are not aberrant of the traditional US policy towards Kurds. Kurds of north-eastern Syria realise they are not among the most important allies for the United States in the Middle East. They try to use diplomacy to ensure their significance.

The relationship between the United States and the Kurds of north-eastern Syria since 2014 epitomises the maturing of Kurdish diplomacy. During this time, Kurdish representatives visited the United States not only to hold private meetings but also to hold public discussions with the policy analysts in Washington, D.C. as well as with the Kurdish diaspora in the United States. These meetings and events increased the visibility of Kurdish demands and interests. Unlike the covert US approach towards the Kurds during the Cold War, the Kurds and the United States now have open relations. Syrian Democratic Council (SDC) as well as the KRG and the pro-Kurdish party in Turkey HDP (Peoples' Democratic Party) have official representation in Washington, D.C.

The US military support for and tacit diplomatic endorsement of Syrian Kurds helped increase international acknowledgment of the Kurds achievement in defeating ISIS on the ground. The US support also moved the focus of overall Kurdish politics to north-eastern Syria. Even though the US withdrawal alarmed many commentators, Syrian Kurds cherished the enduring recognition from the United States. They hope that it will eventually contribute into achieving their political and social goals for AANES. To this end, Kurds use all possible means to communicate their political project for this region, underlining their model of democracy—as developed in AANES—based on principles such as secularism, religious freedom, ethnic diversity, gender empowerment, and non-statist agenda. If they successfully convey this message of a model democracy to the global public, it will also be a force to push the United States to adopt a Kurdish policy based on idealism instead of instrumentalism.

References

Agence France Press. 2015. 'Turkish Journalists Charged over Claim That Secret Services Armed Syrian Rebels' | Turkey | *The Guardian*. November 26, 2015. https://www.theguardian.com/world/2015/nov/27/turkish-journalists-charged-over-claim-that-secret-services-armed-syrian-rebels.

Akbas, Mehmet. 2018. Interview with former NEKA president Mehmet Akbas, Rhode Island, USA.

Atwood, Kylie. 2019. 'Trump Tells Worried Ally 'I Love the Kurds' in Hotel Meeting.' CNN. January 29, 2019. https://www.cnn.com/2019/01/29/politics/trump-kurds-hotel-meeting/index.html.

Barnes, Julian. 2014. 'US Airdrops Weapons and Supplies to Besieged Syrian Kurds in Kobani' - WSJ.' October 20, 2014. https://www.wsj.com/articles/us-airdrops-weapons-and-supplies-to-besieged-syrian-kurds-in-kobani-1413761080.

BBC News. 2014. 'Air Strikes Help Syria Town Curb IS,' October 8, 2014, sec. Middle East. https://www.bbc.com/news/world-middle-east-29526783.

Brice, Makini, Susan Heavey, and Doina Chiacu. 2019. 'US Republicans Join Democrats to Blast Trump's Syria Withdrawal.' *Reuters*, October 7, 2019. https://www.reuters.com/ article/us-syria-security-turkey-usa-congress-iduskbn1wm1zo.

Burns, John F. 2002. 'Kurds, Secure in North Iraq Zone, Are Wary About a US Offensive.' *The New York Times*, July 8, 2002, sec. World. https://www.nytimes.com/2002/07/08/world/kurds-secure-in-north-iraq-zone-are-wary-about-a-us-offensive.html.

Cavusoglu, Mevlut. 2018. 'The Meaning of Operation Olive Branch.' *Foreign Policy* (blog). 2018. https://foreignpolicy.com/2018/04/05/the-meaning-of-operation-olive-branch/.

Charountaki, Marianna. 2011. *The Kurds and Us Foreign Policy: International Relations in the Middle East Since 1945*. Taylor & Francis Group.

CJTF-OIR. 2017. 'Combined Joint Task Force Operation Inherent Resolve Fact Sheet.' US Department of Defense. https://www.inherentresolve.mil/Portals/14/Documents/Mission/20170717%20Updated%20Mission%20Statement%20Fact%20Sheet.pdf?ver=2017-07-17-093803-770.

CNN. 2018. 'READ: James Mattis' Resignation Letter.' CNN. December 21, 2018. https://www.cnn.com/2018/12/20/politics/james-mattis-resignation-letter-doc/index.html.

Costs of War. 2019. 'Budgetary Costs of Post-9/11 Wars Through FY2020.' Brown University. https://watson.brown.edu/costsofwar/figures/2019/budgetary-costs-post-911-wars-through-fy2020-64-trillion.

Dent, Joseph Votel, Elizabeth. 2019. 'The Danger of Abandoning Our Partners.' The Atlantic. October 8, 2019. https://www.theatlantic.com/politics/archive/2019/10/danger-abandoning-our-partners/599632/.

Department of Defense. 2017. 'About CJTF-OIR.' https://www.inherentresolve.mil/About-CJTF-OIR/.

Department of State, US 2020. 'Caesar Syria Civilian Protection Act.' *United States Department of State* (blog). June 17, 2020. https://www.state.gov/caesar-syria-civilian-protection-act/.

Dunn Tenpas, Kathryn. 2020. 'And Then There Were Ten: With 85% Turnover across President Trump's A Team, Who Remains?' *Brookings* (blog). April 13, 2020. https://www.brookings.edu/blog/fixgov/2020/04/13/and-then-there-were-ten-with-85-turnover-across-president-trumps-a-team-who-remains/.

Engel, Eliot L. 2019. 'Text - H.R.4695 - 116th Congress (2019-2020): PACT Act.' Webpage. 2019/2020. October 30, 2019. https://www.congress.gov/bill/116th-congress/house-bill/4695/text.

Entessar, Nader. 2019. 'Iran and the Kurds.' In *Routledge Handbook on the Kurds*, edited by Michael M. Gunter, 399–409. London and New York: Routledge.

Erdoğan, Recep Tayyip. 2019. 'Recep Tayyip Erdoğan on Twitter:' Twitter. October 9, 2019. https://twitter.com/RTErdogan/status/1181921311846735872.

Galbraith, Peter W. 2019. 'The Betrayal of the Kurds,' November 21, 2019. https://www.nybooks.com/articles/2019/11/21/betrayal-of-the-kurds/.

Gibson, Bryan R. 2015. *Sold Out? US Foreign Policy, Iraq, the Kurds, and the Cold War*. New York: Palgrave Macmillan. https://www.amazon.com/Foreign-Policy-Kurds-Middle-Today/dp/1137487119.

———. 2019. 'The Secret Origins of the US-Kurdish Relationship Explain Today's Disaster.' *Foreign Policy* (blog). October 14, 2019. https://foreignpolicy.com/2019/10/ 14/us-kurdish-relationship-history-syria-turkey-betrayal-kissinger/.

Gilman, Nils. 2004. *Mandarins of the Future: Modernization Theory in Cold War America*. The Johns Hopkins University Press.

Global Coalition, Office of Spokesperson. 2020. 'Joint Statement by the Political Directors of the Global Coalition to Defeat ISIS.' *United States Department of State* (blog). January 29, 2020. https://www.state.gov/joint-statement-by-the-political-directors-of-the-global-coalition-to-defeat-ISIS-2/.

Goldberg, Story by Jeffrey. 2016. 'The Obama Doctrine.' *The Atlantic*, April 2016. https://www.theatlantic.com/magazine/archive/2016/04/the-obama-doctrine/471525/.

Graham, Lindsey. 2019. 'Text - S.2644 - 116th Congress (2019-2020): Countering Turkish Aggression Act of 2019.' Webpage. 2019/2020. October 21, 2019. https://www.congress.gov/bill/116th-congress/senate-bill/2644/text.

Gunter, Michael M. 2016. *The Kurds: A Modern History*. Markus Wiener Publishers.

Haberturk. 2014. 'Erdoğan: Kobani düştü düşecek!' *www.haberturk.com*, October 7, 2014. https://www.haberturk.com/gundem/haber/997321-erdogan-kobani-dustu-dusecek.

Hiro, Dilip. 2002. 'When US Turned a Blind Eye to Poison Gas.' *The Guardian*, August 31, 2002, sec. World news. http://www.theguardian.com/world/2002/sep/01/iraq1.

Holmes, Amy Austin. 2019. 'SDF's Arab Majority Rank Turkey as the Biggest Threat to Northeast Syria: Survey Data on America's Partner Forces.' Wilson Center.

Ignatius, David. 2019. 'Opinion | Trump's Betrayal of the Kurds is Sickening to US Soldiers.' *Washington Post*, October 14, 2019. https://www.washingtonpost.com/opinions/for-us-soldiers-its-a-dagger-to-the-heart-to-abandon-the-kurds/2019/10/14/f0a1db60-eecf-11e9-89eb-ec56cd414732_story.html.

Khalidi, Rashid. 2009. *Sowing Crisis: The Cold War and American Hegemony in the Middle East.* Boston, United States: Beacon Press. http://ebookcentral.proquest.com/lib/well/detail.action?docID=3118040.

Krieg, Andreas. 2016. 'Externalizing the Burden of War: The Obama Doctrine and US Foreign Policy in the Middle East.' *International Affairs* 92 (1): 97–113. https://doi.org/10.1111/1468-2346.12506.

Labott, Elise and Veronica Stracqualursi. 2018. 'US Envoy in ISIS Fight, Brett McGurk, Resigns over US Withdrawal from Syria.' CNN. December 22, 2018. https://www.cnn.com/2018/12/22/politics/brett-mcgurk-resignation/index.html.

Landler, Mark. 2011. 'US Troops to Leave Iraq by Year's End, Obama Says.' *The New York Times*, October 21, 2011, sec. World. https://www.nytimes.com/2011/10/22/world/middleeast/president-obama-announces-end-of-war-in-iraq.html.

Landler, Mark, Helene Cooper, and Eric Schmitt. 2018. 'Trump to Withdraw US Forces From Syria, Declaring 'We Have Won Against ISIS.'' *The New York Times*, December 19, 2018, sec. US https://www.nytimes.com/2018/12/19/us/politics/trump-syria-turkey-troop-withdrawal.html.

Latham, Michael E. 2011. *The Right Kind of Revolution: Modernization, Development, and US Foreign Policy from the Cold War to the Present.* Ithaca, United States: Cornell University Press. http://ebookcentral.proquest.com/lib/well/detail.action? docID =3138155.

Lead Inspector General. 2019a. 'Lead Inspector General for Operation Inherent Resolve I Quarterly Report to the United States Congress I October 1, 2018 – December 31, 2018.' Washington, D.C.: Department of Defense, Department of State, USAID. https://www.dodig.mil/reports.html/Article/1747137/lead-inspector-general-for-operation-inherent-resolve-i-quarterly-report-to-the/.

———. 2019. 'Lead Inspector General for Operation Inherent Resolve | Quarterly Report to the United States Congress | April 1, 2019 – June 30, 2019.' Department of Defense Office of Inspector General. 2019. https://www.dodig.mil/reports.html/Article/1926689/lead-inspector-general-for-operation-inherent-resolve-quarterly-report-to-the-u/.

Little, Douglas. 2010. 'The United States and the Kurds: A Cold War Story.' *Journal of Cold War Studies* 12 (4): 63–98. https://doi.org/10.1162/JCWS_r_00048.

Mattis, Jim. 2018. 'Summary of the 2018 National Defense Strategy of the United States of America: Sharpening the American Military's Competitive Edge.' United States Department of Defense.

Middle East Monitor. 2019. 'US Hits Turkey with New Sanctions.' Middle East Monitor. October 15, 2019. https://www.middleeastmonitor.com/20191015-us-hits-turkey-with-new-sanctions/.

Mulroy, Michael. 2020. 'Governance and Security under the Kurdish-Led Autonomous Administration and Turkish-Backed Groups in Syria.' In . Washington, D.C: Washington Kurdish Institute. https://www.youtube.com/watch?v=h4ufpzeu1f8.

Neuman, Scott. 2018. 'Trump And Erdoğan Talk, But There's Disagreement Over What Was Said.' *NPR.Org*, January 25, 2018. https://www.npr.org/sections/thetwo-way/2018/01/25/580578367/trump-and-erdogan-talk-but-theres-disagreement-over-what-was-said.

Pompeo, Michael. 2020. 'Syria Sanctions Designations.' Department of State Press Statement. https://www.state.gov/syria-sanctions-designations-2/.

Rodionov, Maxim. 2019. 'Kremlin Says US Betrayed Kurds in Syria, Tells Kurds to Withdraw or Be Mauled.' *Reuters*, October 23, 2019. https://www.reuters.com/article/us-syria-security-turkey-kremlin-iduskbn1x20lw.

Roosevelt, Archie Jr. 1947. 'The Kurdish Republic of Mahabad.' *Middle East Journal* 1 (3): 247–69.

Trump, Donald jr. 2017. 'The Inaugural Address.' https://www.whitehouse.gov/

briefings-statements/the-inaugural-address/.

United States. 2017. 'National Security Strategy of the United States of America.' Washington: President of the US

United States Department of Defense. 2019. 'Justification for FY 2020 Overseas Contingency Operations (OCO) Counter-Islamic State of Iraq and Syria (ISIS) Train and Equip Fund (CTEF).' Unclassified Document D-C8660C0. Department of Defense Budget Fiscal Year (FY) 2020.

UNSCR. 1991. *Security Council Resolution 688 - UNSCR.* http://unscr.com/en/ resolutions/688.

USCIRF. 2020. 'Syria Chapter 2020 Annual Report.'

Voller, Yaniv. 2014. *The Kurdish Liberation Movement in Iraq: From Insurgency to Statehood.* Routledge.

Wilgenburg, Wladimir van. 2019. 'SDF Says over 11,000 of Its Forces Killed in Fight against the Islamic State.' Kurdistan24. March 23, 2019. https://www.kurdistan24. net/en/news/0dafe596-6536-49d7-8e23-e52821742ae9.

Zanotti, Jim, and Thomas Clayton. 2020. 'Turkey: Background and US Relations In Brief.' R-44000. CRS Report. Washington, D.C: Congressional Report Service. https://fas. org/ sgp/crs/mideast/R44000.pdf.

CHAPTER 10

RUSSIAN POSITIONS ON SYRIA AND SYRIAN KURDS

Konstantin Truevtsev

Russian foreign policy initially did not place a high priority on the issue of Syrian Kurdistan. Relations on the governmental level with Iran, Turkey, Iraq, and Assad's Syria overshadowed this issue that remained extremely marginal until 2011 despite the Kurdish ties of the long-time leader of the Syrian Communist Party, Khaled Bakdash.

In April 2011, Russian political analysts specialising in the region first became interested in Syrian Kurds when they became an important factor of domestic Syrian politics. The opposition's slogan 'power for Sunni majority', meaning only Arab Sunnis excluding Kurds, also excluded them from the general leadership of the anti-government activities even though the Kurdish movement had opposed Damascus since the first stages of the Arab Spring in Syria. That paved a road towards building alternative political structures in Rojava. The narrow Russian interests include, in addition to the previously mentioned specialists, some young intellectuals looking at the anti-globalist and anti-authoritarian aspects of the Rojava project.

This phase lasted until 2014 when the predominantly Syrian Kurdish People's Defence Units (YPG) became the first forces to defeat ISIS in Kobani before any regional government or international military actors. Therefore, Moscow started considering Syrian Kurds as an important factor in the entire dynamics of the Syrian conflict.

After Russia decided to intervene in the Syrian conflict in 2015, the deterioration of relationships with Turkey pushed Russia into building links with Kurds. Also, Russia's political class accepted—some analysts even sympathised with—Rojava's political structure based on the principles of democratic confederalism.[1]

During this period, Syrian Kurdish and Russian politicians started to

---

[1] One of the most interesting analyses of 'democratic confederalism' principles and their practical application in Rojava can be found in the book: Haytham Manna Ogalanism. *Ideological Construction and Practice*. The Scandinavian Institute for Human Rights, Haitham Manna Foundation, Geneve, 2017. Chapter 'The Rights of Persons and the Rights of People', pp. 61 – 83; Chapter 'Democratic Civil Resistance and the Syrian Wars', pp. 87 -98.

contact each other.[2] The co-chairman of the Democratic Union Party (PYD) at that time, Saleh Muslim, visited Moscow.[3] Irregular, but frequent, contacts occurred on various levels in Kamishli, Afrin, and other places. Russian representatives tried to help coordinate political and military efforts between the Kurds and the official government in Damascus. These contacts had some positive results during the battle in Aleppo and some episodes in Tal-Rifaat[4] and Manbij[5]. However, the two parties' incompatible positions complicated the connections.

Russia tried to include representatives of Kurds, in particular of PYD in the Geneva and Astana peace processes[6] but failed because of the refusal of the Syrian government, all factions of Syrian military and civil opposition, and Turkey[7] (in the Geneva negotiations, the USA and some Arab countries also blocked the Kurds). During the Syrian National Dialogue Congress in Sochi in 2018, the Russian government presented a draft of a new constitution of the Syrian Republic (excluding the word 'Arab') that included an autonomy for Kurds. The official Syrian government and the opposition unanimously rejected it.

Moscow positively reacted to the Kurdish offensive in Jarablus and

---

[2] 'The Russian position was: our country considers to have right and obligations to provide military-technical aid to Iraq, Syria, and among others to Syrian Kurds'. Andrey S. ODINOKOV Lomonosov Moscow State University Moscow, Russia GERQO@yandex.ru KURDISH ISSUE IN RUSSIAN-TURKISH RELATIONS. Историческая и социально-образовательная мысль. Том 11 №1, 2019 Historical and Social-Educational Idea Volume 11 #1, 2019, p. 33.

[3] Saleh Muslim visited Moscow in August 2015. https://thearabweekly.com/will-putin-play-kurdish-card-against-turkey

[4] Tal-Rifaat was taken under joint control by Syrian Republican Guard and Russian Military Police on 30 March 2018 according to an agreement with YPD in order to prevent invasion of the Turkish army and pro-Turkish Syrian militants. https://www.almasdarnews.com/article/video-confirmation-tal-riffat-under-control-of-syrian-army-republican-guard-and-russian-army/. This joint control did not exclude preserving YPD presence in the surrounding area.

[5] Starting from 2017, Turkey tried to attack Manbij controlled by PYG formed city council several times using its Syrian proxies. In December 2018, the Syrian Arab army (SAA) announced they would enter the city in order to prevent Turkey threats. https://www.almasdarnews.com/article/video-confirmation-tal-riffat-under-control-of-syrian-army-republican-guard-and-russian-army/. In fact, SAA has not advanced into the city itself limiting its move by occupying its suburbs, but this action still prevented Turkish invasion. Later, in October 2019, Russian Military Police together with SAA entered the city in order to prevent a new Turkish threat. https://www.washingtonpost.com/world/middle_east /syria-says-government-soldiers-enter-manbij-after-us-troops-withdraw/2019/10/15/d494405a-eeb8-11e9-bb7e-d2026ee0c199_story.html

[6] 'Russia insisted on involving all Syrian groups into resolution of the conflict including Kurds without whom according to Moscow opinion it is impossible to solve the Syrian problem'. А. Р. Вахшитех Роль России в урегулировании сирийского конфликта. Известия Саратовского университета. Новая серия. История. Международные отношения. 2018. Т. 18. Вып.4, с. 515. https://cyberleninka. ru/article/n/rol-rossii-v-uregulirovanii-siriyskogo-konflikta/viewer;

[7] 'It became known that Russia expressed the necessity of including PYD into the list of Syrian opposition...The Syrian opposition was against this proposal since the beginning... Cavusoglu admitted that it was unacceptable for Ankara too' https://mk-turkey.ru/blog/cumhuriyet/2017/08/10/rossiya-vyrazila-neobhodimost.html.

Manbij against ISIS because it did not interfere with joint Russian-Syrian operations at the starting battle in Aleppo. Russia also did not oppose the Turkish 'Euphrates Shield' operation because it was officially declared as an offensive against ISIS although the operation's main task was to prevent Kurds from uniting eastern Kurdish territories with Afrin. Russia's position became understandable when Turkey withdrew some of the most important pro-Turkish militias like Ahrar al-Sham and Nureddin el-Zenki from inside Aleppo in the direction of 'Euphrates Shield' operation during the most decisive stage of the battle in the city. However, when the Syrian Arab Army (SAA) moved to the northeast after the victory in Aleppo, Kurds had a chance to use this newly liberated area as a corridor linking with Tal-Rifaat and through it to Afrin. The SAA would not have objected to that and Russians could have played a broker role.

This did not happen because the main Kurdish military resources went in the opposite direction—towards south Raqqa and Deir ez-Zur. The Kurdish-US cooperation in Syria shaped this choice. The Kurdish leaders explained this cooperation: 'We needed arms and we first appealed for arms supply to our Russian friends. They agreed but insisted that the only way for this supply should be through Damascus. It was unacceptable for us. Therefore, we agreed to the American proposal of direct supply through Iraq. That's how our cooperation with Americans started.'

No matter whether this served as a real or a main reason for Kurdish-American cooperation, this became one of the most important factors of the war in Syria. The SAA with its Russian, Iranian, and other allies, on the one hand, and the Kurdish-led Syrian Democratic Forces (SDF) together with American-led international coalition, on the other, waged parallel battles against ISIS until the terrorist enclave collapsed in late 2018. The two sides had competing battles that led to a common victory against terrorists.

Russia took this victory as the most principle achievement with undoubted contributions from the Kurds. Despite fierce competition between the two sides in a common struggle against ISIS, they did not clash seriously with each other. Therefore, according to the Russian perspective, what deep and sharp contradictions that may exist between the current Syrian government and the Kurds do not represent an inevitable antagonism. More than that, the current government in Damascus and the Kurds have exactly the same enemies inside Syria and share a mutual conflict with Turkey.

At the same time, after the defeat of ISIS, it became increasingly apparent that the most important issue in Syria should be a deal between Damascus and Kurds. The Astana process helped bring together the contradicting positions of Russia and Iran, on the one hand, and Turkey, on the other, in order to prevent further escalation of the Syrian conflict. It involved Turkey in the peace process and divided Turkish-backed oppositional militants from the most dangerous terrorists. This clearly short-term transitional agreement during 2018 helped clean terrorists out of three of the four Astana determined de-escalation zones; factions of other militant opposition shifted to Idlib.

The Turkish 'Olive branch' operation that occupied Afrin overshadowed this process. This proved to be the most painful episode for the Syrian Kurds during the entire conflict and it led to negative Russian-Kurdish relations. Some Kurds accuse Russia of not defending them from Turkish aggression and even more, 'giving a green light for it'. Therefore, the Russian position in that case still need an explanation.

1. After the Kurdish alliance with US-led coalition in operations in South Raqqa and Deir el-Zor, some in the Syrian and Russian military regarded the YPD and the SDF negatively because their operations prevented the Syrian Arab Army (SAA) from liberating these territories and led to disintegration of these parts of the country. Non-military Russian political analysts did not share this perspective but did feel that the Kurds, although definitely not enemies, cannot be considered among Russia's main allies in Syria. Some take a non-partisan and realistic view that Kurds committed a strategic mistake when they concentrated their force in the south-east of their main area instead of moving to the west. That prevented them from having more military power to defend Afrin.

2. Turkish intervention coincided with an SAA and Russian operation in western Gouta to secure Damascus. According to the Astana decision, Turkey indirectly participated in this operation to guarantee transferring some terrorists and military opposition to Idlib.

3. However, Russia had made some efforts to prevent a Turkish invasion. One of its last proposals to Kurds was to let SAA enter Afrin. But Kurds rejected this because of the fear that Damascus authorities would destroy the Kurdish local government after obtaining full control over Afrin. These fears were quite understandable but what happened later was still much worse.

4. The story of a 'green light' is an ordinary Turkish lie. What really happened during the visit of the Turkish military delegation to Moscow before the invasion was that it simply informed the Russian side about the coming operation without getting a 'yes' or 'no'.

This spoiled Russian-Kurdish relations in Syria for a certain period. However, that didn't mean that Russian analysts and decisionmakers engaged with Syrian issue stopped thinking of what to do with the Kurds.

At the beginning of summer 2018, after completely cleansing terrorists and military opposition from three of the four de-escalation zones, three major problems needed resolution for finally solving the conflict: the problem of Idlib, the problem of two Turkey occupied territories, and the problem of the northeast.

The northeast clearly became the most important problem, not only because its territorial and resource dimensions but also because of its human dimension unresolvable through military actions.

Thus, a strategic deal between Damascus and Kurds must have a high priority when seeking to solve the entire Syrian conflict. However, the two sides seem to have incompatible positions. While the Kurdish side insists on a full-scale territorial autonomy of the regions controlled by the PYD and the SDF, the Syrian government will not accept any discussion over territorial autonomy.

Therefore, all negotiations between Kurds and Damascus during 2019 ended in a deadlock. Kurds insisted on their rights and tried to prove that their implementation of political structures based on ideas of Abdullah Ocalan demonstrated their effectiveness and that they, including their YPG military, could not be destroyed. Representatives of the central power in Damascus stated that the system drastically contradicted the principles and essence of Syria's entire political system and would lead to the country's disintegration. While Kurds stressed that they identified themselves as Syrian citizens with no intentions to separate from the country, the Syrian authorities could not explain Kurdish intentions in any other way than separatism. This official Damascus position rests on an absolute denial of any possibility of federalisation of the country and points to negative experiences in Lebanon and Iraq.

Still, I believe, we Russian analysts are trying to find a way out of this situation. A Russian proposal to various levels to both sides during 2019 did not use the principle of autonomy but of local governance.

In 2010, Bashr Assad issued Law No. 107 on local governance and postponed implementation because of the civil conflict. The president revived it in December 2018. According to this law , local communities have broad rights that cannot be interpreted for separatist goals. That gives a possibility for substantial convergence of the two sides' positions: on the one hand, this corresponds to the Syrian president's position, while, on the other, it corresponds to Abdullah Öcalan's ideas of local governance. Most important, the Law No. 107 opens the possibility to preserve political structures already existing in Rojava.

The two sides did not initially accept the proposal. Damascus coldly considered it and most Kurds rejected it. However, the Turkish invasion in north-eastern Syria in October 2019 pushed the two sides towards the necessity of reaching an agreement.

Even more important, Russia found an original solution that not only helped stop a Turkish invasion but also prevented a major disaster to Kurds and led to deeper communication between them and Damascus.

On 22 October 2019 in Sochi, Vladimir Putin and Recep Erdoğan signed an agreement to stop the Turkish invasion to within 100 kilometres of the Syrian territory in the Kurdish area. This helped preserve the main political and military Kurdish structures. Thus, Putin addressed Kurds later the same month and characterize the Russian attitude towards Syrian Kurds as: 'All that was achieved on the border between Syria and Turkey is made with the help of Kurds and in their interests.'[8]

Some Kurdish political leaders highly approved of the agreement. Ahmed Suleiman, representative of the Kurdish Democratic Progressive Party (KDPP) admitted that it showed Russia's key role in providing a political solution at the border of Syria. He said, 'I consider that this agreement prevented Turkey from deciding the issue of military intervention.'[9]

This agreement also helped the Syrian government to achieve what it had not dreamed about before—the SAA reaching the north-eastern lands up to the border with Iraq. At the same time, the growing confidence between Damascus and the Kurds increased the possibility of a joint attack on pro-Turkish proxies and Turkish forces occupying Syria. Future SAA and SDF actions in northeast Syria could include Aisha Hasso, the co-chair of PYD, as he acknowledged in an interview with a Syrian journalist Mohammed Ibrahim. However, he insisted that such a scenario would depend on an agreement about the SDF's role in the Syrian military forces.[10]

That increases hope for further progress in the current Syrian government's relations with the Kurds, although a principle strategic agreement still needs long and difficult negotiations. The Kurdish leaders noted that Russia served as a mediator several times in efforts to bring closer the Syrian government and the Kurdish administration of the northeast.[11]

---

[8] https://rg.ru/2019/11/29/reg-skfo/putin-zashchitil-kurdov-ot-televizionnoj-ahinei.html
[9] https://ria.ru/20191023/1560130935.html
[10] https://riataza.com/2020/03/24/sopredsedatel-pyd-sdf-mozhet-prisoedinitsya-k-pravitels tvenn ym-silam-v-idlibe-posle-soglasheniya-o-roli-v-sirijskih-vooruzhennyh-silah/
[11] Ibid

After the Sochi agreement in October 2019 allowed a Russian presence in Raqqa and Hasaka, new possibilities opened for Russian mediation in reaching a reasonable solution of Syria's Kurdish problems. Certain complications in solving the problem of northeast Syria have an objective character and include:

1. The problem of the northeast is not only the problem of Kurds.

2. The problem of the PYD/YPG[12] vis-à-vis the SDF: who will be the main counterpart in negotiations with the Syrian government?

3. If the Syrian government recognises the local political structures built by PYD in the Kurdish regions as legal structures of local governance, what about local governance in southern Raqqa and Deir-ez-Zor?

4. Is the SDF only a military formation or also a political body?

Russia agrees with the Syrian government's position[13] of seeking separate solutions to the problems of the Kurdish regions (northern Raqqa, northern parts of Aleppo, and Hasaka) and the mainly Arab-populated southern Raqqa, and Deir-ez-Zor. This position results from fear of losing sovereignty in territory occupied by the alliance of YPG and the US-led international coalition. Following this logic, the Syrian government negotiates separately with the representatives of PYD/Kurdish administration,[14] and with the representatives of the Arab tribes of Raqqa and Deir-ez-Zor.[15] Thus, these territories could possibly be designated as (1) Kurdish-dominated areas with future complete or partial recognition of the established political structures and (2) Arab-dominated territories with self-determination of the existing

---

[12] PYD is the Kurdish abbreviation for the Democratic Union Party (DUP), the dominant political party of Syrian Kurds. YPG is the Kurdish abbreviation for the People's Protection Units (PPU), military forces created by PYD. YPG refers only to male military forces, while the military structure of the Syrian Kurds also include YPJ – Women's Protection Units (WPU), female military forces parallel to male ones. For convenience, I use only the abbreviation YPG to refer to all the military forces created by the PYD.

[13] Some observers stated that Russia not only shared Syria's position on negotiating with PYD but pressured the Syrian government to intensify these negotiations. https://riataza.com/2019/12/23/putin-okazyvaet-davlenie-na-asada-trebuya-sereznyh-peregovorov-s-sdf/

[14] https://nsn.fm/policy/rossiya-uchastvuet-v-peregovorah-mezhdu-siriiskim-pravitelstvom-i-kurdami, https://tass.ru/politika/7002615, https://tass.ru/mezhdunarodnaya-panorama/6995274

[15] Russian representative Alexander Lavrentiev for the first time admitted to separate talks with Syrian tribes of the northeast in April, 2019. https://sputnik-abkhazia.ru/world/20190426/1027199640/ Spetspredstavitel-prezidenta-Rossii-po-Sirii-podvel-itogi-Astany-12.html. In December, 2019 Bashar Assad security adviser Ali Mamluk held negotiations with representatives of Syrian tribes in Kamishli. http://hawarnews.com/ru/haber/22vizit-ali-mamlyuka-prikryvaet-massovye-ubijstva-okkupantov-i-raskalyvaet-obshestvo22-h7484.html

Arab tribes under the authority of the Syrian government.[16]

During the negotiations between Ali Mamluk and the Syrian tribes, the Syrian president's adviser tried to persuade the Syrian tribes to distance themselves from the SDF. He had met with the tribes previously,[17] but had not openly challenged them to separate from the SDF.

This issue needs more detailed analysis to see the most proper way to solve the entire situation in the northeast. As noted previously, both Russia and Syria believe in separate solutions for Kurdish- and Arab-dominated areas. But does that mean that the Syrian government and its Russian allies should seek to divide the SDF?

The SDF is one of the most important military actors in Syria even considering its size[18] compared to the SAA[19]. Despite differences in estimations of its strength, the SDF doubtlessly remains, after SAA, the second military actor in the country.

Since its foundation in 2015, many have considered the SDF as a predominantly Kurdish power. Since 2017 or even 2018, non-Kurdish personal of the SDF started to at least equal to the Kurdish personnel while some estimations consider non-Kurdish fighters as in the majority.[20] Thus, the SDF cannot be considered now as predominantly Kurdish power but should be regarded as a multinational alliance[21] including, in addition to Kurds, also Arabs, Syriacs, Turkman, and others.

No less important than Kurdish members of SDF are the Arab members that include tribal forces such as Al-Sanadid Forces[22] and Liwa Thuwwar al-

---

[16] The official Syrian representative have never openly expressed this detailed attitude. I reconstructed this based on the logic of the negotiations during the last months of 2019 and the beginning of 2020.

[17] His first meeting with the tribes in 2019 took place in January in Itria, Hama. https://regnum.ru/news/polit/2560110.html

[18] CNN military reporter Ryane Browne estimated about 100,000 fighters in 2019. https://twitter.com/rabrowne75/status/1158818755390189569 . The ANTI-EMPIRE site quoting Brown's Tweet doubted that figure saying that a more realistic figure was 60,000. https://www.anti-empire.com/us-claims-its-syria-proxy-force-is-100000-strong-as-turkey-threatens-to-invade/. I believe that Wladimir van Wilgenburg derived a more accurate figure (80,000) in his report 'The Struggle against ISIS and the Integration of Arab Territories to the Autonomous Administration' at the conference on history and future of Northern Syria in Vienna on 6 March 2020.

[19] The official number of the total military personal in Syria in 2020 is 142,000. https://www.globalfirepower.com/country-military-strength-detail.asp?country_id=syria According to The Military Balance, 2019, p. 368 the number of personal of SAA was 100,000. https://www.iiss.org/publications/the-military-balance/the-military-balance-2019.

[20] Wladimir van Wilgenburg, ibid.

[21] 'A multi-ethnic 50,000 strong coalition, the SDF includes around 30,000 Arab fighters organized by Syrian Arab Coalition, forming around 60 percent of SDF'. Hassan Hassan The Battle of Raqqa, p.2. (The figures driven in the article refer to 2016). https://ctc.usma.edu/v2/wp-content/uploads/2017/06/CTC-Sentinel_Vol10Iss6-4.pdf

[22] Ibid, p. 3.

Raqqa.[23]. The SDF started creating multi-ethnic, military councils in different areas. One of the most significant is Deir ez-Zor.[24] The predominantly Arab military council created in 2016 cannot be regarded a tribal force because it consists of individual fighters coming from different regions.

These features of the SDF indicate that (1) it cannot be regarded as a merely military force but should be considered a military-political alliance and (2) it cannot be regarded as a simple alliance between Kurds and Arab tribes because its ideo-political dimension cannot be easily excluded or ignored by simply separating different Kurdish and Arab interests and motivations. The USA apparently noticed this when they tried to create the Syrian Arab Coalition inside the SDF that consisted exclusively of Arab groups such as the Sanadin Forces and the Deir ez-Zor Military Council. This new council would practically separate them from the SDF.[25] Russians also noticed this ideo-political dimension, especially after the US decided to leave Syria and then Turkey invaded the northeast. In December 2019, Russian representatives met Mazloum Abdi, the General Commander of the SDF. This showed a definite Russian desire to build direct relations with the SDF[26] without sacrificing relations with the PYD.

This meeting became possible after American decided to withdraw from the northeast; an announcement taken by the Turkish leadership as a 'green light' to its invasion. The SDF leadership initially had a sharply negative reaction. General Mazloum Abdi to Deputy Special Envoy told the US-led Global Coalition, William Roebuck, 'You have given up on us. You are leaving us to be slaughtered.' He added, 'You are not willing to protect people, but you don't want another force to come and protect us. You have sold us. This is immoral.'[27] Soon after that declaration, the PYD co-chair, Aisha Haso, stated that the SDF might join the SAA in its operations under certain conditions.[28]

In spite of these and other signs, the Syrian government continued negotiating with Kurds as well as with other elements of the northeast's political landscape. The SAA's field operations even cooperated with local military structures in confronting Turks and their proxies. However, it will

---

[23] Ibid.

[24] https://www.reuters.com/article/us-mideast-crisis-syria-deiralzor-idUSKCN1B516W

[25] https://www.reuters.com/article/us-mideast-crisis-syria-kurds/new-syrian-rebel-alliance-formed-says-weapons-on-the-way-idUSKCN0S60BD20151012

[26] https://riataza.com/2019/12/23/putin-okazyvaet-davlenie-na-asada-trebuya-sereznyh-perego vorov-s-sdf/

[27] https://www.msn.com/en-us/news/world/leader-of-syrian-kurds-tells-us-you-are-leaving-us-to-be-slaughtered/ar-AAIGet1.

[28] https://www.dailysabah.com/politics/us-backed-ypg-signals-possible-cooperation-with-syrian-regime-russia-in-idlib/news

not be easy to include regional political and military structures into a unified Syrian political order.

Russia and Syria have different positions towards the northeast: the Syrian government prefers to have separate talks with the PYD and with the tribes while Russian representatives do not hesitate to directly speak with the SDF. These differences should not be seen as conflicts between the two allies.

Russia has indicated its readiness to mediate between Damascus and the entire northeast. Therefore, it seems quite natural for its representatives to deal not only with PYD but also with the SDF. As for the Syrian government, it seems quite impossible for it to start a direct deal with the SDF, at least in the short-term.

This position has two reasons. The first reason is structural-organisational. As noted previously, the SDF's size is comparable to the SAA. An SDF force built on principles of autonomy cannot practically be included into an SAA using the principles of hierarchical armed forces, especially the principle of unity of command. At the same time, the SDF does not accept the idea of fragmental inclusion of its military units into SAA, promoted by the Syrian authorities, because it would lead to the loss of the SDF's independence.

The second reason connects to the essence of the Arab forces included in the SDF. Damascus only accepts part of them, the Al-Sanadid forces. This militia, formed by the al-Shammar tribe located mainly in Hasaka, has a long history of co-existence with Kurds (at least since the 17th century). The tribe is uniformly anti-Turkish, anti-Saudi, and anti-Wahhabi because of historic confrontation of the tribe with Al-Saud and al-Tamim tribes.[29] From the very beginning, the tribe and the Kurds fought together against ISIS.[30] This background makes al-Sanadin even more ready than the Kurds to ally with Damascus.

At the same time, Damascus will not accept SDF elements such as Liva Thuwwar al-Raqqa and The Military Council of Deir ez-Zor because of historical hostility between them and the Syrian government. Liva Thuwwar al-Raqqa was involved in anti-government military activity since 2011 and allied with Nusrah.[31] The Military Council of Deir ez-Zor includes individuals and structures that had a temporary alliance with ISIS in addition to directly

---

[29] https://raseef22.com/article/1071038-story-shammar-tribe-understand-indigenous-inhabitants-region

[30] Haian Dukhan State and Tribes in Syria. Informal Alliances and Conflict Patterns. NY, by Routledge, 2017. https://books.google.ru/books?id=zAB-DwAAQBAJ&pg=PT206&lpg=PT206&dq=syrian+arab+tribes&source=bl&ots=0hlAdjKgly&sig=ACfU3U28JmAawqQZP0RK0y9v9j1W2E72A&hl=ru&sa=X&ved=2ahUKEwjSrOSIk9LoAhU6zM

[31] https://syria.chathamhouse.org/research/division-defines-syrias-tribes-and-clans

or indirectly including Deir ez-Zor tribes[32] still hostile to the government in Damascus.

These elements influence the SDF's political positions. Despite the will of its leadership, they will still oppose any attempts of its rapprochement with Damascus because the best choice for them in current circumstances remains an alliance with the US-led coalition.

That was quite evident during Russian contacts with the tribes of Deir ez-Zor in December 2019 when the latter did not accept Russia's offer to mediate between them and the Syrian government.[33]

That shows the complications of rapprochement between the Syrian government and political structures of the Autonomous Administration of the North East including the role of the Russian mediation in this process. But despite all these complexities, the process continues without any expectations of a quick solution to the region's problems.

References

Dukhan, Haian 2017: State and Tribes in Syria. Informal Alliances and Conflict Patterns. New York: Routledge.

Manna, Haytham 2017: Ocalanism. Ideological Construction and Practice. Geneve: Haitham Manna Foundation, The Scandinavian Institute for Human Rights.

Odinokov, Andrey S. 2019: Kurdish Issue in Russian-Turkish Relations Историческая и социально-образовательная мысль. Том 11 №1, 2019 Historical and Social-Educational Idea Volume 11 #1, 2019

Wilgenburg, Wladimir van 2020: Report 'The Struggle against ISIS and the Integration of Arab Territories to the Autonomy" at the Conference on history and future of Northern Syria, in Vienna on the 6 March 2020.

Вахшитех, А. Р.: Роль России в урегулировании сирийского конфликта. Известия Саратовского университета. Новая серия. История. Международные отношения. 2018. Т. 18. Вып.4, с. 515.

---

[32] https://syria.chathamhouse.org/research/arab-tribes-in-al-hasakah-and-deir-ez-zor-choose-their-allies

[33] Ibid.

CHAPTER 11

WEAPONS, BORDERS, AND HUMAN RIGHTS: THE COMPLICATED RELATIONSHIP BETWEEN THE EUROPEAN UNION AND THE AUTONOMOUS ADMINISTRATION OF NORTH AND EAST SYRIA

Francesco Marilungo

Introduction

When we consider the European Union's general policy towards the Autonomous Administration of North and East Syria (Kurdish: Rêveberiya Xweser a Bakur û Rojhilatê Sûriyeyê, hereafter simply NES), we must assume that the European Union (EU) does not have any single policy towards the NES. Indeed, it is hard to speak of a EU coherent foreign policy on any issue.[1] In recent years, we became accustomed to complaints about the lack of a broad European policy on defence and foreign affairs, as well as exhortations to create a common continental approach to international security issues. Presently, each Member State moves with considerable autonomy, taking care primarily of its national interests and reacting mostly to domestic grievances, whilst the European bloc in itself seems to move steadily towards irrelevance in the Middle East and North Africa (MENA) region, where global and regional powers have reduced European influence. Recent events, such as the Turkish invasion of areas of northern Syria in October 2019, have only confirmed what analysts have been saying about EU foreign policy in the last years: 'that the EU has little influence over the course of events in Syria' (Pierini, 2016).

This article argues that despite declarations and formal acts, the EU's attitude towards the Syrian Kurds is inadequate and insufficient if it wants to provide concrete support for Kurdish rights in Syria; the EU approach towards the Kurds is substantially weakened by the increasing irrelevance of the EU bloc in the larger region, as well as by the awkward economic, military and political relationship the bloc holds with Turkey. I will try to show in this article that analysing the response against the Turkish recent offensive in

---

[1] https://www.euractiv.com/section/european-external-action-service/interview/there-is-no-real-european-foreign-policy-says-former-eu-diplomat/

northern Syria reveals that the EU has a considerable gap between strongly worded declarations and effective actions; this significantly affects the EU's approach towards the Kurdish-led administration of northern Syria. Beyond declaring support for the democratic, inclusive, gender egalitarian, and ecologic model realised by the Movement for a Democratic Society (Tev-Dem) in north-eastern Syria, there are other real and substantial issues that weigh on the EU Member States' policies towards Rojava. I refer here to chiefly two key issues that have to do with the archenemy of Rojava and a strategic, although in recent years boisterous, ally of Europe, namely Turkey, its government, and its nationalist constituencies. Apart from the Kurdish dossier, Turkey and EU share objectives in the Syrian crisis and are deeply interconnected by migration policies. Therefore, the EU policies towards the NES are inextricably linked and intertwined with the policies and the relationships with Turkey. This relationship has two crucial issues at stake: arm sales and refugee flows. In fact, Turkey, despite its recent tactics of diversifying suppliers by, for example, turning to Russia, remains a major buyer of European weapons (and the weapons industry in some EU countries has been a reliable industrial sector in years tormented by the economic crisis). Secondly, the other issue, the refugee crisis, clearly influences EU policies towards Rojava and the conflict in that part of Syria. Notoriously, in 2016, the European Union asked Turkey to patrol EU borders, choosing to pay six billion euros to the Turkish Government, outsourcing border control in exchange for money, instead of opening its doors to shelter the asylum seekers. This has obviously provided Turkey with an ace up its sleeve in negotiating with EU and leeway in its operations in Syria. Perhaps it is not a coincidence that the first Turkish operation in Syrian territory, Euphrates Shield Operation (Fırat Kalkanı Harekatı), launched in August 2016, took place just months after the EU and Turkey signed an agreement on refugees (March 2016). As I will show, almost every analyst points at the 2016 EU-Turkey Statement on Refugees as a move that drastically disempowered the European Union regarding Turkey, Rojava, and the Syria crisis at large. As the latest developments show, Turkey has learned to blackmail Europe by using the lives and bodies of the millions of Syrian refugees hosted in the country. Therefore, I argue that the EU has lost the capability to provide substantial political and infrastructural support to the very actors that concretely managed to defeat the so-called Islamic State (IS). Furthermore, the various EU Member States have different policies on another crisis area, Libya, where issues intersect at different levels with the Syrian crisis. The interconnection between the two conflicts clearly go beyond the scope of this article, but the Libya crisis provides another example of foreign policy divergence among EU Member States. The fault lines crossing Europe prevent the construction of a united approach to foreign affairs; this disunity results in regional powers considering the EU as less and less important, in this way providing space for global powers, such as Russia, to gain more leverage. In Libya, for example, Italy and Turkey both support the UN-recognised Government of National Accord (GNA) of Fayez Al-Sarraj, and oppose French and Russian support for General Khalifa Haftar. Therefore, it is difficult, if not impossible, to speak of a broad EU policy and particularly concerning the NES, as this policy would have to do primarily with the policy towards Turkey (a major ally within the NATO) and its regional interests. Notoriously, Turkey considers the Democratic Union Party (PYD) and its military branches in the same manner as the EU considers the so-called Islamic State, an enemy with whom no dialogue whatsoever is possible.

The awkward triangle: The EU, Turkey, and the Kurds

Unquestionably the EU, in recent years, has seen the Syrian Kurdish forces as a reliable ally in the fight against the so-called Islamic State or DAESH and has provided a large amount of resources for stability and reconstruction in that part of Syria. In recent years, with its constitutional reforms, political trials, crackdown on media and freedom of speech, and violent repression of the Kurdish political movement, Turkey has moved away from the democratic values that the European institutions flaunt and claim to protect. The complete halt of Turkey's EU accession process and its subsequent slide towards autocracy has made it substantially unrealistic to restart the process. Erdoğan would have to relinquish some of his powers and launch a process of democratisation, which is now unlikely, to say the least. The dismantlement of democratic and judicial independence in Turkey represents an obstacle and a problem for the EU, not only in terms of democratic rights and institutional reform, but also in terms of economics: the European firms, banks, and investors in Turkey have increasing worries about the unpredictable judicial system, have security concerns because of the military operations, and remain preoccupied with Turkey's dwindling sense of social cohesion. Turkish belligerence in northern Syria strains relationship with European businesses. For example, the German firm Volkswagen paused its plan to open a factory in Manisa, after Turkey invaded north-eastern Syria.[2]

The triangular relationship between the EU, the Kurds, and Turkey must be reconnected with the negotiations for Turkey's accession to the European Union. Broadly speaking, the Kurds always favoured the rapprochement of Turkey to the European democratic standards (see Samur and Ekinci 2018), as this process granted, in the decade 2005-2015, a relative liberalisation of

---

[2] https://www.reuters.com/article/us-volkswagen-turkey/volkswagen-delays-final-decision-on-turkey-plant-handelsblatt-idUSKBN1WU0GW

the Turkish State's policies towards the Kurds, the acquisition of some liberties, and 'new spaces of political engagement' (Casier 2010) by the latter. From Ankara's perspective, as famously synthesised by former Prime Minister Mesut Yılmaz in 1999, 'the road to the EU passes through Diyarbakir'. Furthermore, as David Romano has also noted (Romano 2013, 191), Turkey's EU membership is not only looked upon with enthusiasm by the Kurds in Turkey but also the Kurds in Iraq, Syria, and Iran have reasons to support Turkey's accession. In 2013, the so-called peace process between the Turkish government and the PKK looked like the beginning of a democratisation process that would grant the Kurds in Turkey with unprecedented political and cultural rights. However, in the following years, this process has been dramatically stopped, the situation of the Kurds in Turkey returned to levels of violence unseen since the mid-1990s, and the distance between the EU and Turkey in terms of democratic reforms and also in terms of foreign policies, has grown significantly. This has to do with various factors: the critical electoral gains of the pro-Kurdish party in Turkey in the 2015 general elections, the growing international military support for the Kurds in Iraq, but most of all, with the, perhaps unexpected, advancement of the Kurds in Syria. The rise of the Kurds in Syria in this respect might be seen as a game-changer (Resch 2017). The Syrian Kurdish defence of Kobane started a process that brought them greater international recognition and support to recover territory from the hands of the Islamic State. This change has pushed Turkey to reverse its policies towards the Kurds, going back to its ageless nationalist approach against the Kurds, but also towards the EU, and perhaps the West in general. As noted by Pierini: 'On a more global level, the broad objective of foreign policy convergence with the West—one of the requirements of Turkey's EU accession negotiations—is out of reach on the key issue of the Syrian conflict' (Pierini 2016, 8). Therefore, when we try to evaluate the relationship between the EU, the Kurds in Syria, and Turkey, we have to keep in mind this recent shift that brought more distance between Turkey and the EU, and made it more complicated for the Kurds to use the EU leverage to achieve political gains. At the same time EU's influence over Turkish domestic politics and over the Syrian crisis has shrunk considerably, as I will discuss further below.

EU reaction to 'Peace Spring'

On the context of EU-Rojava policies, it is quite enlightening to look at the European reaction to the Turkish military operation called, with a lack of taste, 'Operation Peace Spring' (Barış Pınarı Harekatı). On 9 October 2019, when Turkey launched its third large military operation in Syrian territory since the beginning of the civil war, the European Union was in a transition: the new Parliament was just installed and the new Commission was still under construction. The Brexit dossier was looming, with UK General Elections due in just two months. Perhaps these facts complicated even further the decision-making process and deprived decisions of any considerable meaning. Despite strong individual reactions, the EU waited several days before issuing a general and unanimous statement. In a joint press conference, French President Emmanuel Macron and German Chancellor Angela Merkel condemned the offensive. Macron spoke of a 'common desire that this offensive end' raising awareness on the likelihood of the re-emergence of IS. Merkel said that the offensive 'should be stopped'.[3] Both countries had already issued a ban on weapons 'susceptible of being employed' in the offensive.[4] As reported by the BBC, nine European countries imposed controls on arms sales to Turkey: Czechia, Finland, France, Germany, Italy, the Netherlands, Spain, and Sweden. Furthermore, the 'UK Foreign Secretary Dominic Raab has said Britain would continue selling arms to Turkey but would not grant new export licences for weapons which might be used in military operations in Syria. Germany and Spain have said that their embargoes would only apply to new contracts.'[5] This statement illustrates the ambiguity and vagueness characterising the declarations on arms sales.

The outgoing High Commissioner for Foreign Affairs and Security Policy, Federica Mogherini, on the very same day of the Turkish invasion, had quite strong words. In her closing remarks of the plenary session of the Parliament, she generally noted a shared understanding of the situation, 'beyond some nuances or differences in tones'. She unequivocally stated that the Turkish operation had to be stopped and that the Kurdish forces should not be considered as terrorists, but she also made clear that any measure the EU would take should not confuse the military issue with the EU-Turkey refugee agreement. Finally, she reaffirmed that the power was not in her hands but 'in the hands of sometimes the European Parliament itself—like in the allocation of funding—or sometimes in the hands of Member States individually—like the export of arms—or the Council—such as the possibility of introducing targeted measures, sanctions, or stopping financial flows'.[6] With that statement the Commissioner also gave a brief inventory of the kind of actions that EU could take against Turkey, and revealed the convoluted and fragmented process of decision-making of EU institutions in times of emergency. The Monday after the beginning of the Turkish invasion, with atrocious crimes already committed on the ground—like the brutal

---

[3] https://www.dw.com/en/eu-offers-measured-reaction-to-turkeys-offensive-in-syria/a-50819018
[4] https://www.ouest-france.fr/monde/syrie/la-france-suspend-son-tour-ses-exportations-vers-la-turquie-d-armes-pouvant-etre-utilisees-en-syrie-6562208?fbclid=IwAR16vqab-e_K9GlDQih0Blcr ZMnIpL9zpS8s-NUkGRXI33CTOOqWrtfRHp0
[5] https://www.bbc.com/news/50125405
[6] https://eeas.europa.eu/headquarters/headquarters-homepage/68651/speech-high-representative vice-president-federica-mogherini-european-parliament-plenary_en

assassination of the politician Havrin Khalaf—the foreign ministers of the European bloc gathered and managed to find an agreement, even persuading the UK that would have preferred a softer wording, and released a statement apparently indicating unity and strong condemnation of Turkey, but that, in my opinion, serves as a masterwork of political procrastination. The Council's statement has six points. It recalls Mogherini's condemnation of the military action, and after some calls to the UN Security Council and exhortations to revive diplomatic means, then declares its two main decisions:

> [...] taking into account the fact that Turkey's military action with its dramatic consequences is still ongoing, the EU recalls the decision taken by some Member States to immediately halt arms exports licensing to Turkey. Member States commit to strong national positions regarding their arms export policy to Turkey on the basis of the provision of the Common Position...

> The EU recalls that it will not provide stabilisation or development assistance in areas where the rights of local populations are ignored or violated.

The statement is not, as it may seem at first reading, an EU-wide embargo on arms sales to Turkey. Instead, individual Member States need to walk the talk and issue ban decrees. The unity looks very superficial, after all it only evokes a 'commitment' to act and each country has the space to apply its own policy.

Such measures have a questionable effect on the ongoing military operation, some commentators have defined them as half-hearted[7] and others have doubted that these measures will have any substantial effect on Turkey's military capability[8] or claimed that they would have only a 'minimal impact'.[9] Turkey itself has shown defiance regarding the issue of an arms embargo.[10] In the opinion of former EU ambassador to Turkey, Marc Pierini, the statement by the EU Foreign Ministers 'was firm and principled, but narrow in scope'. For him 'the upcoming European Council meeting should reinforce a strong and cohesive EU attitude. Actions should be launched as the EU, not just as France or Germany.... Arms embargoes, as symbolic as they are, will not impress much unless they are EU-wide.'[11] Some country

---

[7] https://global.ilmanifesto.it/di-maio-promised-an-arms-embargo-against-turkey-it-never-happened/

[8] https://thewire.in/world/temporary-ban-european-arms-exports-turkey-erdogan-syria

[9] https://www.defensenews.com/global/mideast-africa/2019/10/24/no-obliteration-western-arms-embargo-has-little-impact-on-turkey-as-it-looks-east/

[10] https://www.dw.com/en/turkeys-foreign-minister-cavusoglu-arms-embargo-just-strengthens-us/a-50808841

[11] https://carnegieeurope.eu/strategiceurope/80093?lang=en

issued the embargoes, but some others, for example, Italy, one of the major arms exporter to Turkey in recent years, did not fulfil its promises. Several months after Turkey's incursion, Italy still had not issued an arms embargo on Turkey. At the end of the meeting, the freshly appointed young Italian Foreign Minister Luigi di Maio told the press: 'We have left to Member States the commitment to do it because this can be done with immediate effect'.[12] On 9 January 2020, Italy had already changed its priorities: Luigi di Maio met with his Turkish counterpart Mevlüt Çavuşoğlu to discuss Libya, a context in which Italy and Turkey support the same side and where the European internal cracks appear more evident.[13] Until now, any Italian arms embargo on Turkey has not been made public or discussed. In 2018 alone, the Italian government authorised 362.3 million euros in arms exports. In 2014-2017, only Spain surpassed Italy in arms shipments to Turkey.[14] This demonstrates the European lack of unity and the non-existence of a European comprehensive foreign policy with any substance beyond words. The official response seems intended to addressing the general sympathy of the European public opinion for the brave Kurdish fighters rather than actually curtailing Turkish aggression against those fighters. The widespread support for the Kurds who have crucially contributed 11,000 lives to defeat IS, seems to have pushed the European politicians to act and react, but too little too late. After all, the EU Member States knew well in advance of a looming Turkish attack. Operation 'Peace Spring' is the third Turkish military operation in Syrian territory and therefore not a novelty. US President Donald Trump had announced months before that he would withdraw US troops, hence giving Turkey the possibility to intervene. Therefore, no European diplomat could be sincerely surprised by the Turkish incursion. If the EU diplomacy wanted to seriously prevent that aggression, it could have acted in advance with serious diplomatic negotiations and economic actions.

Ten days after the first Council Statement on 14 October, the European Parliament adopted a text entitled 'The Turkish military operation in northeast Syria and its consequences' that seems like a strong condemnation of Turkey's actions. The new President of the Parliament, David Sassoli, had already said a few days before that he 'emphatically and unreservedly condemn[ed] Turkey's military action', welcoming the arms embargoes of the Member States and calling for tougher provisions, such as the suspension of the accession negotiation with Turkey and a EU-wide arms embargo.[15] In the

---

[12] https://www.politico.eu/article/eu-finds-agreement-on-turkey-but-only-just-bloc-foreign-ministers-incursion-north-syria/

[13] https://global.ilmanifesto.it/di-maio-promised-an-arms-embargo-against-turkey-it-never-happened/

[14] https://www.ecfr.eu/specials/mapping_eu_leverage_mena#menuarea

[15] https://www.europarl.europa.eu/news/en/press-room/20191017IPR64557/european-parliament-president-david-sassoli-s-speech-to-the-european-council

text adopted on the 24 October, the Parliament used an even stronger wording. It assessed the operation 'Peace Spring' as unmistakably 'a military invasion in breach of international law' and a 'unilateral operation with no legal basis'. It clearly mentioned the 'killings, kidnappings, and looting' by the Turkish-backed armed groups' and the alleged use of 'white phosphorus'. Furthermore, according to the text, the demographic change projects announced by President Erdoğan at the UN Assembly 'constitute a clear breach of international humanitarian law, and amounts to a crime against humanity'. The statement also strongly criticised the severe Turkish crackdown on internal dissent. In the text, the European Parliament undeniably called things with their proper name. However, the assertive assessment melts away in the document's recommended actions; the wording reveals the European Parliament's lack of diplomatic instruments. In the 21 points for action, the European Parliament 'strongly condemns', 'urges Turkey to put an end', 'expresses solidarity', 'calls on the High Representative', 'reiterates the gravity', 'calls for sanctions', 'calls on Turkey to ensure accountability', 'is extremely concerned about reports that hundreds of IS prisoner are escaping', and 'recognises the fact that Turkey has legitimate concerns'. These sentences and phrases show the inability of the European Parliament to produce anything requiring specific action. In other words, the Parliament can only express a will, a preoccupation, an urgency, perhaps appeal to other institutions, but it could not take any specific step to pressure Turkey to stop its operations. Concerning the sale of weapons, the text 'regrets the fact that the Foreign Affairs Council of 14 October 2019 was unable to agree on an EU-wide arms embargo on Turkey; welcomes, nonetheless, the decision by various EU Member States to halt arms exports licencing to Turkey, but urges them to ensure that the suspension also applies to transfers that have already been licensed and to undelivered transfers'.[16] This text, although accurately and honestly assessing the situation on the ground, clearly reveals that the European Union's only democratically elected institution has little power to make decisions in matters of foreign policy and foreign relations. Perhaps this exposes the European Union's marginal role in Middle Eastern affairs.

The EU influence in the Middle East

Indeed, allies, partners, and adversaries alike, in recent years have observed the EU's marginality in the key issues concerning the MENA region. Most commentators notice the inaction of the old continent's institutions. For Thorsten Benner, 'Germany's and Europe's impotence to have a proper discussion on the whole Syrian conflict is staggering'.[17]

---

[16] https://www.europarl.europa.eu/doceo/document/TA-9-2019-0049_EN.pdf
[17] https://carnegieeurope.eu/strategiceurope/80176

According to recent analysis by Jeremy Shapiro: 'In private, former and current US officials are derisive about European influence in the Middle East. Broadly, they feel that Europeans talk a lot about the region but do very little.'[18] On a similar note, Aslı Aydıntaşbaş notes the 'Turkish perception that Europeans, though sympathetic to some of Turkey's concerns, are largely irrelevant on the ground in the region. Turks broadly share the US view that Europeans talk about challenges in the Middle East but will not do anything about them.'[19] Krzysztof Bledowski sees a substantial military dependence of the EU on the US, saying that: 'As at times in the past, the absence of America lays bare Europe's inability to act independently. The EU does not exercise true foreign policy because it cannot back it up by military force.'[20] In conclusion: 'The EU's reluctance to engage in deeper or more sustained political involvement in the region has allowed Russia—as well as powers such as Iran, Saudi Arabia, Turkey and the United Arab Emirates—greater freedom to strengthen their alliances. Unless they adjust, Europeans will become increasingly irrelevant.'[21]

What condemns the European Union to this irrelevance? Are there other substantial factors beyond the already mentioned disunity and lack of coherent foreign policy? The answers to these question in recent years have probably more to do with the domestic politics of the European Member States and the surge of far-right populism, which in turn tends to break apart the EU institutions. Specifically with Syrian issues, the disruptive effect of each Member State's migration policies serves as a key element hindering EU's capability to make a decision and act . After all, what clearly pushed the EU to issue a declaration concerning Turkish hyperactivity in Syria did not result from the genuine social and political achievements of the Kurdish-led forces in north-eastern Syria. The EU Member States mostly worried about two possibilities: renewed IS activity and a new flow of refugees that would either pour over the EU borders or prompt Turkey to ask for more support. This also brings in the key issue of Kurds holding captive IS fighters with citizenship in an EU Member State. During the Turkish operation, analyst Heather A. Conley commented that the 'events in northern Syria underscore the European Union's relative weakness when it comes to putting forward new policies to address a grave risk and demonstrates the Union's continued political vulnerability to increased migration flows from Turkey to Europe as well as concerns about the release of Islamic State fighters'. [22] Similarly, Gilles Kepel, while remarking on the lack of an EU foreign policy, particularly after the exit of the UK and its army, adds his doubts 'about Europe's capability

---

[18] https://www.ecfr.eu/specials/mapping_eu_leverage_mena/united_states
[19] https://www.ecfr.eu/specials/mapping_eu_leverage_mena/turkey
[20] https://carnegieeurope.eu/strategiceurope/80176
[21] https://www.ecfr.eu/specials/mapping_eu_leverage_mena#menuarea
[22] https://www.csis.org/analysis/experts-react-turkeys-intervention-us-diplomacy-and-crisis-syria

to intervene, as the EU lives in the fear of a new massive wave of refugees'.[23] This perspective considers the Kurds as essential instruments to control IS and serve as an element of regional stability. Somehow, Europe has come out of the Syrian quagmire with the noteworthy paradox of having outsourced its perceived security to two fiercely inimical actors: the Republic of Turkey, for constraining migrations flows, and the PYD, seen by Turkey as a branch of the PKK, for containing IS terrorists.

Many have noticed how the 2016 EU-Turkey Statement on refugees has resulted in the weakening of the EU vis-à-vis Turkey. Caroline De Gruyter, for example, rightly maintains that:

Europe is not endangered by its impotence in Syria. It is, by contrast, endangered by its impotence to welcome refugees—thereby exposing itself to geopolitical blackmail. What happens in Syria is a tragedy. But I don't believe Europe can solve it by intervening. Our military might is limited and ineffective, our decision-making process is complicated and slow. Against better judgment, Europeans tried to intervene in Libya. The effect was disastrous, both for Libya and for Europe. At least we learned one lesson: not to intervene in Syria.[24]

Sinem Adar has also noticed recently that 'for Ankara, threats to open the borders have increasingly become a not-so-uncommon diplomatic practice that has led to public anxiety in Germany'.[25] This attitude extends to Europe at large. In Italy for example, between 2015 and 2019, much of the public discourse expressed angst and hostility against migrants, stirred up by populist and far-right parties such as Matteo Salvini's Northern League and Giorgia Meloni's Brothers of Italy. Even during the operation 'Peace Spring', President Erdoğan threatened to open the borders.[26] Despite former President of the European Council Donald Tusk's resentful answer, 'we [Europe] will never accept that refugees are weaponised and used to blackmail us',[27] many analysts believe the 2016 Statement on refugees provides Turkey with a powerful bargaining card. Branislav Stanicek wrote a briefing by the European Parliament Research Service that clearly stated the crucial preoccupations of most EU politicians:

Despite positive cooperation on migration and the EU-Turkey agreement, under which a total of €6 billion has been allocated for

---

[23] https://www.cdt.ch/mondo/un-europa-impotente-subisce-i-contraccolpi-dei-conflitti-in-medio-oriente-NL2379096

[24] https://carnegieeurope.eu/strategiceurope/80176

[25] https://www.swp-berlin.org/en/publication/eu-turkey-cooperation-over-migration/

[26] https://www.independent.co.uk/news/world/europe/erdogan-syria-turkey-refugees-safe-zone-kurds-trump-europe-borders-a9172311.html

[27] https://www.reuters.com/article/us-eu-turkey-tusk-erdogan/tusk-says-erdogans-threats-of-flooding-europe-with-refugees-totally-out-of-place-idUSKBN1WQ18X

around 3.6 million Syrian refugees, Turkey's incursion into north-east Syria could further damage its EU membership perspective and lead to a new wave of internally displaced persons and refugees, as well as to security threats linked to ISIL/Da'esh foreign fighters present in Syria.[28]

Analyst Mohanad Hage Ali may be added to the choir when observing that since 'the EU's approach has consistently avoided any direct involvement' in the Syria crisis, 'this passive role of the EU in Syria turned into vulnerability with the 2015-2016 refugee crisis and the ensuing March 2016 deal with Turkey'.[29] For Sinan Ülgen, 'Europe's biggest failure was outsourcing its Syrian refugee policy to Turkey'.[30] As this article was being written, a Turkish senior official told Reuters that Turkey would allow refuges to cross sea and land borders, whilst nearly a million people push to the Turkish border from the Syrian province of Idlib, where almost three million civilians are caught in the fight between Ankara and Damascus, with the support of Moscow.[31] The new refugee crisis boiling in Idlib and pushing on to the Greek border, presents the EU with yet another dilemma. Its advocacy for human and civilian rights must be weighed against the possibility of new huge wave of people escaping the war. As suggested by Fabrice Balanche, if Turkey decides to open the Idlib border, then the EU would have to accept a mass of refugees storming to its borders, provide new financial support for Turkey, or eventually accept the relocation plan on the strip of land that Turkey has already seized in north and north-eastern Syria. In this latter case, the Kurds would pay the price.[32] According to Balanche, 'European officials have been careful not to condemn or punish Ankara for human rights violations stemming from its military operations against Kurds in Syria, if only because they do not have an alternative plan at ready if Erdogan decides to retaliate by opening the Pandora's box of mass migration'.[33] The hypocrisy of the EU-Turkey Statement on refugees, reached its climax in early March 2020, when Turkish authorities pushed migrants towards the Greek border as a way to protest EU Member States inaction in Idlib and Greece violently blocked the border crossing. The Commission President Ursula von der Leyen thanked the Greek police and referred to it with the Greek word

---

[28] https://www.europarl.europa.eu/EPRS/EPRS-Briefing-642284-Turkeys-military-operation-Syria-FINAL.pdf

[29] https://carnegieeurope.eu/strategiceurope/80176

[30] https://www.nytimes.com/2019/10/16/opinion/syria-turkey.html?smtyp=cur&smid=tw-nytopinion

[31] https://www.reuters.com/article/us-syria-security/turkey-says-will-not-stop-syrian-refugees-reaching-europe-after-troops-killed-idUSKCN20L0GQ

[32] https://www.washingtoninstitute.org/policy-analysis/view/latest-battle-for-idlib-could-send-another-wave-of-refugees-to-europe#.XljZlBBh7qs.twitter

[33] https://www.washingtoninstitute.org/policy-analysis/view/latest-battle-for-idlib-could-send-another-wave-of-refugees-to-europe#.XljZlBBh7qs.twitter

'*aspida*' – 'shield'. If Erdogan uses refuges as weapons, Europe seem to need border police as a shield.[34] The European Council President Charles Michel in a tweet complimented the 'protection' of the European borders by the Greek police.

In any case, according to most analysts and commentators, national rather than continental issues shape the EU policy towards the MENA region, the Middle East, Syria, and the NES. Rather than being concerned with the living condition of the people of the region, not to mention the socio-political experience of Rojava, EU politicians look at domestic issues such as the fear of new waves of refugees and the impulse they would give to right-populist parties. For European governments and for the Commission, the support to the Kurds has value because it keeps at bay the problem of IS terrorism and of the foreign fighters with citizenship in the EU. Europe therefore lives in a kind of paradox, being threatened by a situation to which it has no power to act beyond defensive responses to threats. Marc Pierini noted that Europe's 'impotence creates a huge paradox: while a witness in diplomatic activities and a subsidiary actor in military activities, the EU is one of the regions most affected by terrorism and refugee waves'.[35] Sinem Adar also claims that Europe's pragmatic approach 'puts interests and values in head-on collision', and most of all 'unintentionally intertwined Turkey's anti-Kurdish security concerns over its Syrian border with the EU's wider concerns over border control, to curb refugee movements',[36] hence Europe's care for Kurdish rights lies below the concerns for its border security. Already on 26 March 2018, just days after the end of the 'Olive Branch' operation in Afrin, Erdoğan met in Varna with President of the European Council Donald Tusk and President of the European Commission Jean-Claude Junker. In the press release, Tusk had the thoughtfulness 'to express [EU's] appreciation for the impressive work Turkey has been doing' in the migration sector, whilst simply asking Turkey 'to ensure the protection of civilians and facilitate access for humanitarian aid' in Afrin,[37] and therefore lightly accepting the policies of ethnic cleansing put into place by the Turkish Army and its allied militias (Schmidinger 2019), reported also by the UN[38].

Make Europe great again

The recent Turkish invasion has also stimulated fresh proposals against

---

[34] https://www.euronews.com/2020/03/03/greece-migrant-crisis-is-an-attack-by-turkey-on-the-eu-austria

[35] https://carnegieeurope.eu/strategiceurope/80176

[36] https://www.opendemocracy.net/en/can-europe-make-it/re-thinking-eu-turkey-co-operation-over-migration/

[37] https://www.consilium.europa.eu/en/meetings/international-summit/2018/03/26/

[38] https://reliefweb.int/sites/reliefweb.int/files/resources/ohchr_-_syria_monthly_human_rights_digest_-_june_2018.pdf

the previously mentioned European dormancy and inactivity, particularly in the Middle East. The criticism expressed by the think-tank analysts cited previously seem to have spurred an attempt at a renovated, although belated, European and, most of all, German international leadership. On 22 October, German Defence Minister Annegret Kramp-Karrenbauer advocated for an internationally patrolled 'security zone'.[39] This proposal would have entailed deploying European soldiers. However, perhaps as a repeated demonstration of EU's marginality, the proposal came on the very same day that President Putin and Erdoğan met in Sochi. At that meeting, Russia and Turkey agreed on their own vision of a 'safe zone', excluding Germany and Europe, and forcing the Kurds closer to the Syrian regime. The memorandum signed by the two Presidents on 22 October mentioned the 'preservation of the established status quo' in Tel Abyad and Ras-al-Ain, joint patrolling, and removing the YPG units to 32 kilometres away from the Turkish-Syrian border. The agreement also mentioned 'joint efforts to facilitate the return of refugees in a safe and voluntary manner'.[40] This forced SDF, EU's partners in stabilising the region and controlling IS foreign fighters, to retreat and give way to Turkish-Russian joint patrols, whilst the stretch of Syrian land now controlled by Turkey could be engineered for the 'return of refugees'. Kramp-Karrenbauer's motion sought to relaunch a leading role for Europe within the framework of the United Nations and international law, but her proposal received varied reactions, mostly negative. These responses reveal the difficulties of forming a cohesive EU foreign policy. Analyst Shimon Stein welcomed the proposal as a move that would 'mark a departure away from posturing and toward actively helping to shape an environment that serves European interests',[41] whilst for Thorsten Benner the 'half-baked' proposal 'cater(s) mostly to a domestic audience'.[42] Nonetheless, the proposal did not at all satisfy the German domestic audience. At the Bundestag, Rolf Mützenich, the SPD party's parliamentary group chair questioned Turkey's membership in NATO. Die Linke Party's parliamentary group chair, Dietmar Bartsch, rejected any type of intervention that could include the presence of German soldiers. German Foreign Minister Heiko Maas put the nail in the coffin when meeting with his Turkish counterpart in Ankara, he called his colleague's proposal 'unrealistic'.[43] Turkish Foreign Minister Çavuşoğlu demonstrated how Turkey has learned to move in the cracks of the European domestic politics when, in a joint press conference, he ironically said: 'We understand that Germany should first clarify its domestic affairs. I do not

---

[39] https://www.youtube.com/watch?v=DkecyJz5AxY
[40] https://www.aljazeera.com/news/2019/10/full-text-turkey-russia-agreement-northeast-syria-191022180033274.html
[41] https://carnegieeurope.eu/strategiceurope/80176
[42] https://carnegieeurope.eu/strategiceurope/80176
[43] https://www.european-views.com/2019/10/maas-faces-criticism-after-ignoring-kramp-karrenbauer/

interfere in German affairs.'[44] The German Foreign Minister Maas was harshly criticised after his trip to Ankara. The episode revealed a new low in German and by extension EU diplomacy. As a further demonstration of the impossibility of forging a connected and coherent policy in the labyrinthine context of EU's foreign relations, in a time of worrisome humanitarian conditions for the population of north-eastern Syria, one of the EU's most important countries, Germany, managed to be surprisingly divided and therefore weak.

Despite stern words from the European Parliament and a scattered policy of national arm-sales embargoes, the EU eventually had to accept the facts on the ground of Turkey having snatched another piece of Syrian land (after Jarablus, Azaz, and Afrin), having negotiated an agreement with Russia, and having involuntarily secured a way for the Syrian regime to enter into north-eastern Syria. With these accomplishments, Turkey prepared demographic engineering on the back of those refugees (as it did already in Afrin) blocked within Turkey because of the unwillingness of the European Union to open its borders. EU foreign policy faced a complete defeat except that Turkey did not 'open the borders' as threatened and IS seems to remain relatively quiet, at least outside of the region. However, now that the Syrian conflict moves towards its last chapter in Idlib, Turkey has resorted again to playing the refugee card and again the EU faces pressure. The Kurds have been forced to slide closer to the Syrian regime strongly opposed by the EU. Both developments do not bode well for the health of the relationship of the EU with the NES.

Conclusions

In this paper, I argued about a deep discrepancy between words and facts, regarding EU policies in support of the Syrian Kurds and specifically the NES and the Syrian Democratic Forces. In the early 2010s the Turkey-EU accession process produced positive results in terms of Kurdish rights, in Turkey and in neighbouring countries. However, since 2015, Turkish foreign and domestic policies have drastically changed, distancing the country from the EU democratic values, whilst also creating fault lines in terms of the EU's international interests. Concurrently, the European Union was progressively made less relevant in the Middle East and specifically in the Syrian crisis. The 2016 EU-Turkey Statement on refugees proved to be a grave mistake for the EU, providing Turkey with a blackmailing tool and exacerbating European weakness on Syrian issues. Therefore, the EU currently has little to offer the Kurds in Syria, beyond a general recognition of principles. With the sudden abandonment of the SDF by the USA, the NES is left to negotiate with the

---

[44] https://www.european-views.com/2019/10/maas-faces-criticism-after-ignoring-kramp-karrenbauer/

Syrian regime and Russia without any powerful international support from the West. The disunited EU has basically sacrificed its influence for the sake of 'protecting' its borders and presently cannot safeguard the democratic experience that in northern Syria successfully tried to locally implement the shared values of democracy and inclusivity that the EU claims to sponsor globally.

References

Casier, Marlies 2010. 'Turkey's Kurds and the Quest for Recognition: Transantional Politics and the EU-Turkey Accession Negotiations'. *Ethnicities* 10 (1), pp. 3–25.

Pierini, Marc 2016. 'In Search of an EU Role in the Syrian War'. Carnegie Europe.

Resch, Eva Maria 2017. 'Syria's Impact on the Kurdish Peace Process in Turkey'. 17 | 24. Working Papers. IAI - Istituto Affari Internazionali.

Romano, David. 2013. 'The Kurds and EU Enlargement: In Search of Restraints on State Power'. In *Divided Nations and European Integration*, edited by J. Tristan Mabry, John McGarry, Margaret Moore, and Brendan O'Leary, 190–209. National and Ethnic Conflict in the 21st Century. University of Pennsylvania Press.

Samur, Hakan, and Mehmet Behzat Ekinci 2018. 'The European Union Dilemma of the Kurds: High Support for Membership despite Lack of Sufficient Trust' 20 (3): 219–40.

Schmidinger, Thomas 2019: The Battle for the Mountain of the Kurds. Self-Determination and Ethnic Cleansing in the Afrin Region of Rojava. PM Press: Oakland.

CHAPTER 12

THE UN AND THE TURKISH INVASION IN SYRIA

Christoph Osztovics

Introduction

On 9 October 2019, Turkey's military launched operation 'Peace Spring' in an area between Tall Abyad and Ra's al-Ayn in the Syrian Arab Republic. Over 200,000 civilians fled their homes amid the initial hostilities, reportedly 123,000 had returned by November (UN Security Council 2019).[1] Syrian Islamist militias aided the Turkish military forces. The so-called 'anti-terror campaign' declared a goal of creating a 30 kilometre-deep 'safe zone' on the Syrian side of the border. The Turkish government has long wanted to establish such a zone to prevent the creation of a Kurdish political entity.

This article aims to analyse Turkey's plan to resettle Syrian refugees in this area and the reactions and possible involvements of the United Nations (UN) and some of its main agencies. Therefore, it mainly focuses on the roles of the United Nations Security Council (UNSC) and the United Nations High Commissioner for Refugees (UNHCR).

Turkey's refugee resettlement plan

After completing operation 'Peace Spring', Turkey reportedly intends to initially 'resettle' 1 million and then up to 3.5 million Syrian refugees from Turkey[2] in specially built villages. To accomplish this, the Turkish government wants to specify areas in northern Syria as so-called 'safe zones' for the resettlement of Syrian refugees. Turkey plans to build these new villages next to already existing villages. The project will cost an estimated $27 billion (Evans 2019). While many criticise this plan as causing a drastic demographic shift in northern Syria, the Turkish government argues it would only correct the demographic engineering done by the YPG (People's Protection Units).

The endeavour has the long-term goal of permanently suppressing Kurdish autonomy through demographic engineering under the guise of an 'anti-terror operation'. It would further relieve Turkey of the economic

---

[1] The reported numbers of displaced persons vary between 160,000 and 300,000.
[2] Currently, Turkey hosts 3,643,700 registered Syrian Refugees (30.4.2020) (UNHCRb).

burden of the Syrian refugees. Also, it would boost Turkish construction businesses, which would profit from building the resettlement villages. In fact, the stock of several cement plants in Southern Turkey has gone up since the announcement of the plan (Evans 2019).

The United Nations Security Council (UNSC)

The UNSC has addressed the Syrian Civil War many times, notably on issues like the use of chemical weapons or border crossings for humanitarian aid (S/RES/2504, 10. January 2020, see Security Council Report). But what about Operation 'Peace Spring'? The UNSC has been officially silent on the Turkish invasion of Syria.

Five European members of the UNSC[3]—France, Germany, Belgium, United Kingdom, and Poland—drafted the only UNSC statement condemning Operation 'Peace Spring'. The USA and Russia vetoed it. Russia's U.N. Ambassador Vassily Nebenzia, whose country is a key ally of the Syrian regime, declared that any council statement on Syria must address broader issues, including the presence of foreign forces in the country (Daily Sabah 2019). U.S. Ambassador Kelly Craft declared that the United States 'has not in any way' endorsed Turkey's decision to invade Syria. According to Craft, the US president has emphasised to Turkey's government that it bears 'full responsibility' for protecting Kurds and religious minorities, and for ensuring that so-called Islamic State (IS) terrorists remain in prison and the terrorist group does not reconstitute itself (Daily Sabah 2019).

While UN Secretary-General António Guterres expressed his 'deep concern' at the spiralling violence in Syria (Al Arabiya 2019), the UN General Assembly did not pass or even draft any resolutions concerning the Turkish invasion in northern Syria. This is astonishing inaction when one considers that a military incursion on the territory of a sovereign nation state has taken place. Furthermore, Amnesty International (AI) has publicised serious allegations of war crimes committed by Turkish forces such as the use of chemical weapons and the killings of civilians (Amnesty International 2019a).

Given the direct involvement in Syria of the U.S. and Russia, these states unsurprisingly vetoed the statement. The UNSC's failure to act on the situation in northern Syria disregards its mandate to maintain international peace and security, to try to end armed conflicts, and to promote respect for human rights.

---

[3] The current non-permanent members of the UNSC are Belgium, Dominican Republic, Estonia, Germany, Indonesia, Niger, Saint Vincent and the Grenadines, South Africa, Tunisia, and Vietnam.

The United Nations High Commissioner for Refugees (UNHCR)

During a meeting in Istanbul on 1 November 2019, Turkish President Recep Tayyip Erdoğan presented the Turkish resettlement plan to the United Nations Secretary General António Guterres. 'The Secretary-General stressed the basic principles relating to the voluntary, safe and dignified return of refugees. He informed the president that UNHCR will immediately form a team to study the proposal and engage in discussions with Turkish authorities, in line with its mandate.' (UN News 2019) No further response or comment has been issued since.

Since the UN made no further statements on the issue, we should look closer at the potential role of the UNHCR and ask: Does the Turkish plan constitute 'resettlement' as defined by the UNHCR? According to the UNHCR, 'Resettlement is the transfer of refugees from an asylum country to another State that has agreed to admit them and ultimately grant them permanent settlement. (…) the relocation of refugees from an asylum country to a third country.' (UNHCRa)

Since the refugees would be resettled in the country of their origin (Syria) and not in a third country, the answer is clearly no—the Turkish plan does not constitute resettlement as defined by the UNHCR. Why hasn't the UNHCR declared so and immediately rejected the proposal? Furthermore, many important questions regarding the implementation of the plan have not yet been answered: Who exactly will be resettled? Is there a neutral application process or will the Turkish authorities choose who will go?

Would the process be completely voluntary? According to Oytun Orhan with the Ankara-based Middle East Research Center (ORSAM), of the current 3.5 million Syrians in Turkey, only 10 to 15 per cent come from east of the Euphrates. If the resettlement is indeed voluntary, probably only several 100,000 refugees would go back (Serdar 2019).

The Turkish government has been eager to assure that the return would indeed be voluntary and claims that over the last years more than 300,000 Syrians have voluntarily left Turkey and returned to Syria. However, an Amnesty International report shows otherwise (Amnesty International 2019b). According to interviews conducted between July and October 2019 with Syrian refugees who have returned from Turkey, Turkish police and officials have tricked refugees to sign papers declaring their voluntary return to Syria. Some report they had been forced onto buses who would transport them to Syria, and that they were beaten during their journey. AI estimates that hundreds of refugees have been forcibly and illegally deported to northern Syria, a still active war zone (Amnesty International 2019b, 4-5).

Although no one had been deported to the 'safe zone' between Tall Abyad and Ra's al-Ayn but instead to the region of Aleppo and Idlib, these incidents of forced deportations show Turkey's willingness to reach their goals by violating international norms. The low number of deported so far shows that the Turkish government has not yet widely used this tool, but perhaps tests it for future implementation.

What would become of the people in the 'safe zone' who did not flee? Will internally displaced persons (IDPs) or people who have fled to Iraq be able to return to their original homes? These questions bring up merely technical details, when considering the potential consequences of a UN and UNHCR involvement that would indeed be highly problematic.

An active UN involvement in the resettlement would give legitimacy to a demographic engineering that would severely alter the ethnic composition of the region and set a dangerous precedent for other conflicts. Other countries could then imitate the mass resettlement of refugees onto the territory of another sovereign state. Furthermore, it would legitimise a military invasion of a sovereign nation state and the mass expelling of civilians. It would support an outright neo-colonial strategy of demographic engineering, which actively undermines the post-Ottoman border regime. In this scenario, the refugees serve as hostages, pitted against the local inhabitants. The UN's involvement would allow Turkey to frame its actions within a narrative of aiding refugees in the wake of a successful anti-terror campaign, instead of the brutal reality of resettling refugees into territory gained after a military invasion forcefully expelled civilians from their homes.

Historically, civilians have often been used in that manner throughout the region. This new approach to ethnic homogenisation uses the guise of resettlement of refugees and openly doing this while seeking support of the international community.

Historical parallels

When analysing the current Turkish resettlement plan, some helpful historical parallels include the genocide against Armenians and Assyrians between 1915 and 1917, the Syrian Arabisation programme of the 1960s and '70s, and the Arabisation campaigns in Iraq of the 1970s and '80s.

The planned resettlement of refugees in northern Syria and especially the reports of forced deportations (Amnesty International 2019b) bear some parallels to the deportations undertaken during the genocide against Armenians and Assyrians. During the genocide, northern Syria was a main area for the mass deportations. Many settlements in the area resulted from this ethnic cleansing (see Schmidinger 2015). To this day, Assyrians living in northern Syria associate the recent Turkish invasion with the genocide of

1915.

In 1962 the Syrian regime issued Decree 93 authorising a census to be conducted only in the Cezîre. It resulted in 120,000 Kurds losing their Syrian citizenship for being 'foreigners, illegally infiltrated into the area' (Vanly 1992: 151). In 1963, the newly established Ba'ath regime continued these anti-Kurdish policies. That year, Lieutenant Mohammad Talib Hilal, head of the secret service in Hasaka, wrote a 'Study of the Jazira Province from National, Social and Political Aspects' in which he formulated a twelve-point plan to eradicate the 'Kurdish threat' and which was 'an outright call for genocide.' (Vanly 1992: 153) The plan included a comprehensive Arabisation programme for the north-east of Syria and the deportation of Kurds from the area. In 1965 the Syrian government adopted the plan and partly implemented it until 1973. It concentrated mainly on creating an 'Arab cordon' (*hizam 'arabi*) by resettling Arab farmers to the northeast of Syria and resettling Kurds in the South. The plan was never fully carried out and the resisting Kurdish population was not forced to leave (Vanly 1992: 157-158). Nevertheless, the Kurdish population suffered from harsh discrimination and the denial of basic rights for decades.

Iraq and its Arabisation programmes offer further parallels. Between 1975 and 1980, 250,000 Kurds from the north-eastern border regions were deported to so-called 'collective towns' (*mujamma'at*) and their villages were razed. The Anfal campaigns between February and August of 1988 largely used this form of forced resettlement (Fischer-Tahir 2004, 179-181). The new villages, the Turkish government wants to build for the resettled refugees in northern Syria, conjure up images of the *mujamma'at*.

In an area, where mass resettlement and demographic engineering has been a regularly used tool, the resettlement of people by a state across an international border into a different state still constitutes a radical change in this area's border politics. Because of the previously mentioned historical parallels, the current Turkish resettlement plan should alarm everyone, especially the UN.

Conclusions

The UN Security Council has not addressed the current situation in northern Syria after the Turkish invasion. From the standpoint of a realist interpretation that is not a real surprise. The UNSC reflects the standpoints and interests of its member states. The parties involved in the conflict want to deal with the situation on an interstate diplomatic level and not through international organisations. From a liberal/idealist perspective on international relations, the silence of the UNSC constitutes a failure to address the violation of a sovereign border and to act as a corrective.

The question remains: why hasn't the UNHCR rejected or condemned Turkey's plan? Is it still studying the proposal? Perhaps, it hopes to shape the process in favour of the civilians involved? More likely, they do not quite know how to react. Because of recent events in the Syrian war and with Turkey having to make concessions to Russia and the Syrian regime, perhaps the UNHCR seeks to avoid the dilemma, hoping the issue might resolve itself. If Turkey faces setbacks in Syria, it might have to call off the resettlement plan. However, Erdoğan will probably not let this opportunity slip away.

By participating in Turkey's resettlement plan, the UNHCR would legitimise deliberate demographic engineering and thus set a dangerous precedent for other conflicts. Even if the UNHCR cannot actively prevent the Turkish government from implementing its plans, denying international approval would have noticeable effects. The UNHCR's reaction would affect other states' willingness to support (or oppose) the plan. However, not reacting also creates problems. Frequently, the UN only has the power of moral legitimacy. The UN would lose its ability to act as a moral leader, if it cannot bring itself to clearly condemn the resettlement plan.

Since there have not been any new developments since November 2019, it remains to be seen if Turkey will actually implement its resettlement plan and what role the UN will eventually play.

References

Al Arabiya. 2019. UN chief expresses 'deep concern' over Turkish offensive in Syria. 11.10.2019. https://english.alarabiya.net/en/News/middle-east/2019/10/11/UN-chief-expresses-deep-concern-over-Turkish-offensive-in-Syria visited 30.01.2020

Amnesty International. 2019a. Syria: Damning evidence of war crimes and other violations by Turkish forces and their allies.
https://www.amnesty.org/en/latest/news/2019/10/syria-damning-evidence-of-war-crimes-and-other-violations-by-turkish-forces-and-their-allies/, visited 03.05.2020

Amnesty International. 2019b. Sent to a war zone. Turkey's illegal deportations of Syrian refugees.
https://www.amnesty.org/download/Documents/EUR4411022019ENGLISH.pdf, visited 03.05.2020

Daily Sabah. 2019. US, Russia veto UN Security Council statement on Turkey's op in Syria. 10.10.2019. https://www.dailysabah.com/war-on-terror/2019/10/10/un-security-council-fails-to-issue-joint-statement-on-turkeys-op-in-syria, visited 27.01.2020

Evans, Dominic. 2019. Turkey's plan to settle refugees in northeast Syria alarms allies. 8.10.2019. Reuters. https://www.reuters.com/article/us-syria-security-turkey-refugees-graphi/turkeys-plan-to-settle-refugees-in-northeast-syria-alarms-allies-idUSKBN1WN28J visited 28.01.2020

Fischer-Tahir, Andrea. 2004: Widerstand und genozidale Verfolgung in Kurdistan (1968-2003). Akteure, Möglichkeiten und Grenzen, Perspektiven. In Kreutzer, Mary & Thomas Schmidinger (eds.), *Irak. Von der Republik der Angst zur bürgerlichen Demokratie?* Freiburg.

Schmidinger, Thomas. 2015. Westarmenien in Kurdistan: Überleben und Exil armenischer Gemeinden in Kurdistan hundert Jahre nach dem Genozid. In Hennerbichler, Ferdinand, Christoph Osztovics, Marianne Six-Hohenbalken & Thomas Schmidinger (eds.), *100 Jahre Völkermord an ArmenierInnen und die KurdInnen. Komplexe Vergangenheit und Nachwirkungen in der Gegenwart.* Wiener Jahrbuch für Kurdische Studien 3/2015. Wien. Caesarpress. 135-182.

Security Council Report. UN Documents for Syria. https://www.securitycouncil report.org/un-documents/syria/ visited 30.01.2020

Serdar, Seda. 2019. Syria: What does Turkey's 'resettlement' plan mean? https://p.dw. com/p/3SKuj, visited 30.04.2020

UN Security Council. 2019. Implementation of Security Council resolutions 2139 (2014), 2165 (2014), 2191 (2014), 2258 (2015), 2332 (2016), 2393 (2017), 2401 (2018) and 2449 (2018). Report of the Secretary-General. S/2019/949. https://www.security councilreport.org/atf/cf/%7B65BFCF9B-6D27-4E9C-8CD3-CF6E4FF96FF9%7D/s_2019_949.pdf

UN News. 2019. Guterres in Turkey: UN to study 'new settlement areas' plan for Syrian refugees. 01.11.2019. https://news.un.org/en/story/2019/11/1050451, visited 27.01.2020

UNHCRa. https://www.unhcr.org/resettlement.html visited 27.1.2020

UNHCRb. Operational Portal. https://data2.unhcr.org/en/situations/syria/location/11 3, visited 05.05.2020

Vanly, Ismet Chériff. 1992: The Kurds in Syria and Lebanon. In Philip G. Kreyenbroek, Stefan Sperl (eds.), *The Kurds. A Contemporary Overview.* London & New York.